THE DICTIONARY
OF DREAM
INTERPRETATION

THE DICTIONARY OF DREAM INTERPRETATION

Including a Glossary of Dream Symbols

Gerald Schoenewolf, Ph.D.

JASON ARONSON INC.
Northvale, New Jersey
London

This book was set in 10 pt. Goudy by FASTpages of Nanuet, NY.

Copyright © 1997 by Jason Aronson Inc.

10 9 8 7 6 5 4 3 2

Library of Congress Cataloging-in-Publication Data

Schoenewolf, Gerald.
    The dictionary of dream interpretation / Gerald Schoenewolf.
        p.   cm.
    Includes bibliographical references and indexes.
    ISBN 0-7657-0041-7 (alk. paper)
    1. Dream interpretation.   2. Dreams.   3. Symbolism (Psychology).
    4. Psychoanalysis.   I. Title.
    BF175.5.D74S36   1997
    154.6'3'03—dc20   96-31855

Printed in the United States of America on acid-free paper. Jason Aronson Inc. offers books and cassettes. For information and catalog write to Jason Aronson Inc., 230 Livingston Street, Northvale, New Jersey 07647-1731. Or visit our website: http://www.aronson.com

To all the patients, friends, and colleagues
who volunteered their dreams
for this project
and to Kim Chau Bui

CONTENTS

PREFACE

This new *Dictionary of Dream Interpretation* has been specially designed to offer both mental health professionals and lay people a concise and wide-ranging reference source on dreams in a convenient and easy-to-use format. It lists, from A to Z, more than 1,000 dreams and their interpretations, emphasizing today's most modern and accepted psychoanalytic techniques of dream interpretation. It is the only psychodynamic dictionary of dreams now available.

Each entry in the *Dictionary* (with the exception of those that come from myths, fairy tales, and certain literary works) is divided into four sections: (1) the dream, (2) the dreamer, (3) the dreamer's associations, and (4) a brief interpretation. This format allows the user to understand each dream in its full context and to form his or her own opinions as to other possible meanings, since it is generally recognized that the only correct interpretation of any dream is the one that the dreamer affirms. Moreover, since associations and interpretations of associations can be endless, this volume attempts to capture only a core meaning of each dream.

Most of the dreams have been taken from the author's own practice. A number of them are the dreams of famous dreamers ranging from Shakespeare to Henry Miller, from Napoleon to Johnny Carson, and from Freud to Dali. Others have been gleaned from notable cases in the psychotherapeutic literature; a few have also been taken from paintings, novels, myths, and fairy tales since these have long been regarded by psychoanalysts as similar to dreams. This wide spectrum is a tool to assist therapists of all persuasions in dream interpretation.

The volume also includes a glossary of dream symbols. This section incorporates not only psychoanalytic interpretations of common symbols, but also the meanings attributed to symbols in myths, fairy tales, philosophy, religion, and literature. When a symbol can be interpreted in more than one way, each meaning is listed, along with its source (i.e., psychoanalysis, mythology, Christianity). In addition, the book also includes an introductory chapter on the history of dream research, and several handy indexes, including an index of dreams according to personality characteristics.

In short, this is an all-purpose reference source on dreams that will serve the everyday needs of all who are interested in dream interpretation as well as the interpretation of myths, fairy tales, and literature.

Introduction:
A History of Dream
Research

Prescientific Notions about Dreams

Until recently, the meanings of dreams were steeped in superstition. From the time humans first began to develop languages, they reported their dreams. Generally they explained dreams as messages from higher powers, either divine or demonic, and saw them accordingly as omens of good or bad fortune.

Primitive people saw dreams as real experiences. Fromm (1951) reports that the Ashanti, in West Africa, assumed that if a man dreamed about having sex with another man's wife, his soul and hers had actually cohabitated; he was therefore fined. The Mohave and Yuma Indians believed that the spirits of the departed appeared in dreams to exhort them, warn them, or give them other kinds of messages. The Kiwai Papuans of New Guinea believed that if a sorcerer caught the soul of somebody while in the state of dreaming, the sleeper would never wake up.

Ancient books are replete with stories of how dreams were used to provide explanations for events that were not readily understandable. In the *Bible*, it is reported that during the time when Joseph and Mary were engaged, Mary became pregnant. Since Joseph and Mary had not yet had intercourse, Joseph was left with a predicament. His way out of this predicament was to have a dream in which the God of the Jews appeared to him: "Joseph, thou son of David, fear not to take unto thee Mary thy wife, for that which is conceived in her is of the Holy Ghost. And she shall bring forth a son, and thou shalt call his name Jesus: for he shall save his people from their sins."

In addition to the superstitious meanings attached to the symbols of dreams, ancients and primitives also offered various explanations of why people dreamed.

Dreams were said to be the result of indigestion, large adenoids, infected tonsils, a full moon, or a shooting star. Or they might be the result of someone being lovesick, visited by ghosts, or stung by insects. If people talked or walked in their dreams they were said to be possessed by spirits.

The word *nightmare* comes from the German word *nachtmar*, which means *night devil*. The witch doctors of old used the Latin terms *incubus* and *succubus* to describe night terrors in which young women or young men were raped by demons during the night—they referred to such events as incubus or succubus attacks. They believed that an incubus was an evil spirit who lies on top of sleeping women and has intercourse with them; a succubus was a spirit who lies under sleeping men and has anal intercourse with them. The popular novel, *Rosemary's Baby*, illustrates this theme.

Indeed, most dream dictionaries are nothing more than compilations of the superstitious meanings historically attached to dreams. One of the first, called *The Dictionary of Dreams* (Miller 1884), came out a few years before Freud's *Interpretation of Dreams* (1900). It boasts of explaining 10,000 dreams. Among the explanations are the following: "Hearing an ass bray is significant of unwelcome tidings or intrusions" (p. 104). "Sickness sometimes follows dreams of old negroes" (p. 399). "To dream of gathering nuts augurs successful enterprises, and much favor in love" (p. 405). "For a woman to dream that she is pregnant denotes she will be unhappy with her husband, and her children will be unattractive" (pp. 456–457). "To see violets in your dreams, or to gather them, brings joyous occasions in which you will find favor with some superior person" (p. 580). "If you yawn in your dreams you will search in vain for health and contentment" (p. 614). Miller's compendium is still a best seller today, which shows that a great many people still believe in such methods of interpretation.

The first systematized research on dreams was conducted by Greek and Roman philosophers. In his work, *On Divination*, Aristotle (312 B.C.) theorized that dreams were of two kinds: some were visualizations of plans and principles of action and could serve predictive functions, while others were simply accidents that did not deserve attention. Artemidorus, in the second century A.D., wrote the first how-to book on the interpretation of dreams (Wood 1947). According to him there were five kinds of dreams: dreams (messages conveyed by symbols), visions (occurring when one sees something in a dream that he later sees on awakening), oracles (messages from angels), fantasies (wish fulfillments), and apparitions (ghosts appearing before weak infants and old people).

Many other philosophers and poets have written about dreams since Aristotle and Artemidorus. Goethe believed that our power of imagination—as well as our innate strivings for health and happiness—were enhanced by our dream life. "There have been times in my life when I have fallen asleep in tears; but in my dreams the most charming forms have come to console and to cheer me, and I have risen the next morning fresh and joyful" (quoted in Fromm 1951, p. 140).

One of the most eloquent speculations on dreams comes from the philosopher Emerson:

Dreams have a poetic integrity and truth. . . . Their extravagance from nature is yet within a higher nature. They seem to us to suggest an abundance and fluency of thought not familiar to the waking experience. They pique us by independence of us, yet we know ourselves in this mad crowd, and owe to dreams a kind of divination and wisdom. [1904, p. 7]

Freud's Contribution

At the time Freud was writing *The Interpretation of Dreams*, the scholarly community had just begun to explore the significance of dreaming. Some scholars considered dreams as representing mental forces that have been prevented from actualizing themselves during waking hours (Volkelt 1875). A vivid dream life was considered by such philosophers to be associated with a sharper memory. On the other hand, empirical scientists such as Binz (1878) considered dreams as nothing more than somatic processes that are not only meaningless but in many cases pathological (a view shared by some scientists today).

With the advent of Freud and psychoanalysis, dream research reached a new, more scientific plateau. Like those who went before him, he analyzed his own dreams, but he also had the advantage of analyzing the dreams of his patients and studying them at length, codifying the patterns and symbols he found there. Freud offered a convincing, detailed explanation of the meaning and function of dreams (although, as previously noted, various philosophers and artists had foreshadowed his views). Basically, he held that dreaming represents one of the most important activities of the unconscious mind.

According to his initial theory, all dreams are symbolic wish fulfillments of desires that are repressed by the conscious mind, usually sexual wishes. He later modified that theory in *Beyond the Pleasure Principle* (1920), noting that dreams occurring in traumatic neuroses (what today we call *post-traumatic stress disorder*) were not wish fulfillments but related to a compulsion to repeat the trauma that caused the stress. However, some modern psychoanalysts have theorized that in such cases there is an implied wish to master the earlier trauma by repeating it in dreams. Shur (1966), for example, suggests that in nightmares the patient's ego wishes to undo the trauma by repeatedly dreaming of it.

In young children the wish fulfillment of dreams is readily apparent: the child dreams that he receives a coveted toy or goes on a trip to an amusement park. In adults, whose repression is stronger than that in children, the wish or desire is clothed in symbols that are more difficult to understand. Nevertheless, Freud attempted to demonstrate that nearly all dreams, including anxiety dreams, are fueled by a conscious or unconscious wish. For example, a man might dream that strange men are chasing him and trying to kill him. Upon analysis, it turns out that the man is feeling guilty about something, and so the wish in this dream is that he might be punished for his wrongdoing.

Just as he coined the terms *conscious* and *unconscious* to depict levels of human awareness and mental functioning, Freud also came up with the related terms *manifest* and *latent* content with respect to dreams. The manifest dream is the dream that is reported and of which the dreamer is immediately aware. The instigating source of this manifest dream can usually be traced to something that happened to the dreamer in the preceding day or days, termed by Freud the *day residue*. The latent content consists of the unconscious associations to the dream, and it will usually lead back to a wish as well as to repressed memories, emotions, and thoughts. Hence, Freud wrote that dreams were the "royal road to the unconscious."

In studying the distorted symbolism of most adult dreams, Freud postulated that the dreamer's original dream thoughts become distorted due to what he called the *dream work*. The dream work is responsible for "transforming the dream thoughts into the dream content" through "condensation and displacement of the material and its modification into pictorial form" (1901, p. 76). That is, the plots of dreams are compressed and feelings and forbidden thoughts are attributed to people other than the dreamer. Freud also added *secondary elaboration* to the functions of the dream work, referring to the changes to the dream content one makes when, in the process of recalling the dream, one tries to make the dream more logical and intelligent.

Another process that affects the manifest content of a dream is the dream censorship. Even though an individual's repression loosens up during sleep, the dream censorship still censors the contents of dreams, obfuscating and rendering them palpable to the ego. Upon waking, the censorship—that is, the resistance to acknowledging forbidden thoughts—is even stronger, and the dream is almost immediately forgotten. Even if a dream is remembered, resistance to the understanding of dreams, the key element of dream censorship (1933), is still ever-present and makes the task difficult.

While, according to Freud, dreams primarily represent unconscious wishes symbolically played out, the function of dreams is to serve as the guardians of sleep and dischargers of frustrated impulses. This role can be seen most clearly in the dreams of children. A child is told he must go to sleep despite the fact that he wants to go on playing. Since his wish to play has been frustrated in real life, he dreams that he is still playing as he sleeps. Dreams are generally believed as they are happening, so the dream shows the wish as fulfilled and enables the boy to sleep on. And, like a night watchman, the dream also awakens the dreamer if the contents of the dream are too full of anxiety. An individual may dream about a tapping at his bedroom door, for example, and imagines that he opens the door and nobody is there (which allows him to continue to sleep). However, if the tapping goes on too long, the dreamer becomes anxious and awakes—and finds that his child is tapping at his door and needs his attention.

Freud's method of interpreting dreams was threefold. First the patient was asked to recall the manifest content of the dream. Then he was asked to associate to it. Only after considering the manifest content and its associations, along with the dreamer's background, was Freud able to interpret a dream.

Other psychoanalysts have refined and extended Freud's theories. Jung (1971) believed that there are certain universal patterns in the unconscious that emerge in dreams, works of art, myths, and fairy tales in all societies. He thought these universal symbols or archetypes—such as "the hero" or "the snake swallowing its own tail"—formed the collective unconscious common to all humankind. Jung criticized Freud for basing too many of his theories on sexual repression, including his interpretation of dreams, and he had a point. However, Jung tended to veer toward mysticism, viewing dreams more abstractly as manifestations either of the collective unconscious—which Ackroyd (1993) describes as a grab bag of human primitive thinking—or other spiritual forces, while minimizing the importance of sexuality. Stekel (1911) also contributed to the understanding of dream symbolism, writing extensively on the language of dreams.

Gutheil (1951) elaborated on Freud's theories about the purpose and meanings of dreams. He saw three purposes of dreaming: (1) protection of sleep, (2) regulation of the affect metabolism (feelings), and (3) protection of the integrity of the ego. He contended that dreams are not only wish fulfillments, but can also represent:

- *discharges of emotional energy*—as when we feel like attacking an adversary and do so in our dreams instead;
- *preventions of shocks*—as when we fear a dear one will die soon and we repeatedly envision him dying in our dreams so as to prepare ourselves for the eventuality;
- *warnings*—as when we dream of potentially dangerous situations (failing an upcoming test, having illicit relations that turn out badly), so as to alert ourselves about them;
- *solutions*—as when we cannot quite solve a problem and then in a dream, through indirect symbolism, we find the answer.

As an example of a solution dream, Gutheil alludes to Kekule, the inventor of the graphic representation of the benzene ring. After many years of fruitless attempts to draw the configuration of atoms in such a ring, he dreamed of a snake biting his own tail. He awakened and immediately drew the formula on paper. Kekule's vision of the benzene ring has been hailed as one of the most brilliant pieces of prediction to be found in organic chemistry.

Regarding the third function of the dream, protecting the integrity of the ego, Gutheil explains that the dream protects the ego by acting as a buffer between sleep (when the ego ceases to exist) and awakening. "[I]t thus preserves the continuity, cohesion, and unity of our mental processes" (1951, p. 37).

Gutheil's expansion of the purposes of dreams is a useful one, harkening back to the classifications of Artemidorus. However, I agree with Freud that there is invariably a wish underneath almost every dream, whether that wish is direct (dreaming of food to satisfy hunger), indirect (dreaming of punishment to atone for guilt), or implied (dreaming of traumatic horror in order to master it).

Most psychoanalysts have noted that dreams can have as many themes as there are literary forms. "The dreaming experience is rather like being a stupe: the dreamed self is an everyman," Bollas notes (1995, p. 233). Dreams often express unconscious desires, but sometimes they also address unconscious fears, frustrations, or doubts; they can be fables or allegories, nonsensical farces or scathing satires, melodramas or tragedies.

Bollas relates a humorous dream, which followed a challenge by a colleague to the effect that Bollas needed courage to take a certain action. In a dream that night he found himself being discussed by a large assembly of medical personnel. He was on an operating table or autopsy bench, covered by a sheet. He lifted the sheet to find that underneath was a chicken. The chicken was himself, a roast chicken, in fact, "rather well done." Bollas interpreted the dream to mean that he was "dead meat," that he had "chickened out." The dream was a comedy, he decided, that expressed his fear that he would not be up to the task. "This dream was a comic event and I was the butt of my own unconscious" (p. 232).

The meaning of any dream, in short, depends very much on who the dreamer is, where he is in terms of his emotional and mental life, and what his associations are to the dream. Only after all this is considered can the dream symbols be interpreted.

Sleep and Dream Research

Psychoanalysts have used their own intuitions and their investigations of the dreams of numerous patients in order to establish their theories. Other researchers have used a more empirical approach.

In recent years physiologists have collected evidence from the electroencephalogram (EEG), an instrument used for recording brain waves, in studying the electrical activity of the brain during sleep. They have found four recognizable stages of sleep, each with a typical brain wave pattern. They run from stage one—the shallowest—to stage four—the deepest, and seem to resemble the stages of hypnotic trances. Throughout the night, an individual passes from one stage to another. It is in the second stage that most dreams occur. This stage has been called REM (rapid eye movement) sleep because of the eye movements that can be observed under the closed eyelids of sleepers during such periods, indicating that the sleeper is dreaming and is actually visualizing his dreams in his "mind's eye."

The stages of REM sleep lengthen during the night, and reach their longest points in the hours just before waking, perhaps because the dream impulses continue to build momentum through the night. While dreaming, the sleeper becomes very still (except for the rapid eye movements), just as does a person hypnotized.

Since the rapid eye movements during the second stage of sleep can be recorded even while the eyes remain closed, they provide an objective method for studying the incidence and duration of dreams. Experiments conducted since the late

1950s have revealed that most dreaming occurs in the latter part of the night, and that dreams last anywhere from several minutes to more than an hour. It has been estimated that the average person has more than 1,000 dreams a year (Faraday 1974).

Although many people do not recall dreams in the morning, the evidence from studies of eye movements proves that everybody dreams, except perhaps some schizophrenics (more on that later). The dreaming state associated with REM sleep is also characterized by a high degree of electrical activity in the brain, together with an unusually relaxed state of musculature, higher levels of male and female hormonal production, and erections in men. It has also been noted that the dreamer is difficult to awaken while in that state.

Greenberg and Pearlman (1974) and McGrath and Cohen (1978) show that the large body of sleep research indicates that sleep is involved in the processing of new information in both humans and animals. In animals, this phenomenon seems to follow the integration of unusual experiences into the animal's behavioral repertoire. Experiments in which dogs were taught to press a knob with their paws in order to get food showed that when they slept their eyes would move and their paws twitch. In humans, the anxiety of starting a new job or marriage often ends up in similar eye and body movements during REM sleep. Greenberg and Pearlman conclude from this evidence that dreams "are part of our struggle to make emotional sense of our experiences," (p. 520) and assert that REM physiology suports the psychoanalytic theories about dreams being stages for wish fulfillments and the symbolic enactment and discharging of pent-up impulses and feelings.

However, not all dreams happen during REM sleep. Keith (1975) distinguishes between the REM nightmare or bad dream and the night terror that appears to occur in the deepest stage of sleep. According to Keith, a night terror happens during stage four, with arousal to an awake, alpha pattern on the EEG. There is pronounced autonomic activity during the attack—fast pulse, perspiration, rapid breathing—as well as increased physical activity, including tossing and turning and somnambulism. In addition, talking and screaming often occur. The night terror, if recalled, is terrifying, violent, aggressive, and quite emotional. If awakened the dreamer is confused, disoriented, and amnesic.

On the other hand, the bad dream, which Keith calls the *anxiety dream* occurs in REM sleep, with only minor autonomic changes, decreased muscle tone, little physical movement, only occasional talking, rare screaming, and elaborate, vivid mental content. If awakened from a REM anxiety dream the dreamer is easily calmed and lucid. The memory of the dream is much more clear.

Broughton (1968) demonstrated that what he called *night terrors* of adults and children, as well as somnambulism and nocturnal bed-wetting, all seem to pertain to the deeper stages of sleep—stages three and four—and all involve a sudden change in the mental stage from that of deep sleep (slow-wave EEG patterns) to an arousal pattern (alpha-wave EEG). Thus, although during this process the person remains asleep, the brain is in a dissociated state of arousal. This arousal state is normal for all people, happening at regular cycles throughout night. Most people sleep through it.

In his investigations, Broughton noticed that those individuals prone to night terrors, bed-wetting, and somnambulism were generally hyperactive during the entire night, not just during the deeper stages. For such individuals, the arousal period merely seemed to push them over the edge. In other words, people prone to the night terrors were people who were already under a lot of distress and carrying the freight of past traumas inside of them. Because of this increased hyperactivity, such invidividuals wake up in terror.

Friedman (1980) postulates that night terrors are related to the most deep-seated kinds of emotional trauma, such as physical or sexual abuse, rape, war, or some other natural or artificial catastrophe, leading to post-traumatic stress disorder. Hence, night terrors would be the result of the "repressed past intruding into the unguarded ego of deep sleep" (p. 314). Perhaps, Friedman adds, the night terror is an aspect of Freud's "compulsion to repeat"—an attempt to master a traumatic situation by continually repeating it in nightmares.

With regard to symbolization in dreams, Bettelheim and Hartmann (1924) conducted some interesting research with sufferers of Korsakoff Psychosis. They presented a group of these patients with erotic texts and then asked them to repeat them from memory. They found that in repeating these stories, their patients tended to use condensation, displacement, and symbolization similar to that occurring in dreams. One of the texts went as follows: "A young girl took a walk alone in a field. Suddenly a man came along and attacked her and threw her down. The girl struggled hard against him, but in vain. The man lifted her skirts and inserted his membrum into her vagina. After the intercourse, he left the girl alone lying on the field and weeping loudly."

One of the patients repeated the story as: "Two girls walked upstairs. Two boys followed them. Then they married the girls because one of them was pregnant; the other went home." Another described the intercourse as the man putting "the knife into the sheath." Another substituted "cigarette" for "membrum." The symbolization of such patients runs along similar lines to that of retarded people, children, and primitive tribes, and appears to be related to the kind of symbolization found in dreams.

The sleep and dream research of physiologists, experimental psychologists, and psychiatrists has confirmed that all people dream (even those who claim they do not). It has also revealed when and how often they dream. It has confirmed that animals also dream and that both humans and animals do so in connection with frustrating events in their lives (day residues of traumatic events). These researchers have also studied the production of symbols as a way of disguising forbidden thoughts. This research augments the theories of psychoanalysis.

Dream Research with Various Character Types

Dream research in more recent times has expanded our understanding of the relationship between dreams and the dreamer. Psychiatrists, studying the dreams of various character types, have discovered that each character type has his or her own typical kind of dream, and each dream has a particular meaning according to the type of character who dreams it. Some character types also have particular ways of relating dreams and associating to them. Generally the more cut off people are from their unconscious, the more abstract and unintelligible are their dreams, whereas during the course of therapy dreams tend to become more intelligible and meaningful.

The schizophrenic, according to Kafka (1980), reports no dreams while caught up in the throes of an acute episode. Whether or not this means that the schizophrenic does not dream during such periods is a matter of debate. Some psychoanalysts have interpreted this apparent lack of dreaming as having to do with the fact that the schizophrenic, when going through the most insane periods, tends to hallucinate (an extreme form of wakeful dreaming), eliminating the necessity of dreaming at night. Kafka also points to an observation made by Freud and Eissler that a schizophrenic's dreams seem more real than his or her daytime delusions. In contrast, the daytime world of neurotics is based more on reality than that of schizophrenics, while their dreams are more unreal.

As an example of this observation, Kafka writes, "I accidentally discovered many years ago that when I woke a hospitalized schizophrenic patient with a complex paranoid delusional system, for five or ten minutes he was apparently free of delusions" (p. 104). Although he was not able to confirm that the patient had been dreaming, he speculates that this might well have been the case, and it is his contention that dreaming, for psychotics as well as for neurotics, serves a reparative function.

While Pao does not believe that dreams of those diagnosed as manic-depressive have specific characteristics, he maintains that "on account of the varying ego organization during a full manic depressive cycle, the dreams during the manic, depressive, and the normal phases could show some differences" (1980, p. 111). He cites the "blank dream" of the manic phase. The literature has shown that it is common for manic-depressives to dream about blankness (like seeing a blank screen) when they are about to erupt out of a depressive mode into a manic mode. Generally, something has occurred during the preceding day that plugs into the manic-depressive's fear of dying (a common theme of individuals suffering from this form of psychopathology). Perhaps a close relative dies, or they lose a friend or lover; this in turn brings to consciousness repressed memories of an earlier trauma. The blank dream represents a wish to die or sleep, and the mania that usually follows such a dream represents the attempt at defending against the dangers of falling asleep.

On the other hand, the dreams of those diagnosed as clinically depressed have typical themes, according to Bonime (1980), that correspond to traits of the depressive personality: manipulativeness, hypersensitivity to coercion coupled with a tendency to interpret the attentions of others as efforts to coerce, unwill-ingness to enhance others, anxiety, and an emotional core of indirectly expressed anger. He sums it up by characterizing the basic affect of depressives as "angry unwillingness" (p. 145).

He describes one dream of a depressive patient: she and her husband were before a fireplace in their living room and the husband was going to put the baby on the fire. (Their real children were of school age.) Although she felt horrified, she did not try to stop him. She walked out of the room, thinking it was up to her husband to rescue the baby. Suddenly she changed her mind and decided to save the baby from the flames.

Bonime interprets this dream as follows: the baby represents the dreamer, who often felt "burned up" (angry at her husband). Her feeling that it is her husband's business to rescue the baby stems from the conviction that becoming pregnant and having the baby in the first place was his fault, and also from her general "angry unwillingness," which related to events in her childhood that had embittered her. Therapeutic movement for her, he claims, would depend on her development of a willingness to make use of her resources and assert herself.

With obsessive individuals, it is not so much the content of their dreams that has a special quality, but their manner of verbalizing it. In treating a number of obses-sives, I have found that their dreams do not tend to conform to any one theme. However, their way of relating the dream is highly avoidant and obsessive about details. This observation is confirmed by other researchers. "Circumstantiality and a circuitous avoidance of direct statement—often to a tortuous degree—recurs throughout treatment," notes Namrow (1980, p. 156). He states that some obses-sives will use dream production as a "handmaiden for resistance," coming up with one dream after another, and relating them in a detached, distracted, intellectual manner, as a way of keeping a distance from the therapist or other primary figures in his or her life. This also accords with my findings.

The dreams of phobics, on the other hand, are quite often anxiety dreams. One of the most famous of such dreams is that of Freud's patient, the Wolf Man (Freud 1918). He had an irrational phobia of being eaten by wolves, and his recurring dream, at age four, was that a tree outside his window was filled with wolves who were calmly looking at him. After listening to the patient's associations, Freud was led to speculate that the Wolf Man had, as a toddler, witnessed his parents having sexual intercourse. He interpreted that the patient's phobia was based on his fear and unconscious wish to be castrated and devoured in the course of seeking homo-sexual gratification from his father. In addition to anxiety, the dreams of phobics, according to Pomer and Shain (1980), show a distinct clarity and lack of disguise that reveal the basic conflicts and dynamics of the phobia.

I have previously written about a woman patient who had a phobia of buttons (Schoenewolf 1994). This woman spent much of her young adulthood avoiding looking at people's buttons, especially men's buttons. Hence her eyes were always staying on people's faces or their feet. If she glanced at a button, she became nauseated. In her dreams there were often images of buttons and also themes of people chasing her. Eventually she was able to remember an incident of her childhood in which she had been sexually abused by a man who had been wearing long under-wear—the kind with buttons from the neck to the crotch. These buttons had come to symbolize not only the phallus but also the incestuous feelings she had had while being abused by this older man.

Borderline personality types have little ability to tolerate anxiety or stress; instead, underlying conflicts are acted out. Hence, the dreams of borderlines may be full of anxiety and stress, yet they do not care to analyze them. Upon recalling the dreams, they will immediately begin acting out, rather than associating to, the dream's contents. Lebe (1980) points out that the dreams of borderlines are replete with memories from a time when they could not yet talk and when acting out was the way in which they expressed themselves (i.e., as toddlers).

People prone to psychomatic illnesses use dreams as a substitute for grief, accord-ing to Levitan (1980). Such people tend to harbor a lot of unconscious grief about the losses of important people or things in their lives (parents, spouses, girlfriends, jobs, etc.), but are unable consciously to acknowledge this grief or to work it through. Hence, the grief gets partially worked on in their dreams, but expresses itself primarily through an illness.

Levitan, who believes that some kinds of arthritis are psychosomatic, cites a case of a 59-year-old woman with severe rheumatoid arthritis. Her condition worsened sharply after her husband's suicide, but at the time she was aware of little feeling about his death. Instead, she was completely bedridden and would lie about with a blank mind. In the midst of this situation, her daughter told her she was going to move to another city. That night the woman dreamed that a neighbor was crying. She rushed up to the neighbor and asked why she was crying, and the neighbor replied that she was crying because "your daughter is going on an airplane." The dreamer answered that there was no reason to be frightened about that, as the daughter was used to flying.

Even in this dream the woman could not allow herself to experience her feelings directly. The feeling of loss was there, but it was projected onto another person and transformed into a fear of flying rather than a sadness at her daughter's departure—and her husband's.

Ravenscroft and Hartmann (1968) demonstrated that nocturnal asthma attacks are more likely to occur during REM periods than other stages of sleep. This may support the thesis that physiological overstimulation, which sets the stage for the development of illness, may occur during dreams. Any chronic state that happens nightly over a period of time would seem to be capable of being a factor in illness formation.

Studying the dreams of perverse patients, Socarides (1980) finds that many of them depict the very same perverse acts for which they seek therapy. However, in the manifest dream, the perversion is experienced without the usual interfering factors, anxieties and frustrations. Hence, the masochist will dream of spanking, a pedophile will dream of sex with children, a glove fetishist will visualize women in gloves, and a voyeur will dream of peeping at a naked neighbor. The dream serves to alleviate anxiety and stabilize the sense of the dreamer's perversion being acceptable.

These are just a few of the personality types that have been observed by researchers. The list could be longer and could also encompass people's predicaments: starving people dream about food, suicidal people have suicidal dreams, amputees dream about regaining their limbs, trauma victims have nightmares about trauma, students dream of passing or failing tests. The bottom line is that the dream is always closely connected to the personality, background, and associations of the dreamer. No interpretation can be made without the full spectrum of such data.

Modern Dream Interpretation

Although there has been a lot of research on dreams and their significance, the interpretation of dreams remains an art, just as does the interpretation of a poem, a parable, or a painting. However, that art can be aided through the rigorous application of knowledge and methodology, just as the interpretation of a poem can be aided by a wide-ranging knowledge of art and the methodology of interpreting art. Yet, even the interpretations of the most learned art critics disagree with one another, and so too do the interpretations of the most well-trained psychoanalysts and psychotherapists.

The main problem arises when the interpreter of a dream is too wedded to a particular school of psychoanalysis or psychotherapy, or to a particular philosophy, political bias, or religion. In the *Bible*, all the symbols were interpreted in terms of Judaeo-Christian teachings. Political radicals will interpret dreams or literary symbols in terms of the struggle of the underdog against the oppressor. Followers of Kleinian psychoanalysis interpret any container as either a good or bad breast. Orthodox Freudians see every cigar as a phallus, despite Freud's often-repeated disclaimer that "sometimes a cigar is just a cigar."

Most of us who do therapy and interpret dreams today tend to be eclectic. Rather than focusing on the symbols of the dream and attempting to fit them into our own theory, we focus on the dreamer and the dreamer's associations. If possible, we do not interpret at all; instead, we guide the dreamer through the process of recalling the dream, associating to it, and making the connections that allow the dream to, in effect, interpret itself. The more initiative the dreamer takes, the more meaningful will be the dream.

There have been many definitions of the aims and functions of dreams. My own way of defining dreams is a bit broader than most and metaphorical: dreams are the dustbins of forbidden thoughts and frustrated desires. They are the night elves of unfinished business. They represent our brain's attempt to process the psychic material that has backed up in our system during waking hours. They are the night-time idea processors.

However, modern dream interpretation is more concerned with the process of interpreting the dream than with definitions of what dreams represent. It does not matter whether or not we determine that dreams represent a wish, a warning, a solution, a punishment, a prediction, or the mastery of a traumatic situation. It does not matter whether dreams are guardians of sleep or, as Faraday (1974) puts it, "watchdogs of the psyche," (p. 14) or the dustbins of forbidden thoughts and frustrated desires. What matters is—how does this particular dream relate to this particular person? What is the unconscious trying to say about the person's inner conflicts? What can the person learn from the dream's latent message? One of the mistakes Freud and other early psychoanalysts made was to get too caught up in the scholarly pursuit of deciphering dreams and lose sight of their actual relationship with their patients, for which dreams can offer a bridge.

The first step across that bridge, of course, is to understand the symbols of the dreams (see Glossary of Dream Symbols), but that is only one step. Even though the symbols in a dream are generally personal, having to do with each individual's associations, the symbolization usually proceeds along a certain path, which we call *symbolic parallelism*. That is, symbols occur as a compromise between two or more opposing ideas. For example, a woman who feels that intercourse with her boyfriend is like being murdered and fears she will die during orgasm, dreams of being shot by a man. In this case shooting symbolizes intercourse, which is to her a kind of soul murder.

Not only do we interpret dreams, but we also use them to help us determine where a patient is in terms of his or her therapy and in terms of development. They help us to know what intervention to use. And once people become proficient in dream interpretation, they can also use dreams to check up on their own unconscious thoughts, feelings, and impulses.

In psychoanalysis it has become a truism that everything a patient says about childhood, work, or home life is at the same time a message to the psychoanalyst. This idea certainly holds true for dreams. Every dream that is brought in not only has a meaning with respect to the patient's life, but also with respect to the analysis. A patient may dream that she is being led by a strange man through a dark hallway into another dark hallway and that people are yelling and hissing at them as they walk by. This dream not only alludes to the dreamer's past and present situations, but also to the therapy. She feels the therapist is leading her down a dark hallway (to her unconscious, which she fears) and feels guilty about doing so, because her parents and siblings (the people who are yelling and hissing) do not want her to talk about them. By understanding such dreams we can better determine what approach to take toward the patient. This kind of dream interpretation can also be applied outside the therapy office. A husband and wife, sharing dreams with one another, may also use them to help bridge a communication gap.

By studying a series of dreams over a period of time, we can determine a patient's progress. Generally speaking, dreams become less censored, less distorted, and less symbolic over time, as that which was unconscious becomes conscious. A pyroma-

niac may at first offer dreams about abstract scenes of burning buildings with
strangers inside. "A building was burning. Many people inside. I went to work and
asked Bill to have lunch with me. . . ." A series of dreams about fire begins to tell
us of this obsession, but not much more. Then the symbols become clearer: "A couple inside their apartment notice a fire in their filing cabinet. It quickly spreads. A
child is standing somewhere." Now the people who are burned become a couple,
and a child is introduced. The filing cabinet denotes some kind of record or history, telling us that this is a memory. Finally, many sessions later: "My mother and
father are lying in bed. Their bed catches fire. I'm outside the building watching.
Somehow, I have started the fire, but now I must put it out." The dream fits in with
what we know about the dreamer's background—his anger at both parents for having to sleep in the same room with them as a child and witness their sexual intercourse, and the recurring dreams and fantasies of burning their bed.

Another technique I use, particularly with those who are artistically inclined, is to
have them sketch their dreams. A man may say, "I dreamed I woke up with a tumor
in my stomach." We cannot be quite sure what he means so I tell him to sketch the
dream. The resulting drawing (see Figure 1–1) helps us to understand. The tumor is
not in the stomach, but lower down, and it has the shape of a fetus. The meaning of
the dream is now more apparent: it expresses his wish to have a baby.

Figure 1–1

Sometimes I encourage *lucid dreaming* to effect change, giving patients assign-
ments to carry out while they are dreaming. Hence, a patient who dreams of falling
is told that the next time he has this dream he is to allow himself to hit bottom in
order to find out what it is that he fears. At the bottom, for example, he may find
his wife, who suspects him of cheating and is thinking of leaving him. Or a woman
may dream of being chased by a dark figure or monster. She is assigned to take a good

look at the figure in the next dream in order to determine who he is. Perhaps she will find her husband, her father, her brother, or some other familiar figure there.

Using dreams in this way is not new. It was quite common for the shamans of primitive tribes to use dreams for curative purposes. The Senoi, a tribe that once lived on an island in the Pacific Ocean, would discuss their dreams every morning. If a child had had a nightmare, the elders would tell him or her to dream the same dream again the following night and to make adjustments to it, such as the ones described above. It was a routine part of their child rearing.

Modern dream interpretation attempts to get people back to the simplicity of our ancestors in the days before technology and overpopulation inundated society. Dreams themselves are a primitive language. Freud referred to the kind of language we find in dreams as *primary process* and called the language that was learned in school *secondary process*. Unfortunately, as modern humans have become more educated and cultured, they have lost touch with their primary process. Many of the ailments of modern man may be traced to this factor. Today we find more and more computer addicts, spending almost all their leisure time (and sometimes work time as well) eyeing their monitors. Their relationship with their computer is more important than those with other people or with themselves. Such individuals have a great deal of difficulty remembering their dreams; the primary process of dreams, and of life, is beyond their reach.

Dreams offer a good way of getting back in touch with it. Despite all the advances in dream research over the years, we may just now be reaching the advanced stage of interpretation that was enjoyed by the Senoi. Only now we have the advantage of having studied dreams clinically for over a century and of confirming that, without any doubt, they have a life and meaning of their own. By understanding the meaning of dreams we have while we are asleep, we can lessen the impact of their undercurrents while we are awake.

Dictionary of Dreams

Abandonment

Dream: I was swimming in a large body of water, like an ocean. It was dark and cold. I felt completely abandoned and terrified. Then I swam into a small cove and the water turned warm.

Dreamer: A 37-year-old man with a schizoid personality who had grown up in a foster home. His real parents had been killed in an automobile accident when he was 4.

Association: He had a quarrel with his landlady the day before over paying the rent (he was always late). He was afraid she would kick him out of the apartment, and he didn't think that was fair. He didn't know why she couldn't be more understanding.

Interpretation: The dreamer's fear of being kicked out of his apartment by his landlady may hark back to memories of having been abandoned by his parents. His foster parents had never understood his feelings of longing for his real parents. Like the landlady, they were not understanding. The cove with warm water may represent the womb, and the wish is to go back to the womb of his mother and get the maternal love that he once lost. He feels he is entitled to pay the rent late without punishment as a recompense for having suffered this original abandonment.

Abdomen

Dream: I'm pregnant, but the fetus is growing in my abdomen instead of my uterus. I am sitting in the hospital getting ready to give birth, but I'm dressed in a man's pin-striped suit. My brother is there and he is frowning at me.

Dreamer: A 38-year-old gender-confused woman who has grown up in a family in which both parents favored her older brother and were overly controlling with her.

Association: She didn't know why the fetus was growing in her abdomen instead of her uterus. She guessed that if she were a man she would have to give birth that way. If her brother gave birth, he would have to do it that way.

Interpretation: The dream shows the dreamer's main conflict—her struggle with respect to her sexual identity. She wants to be a woman (give birth), but she also wants to be a man like her favored brother (who often wears a pin-striped suit), so she has to give birth by using her abdomen. Her brother is frowning because she has in effect done something he cannot do, worn "the pants" and had a baby, hence finally surpassing him. The dream suggests her wish to have the best of both masculine and feminine worlds.

Abortion

Dream: I was very sick and then I had an abortion and felt better. I had the feeling that something evil had been removed from me.

Dreamer: A 30-year-old woman suffering from obsessive-compulsive disorder.

Association: When she had sex with her boyfriend the day before, she began worrying about becoming pregnant.

Interpretation: This dream may be a warning about getting pregnant on one level, and on another it is a wish to have an abortion. The evil fetus represents the dreamer's conscious sense of something evil inside her, and the wish is that it could be removed. In this case the evil may be the woman's rage at her mother pertaining to her feelings about having been an unwanted infant. In the dream, this rage gets displaced onto herself (the evil in herself) and to her own growing offspring.

Dream: I was sitting on the toilet when suddenly I heard a plop and looked down and saw a fetus floating in the water.

Dreamer: A 21-year-old single pregnant woman.

Association: She had become pregnant by mistake and her boyfriend had left her. She wished she were not pregnant.

Interpretation: Sometimes dreams have literal meanings. In this dream, the dreamer avoids the dilemma of having to decide between an abortion or bringing up the baby as a single mother.

Accident

Dream: I was standing on the corner near my house. I saw a woman across the street and she ran toward me. I stepped into the street to kiss her, but I did not become erect. Suddenly there was an accident; a car whirled around the corner and hit the woman, killing her. I felt very guilty, as if her death were my fault.

Dreamer: A 40-year-old man who had a conflict about his sexual orientation. He had been an only child of rich parents, who had left him in the care of servants. His mother had treated him coldly, and his father had been absent much of the time.

Associations: He recalled looking at a woman in his office the day before with mild interest, and then thinking to himself that he would not be able to get an erection with her. Then he recalled his mother's disapproving face.

Interpretation: The dream may be an allusion to his present conflict between heterosexuality and homosexuality, and to his past problems with his mother. The woman represents both the woman he had seen the day before and all women, toward whom he is ambivalent. She also represents his mother, who originally engendered this ambivalence (her disapproving face). The accident suggests a displacement of this ambivalence toward his mother in the form of murderous wishes, for which he feels guilty. The dream may also be a warning that if he shows interest in a woman something bad will happen.

Acting

Dream: I'm watching a movie on TV. Suddenly I'm also acting in the movie. I'm acting two roles, those of the hero and the villain. Afterwards I discuss the movie with my friends and ask for their comments about my acting. Nobody has detected that I was playing both parts.

Dreamer: A young man with a borderline personality and a tendency to project and depersonalize.

Associations: He remembered going to see a movie the night of the dream that had a plot similar to the one in his dream movie. As he had watched the real movie, he had sensed that he was not inside his body.

Interpretation: The movie or theatrical performance a patient sees in a dream is generally the story of his own life or the life he wishes to have. It is a projection of his primary conflicts. In this instance, the dream shows the split in his personality between good and bad (as if he were two different people). In reality, he generally splits off his aggressive (villainous) impulses and projects them onto others, viewing others as bad and himself as a victim. The fact that nobody detects that he has played two roles may be an indication of how much he feels he is acting in his daily life. His association of not being in his body as he watched the original movie describes his depersonalization. The dream could be an attempt to integrate his two sides.

Admiration

Dream: I'm skiing down a hill, racing with several other skiers. I soar ahead of them. Many beautiful girls are standing on the sides, smiling at me with admiration. I pass them by.

Dreamer: A 32-year-old postal worker with narcissistic and masochistic features in his personality.

Association: I went skiing this weekend but I felt very lonely. I kept comparing myself to the other men.

Interpretation: Skiing downhill and outracing other men expresses the dreamer's competitive drive (comparing himself to other men). His passing by a string of admiring girls could indicate both his narcissistic wish for the admiration of beautiful girls and his fear of getting close to them. The skis may be phalluses, and skiing alone may be masturbation.

Advice

Dream: A couple was in trouble with the law. They asked me for advice. I told them not to tell the truth.

Dreamer: A 40-year-old businessman.

Association: He had had a quarrel with his wife the night of the dream because he had acknowledged flirting with another woman.

Interpretation: The dreamer appears to wish that he had not told his wife the truth, and therefore advises the couple not to tell the truth in his dream.

Aging

Dream: I am suddenly 50 years old and have had a good job for about 30 years. My boss gives me a raise. The secretaries love me. Then I have to leave and everybody is sorry to see me go.

Dreamer: A boy of 9, whose father, at age 50, had divorced his mother. At the time of the dream, the mother was angry at the boy because he was neglecting his schoolwork.

Association: He could never forgive his mother for allowing the marriage to collapse. He was always studying his father's old pictures, trying to imitate him.

Interpretation: This is a revenge dream. In it, the dreamer has become like his father, 50 years old and a successful businessman. And, like his father, he also leaves his mother. (His mother had also nagged his father, just as she now nagged him about school.) The father went away (divorced his mother) at a time when the boy most admired and needed him. In the dream he emulates him. His mother (perhaps one of the secretaries) is sad to see him go.

Dream: I looked in the mirror and I was 21 years old again.

Dreamer: A 42-year-old man who had grown impotent with his wife.

Association: When he thought about the age of 21, he thought about his daughter, who had turned 21.

Interpretation: The man had an unconscious erotic fixation toward his daughter. If he were her age, he could actualize it.

Airplane

Dream: My friend Michael and I were in the subway and we were trying to get to the airport. But there were crowds of people in the subway, getting in our way. Michael was running ahead, knocking people down. Finally we got to the airport, but we missed our plane. I was so disgusted I threw up.

Dreamer: A 40-year-old woman from a large dysfunctional family, whose parents had been alcoholics.

Associations: Michael reminded her of the boy who lived next door to her when she was a child. Throwing up in the dream reminded her of a time when her parents were fighting and she felt the same disgust as in the dream and threw up.

Interpretation: The dream is an anxiety dream that reenacts the trauma of her early childhood. The subway may symbolize her subterranean family life, as well as her mother's womb, which to her was not a comforting place. The crowds of people that had to be pushed aside represent the traumas of her childhood caused by her abusive older brothers and her parents. Missing the plane may reflect her inability to escape from her dependency on her mother, as well as the feeling of having missed out on life. Her disgust and throwing up hark back to her disgust with her parents' fighting. Her friendship with the neighborhood boy (Michael in the dream), appears to symbolize the innocence of childhood.

Alarm Clock

Dream 1: One spring morning I was going for a walk through the green fields when I came to a neighboring village, where I saw villagers flocking to church. While I was reading some of the tombstones surrounding the church, I heard the bell ringing.

Dream 2: It was a winter's day and the streets were covered with snow. I was to join a party for a sleigh ride. I had to wait a long time. I took my place in the sleigh, spreading out the fur rug as a foot-muff, and soon the horses took off and the bells began to jangle.

Dream 3: I saw a kitchen maid carrying several dozen plates. I said "Be careful." She replied, "I'm used to doing this job." Soon the plates all fell to the floor, making an awful rattling.

Dreamer: F. W. Hildebrandt, nineteenth century German psychologist. Reported in Freud's *The Interpretation of Dreams* (1900).

Association: Hildebrandt conducted an experiment using an alarm clock. He interrupted his sleep with the alarm clock repeatedly to see what kind of dreams resulted. He discovered that the dreams always varied, but they all ended with some kind of noise.

Interpretation: While an immediate external event such as sound or smell or bright light can influence a dream, the actual symbolism in a dream comes from our own psyche. In the above three dreams, the dreamer works through an aversion to church, visualizes a wish for winter companionship (sleigh ride), and has an "I told you so" experience with the maid (perhaps his mother).

Dream: I rush to school but I'm late for class. The teacher is waiting for me. He says I'm late and asks what's wrong with my alarm clock. Then he tells me I'm going to flunk his course.

Dreamer: A male high school student.

Association: He had turned off his alarm clock and gone back to sleep, then had woken up again after having this dream.

Interpretation: This is a warning dream. On one level it is a simple warning to wake up. On another level it alludes to problems he is having with his classwork. The dream in this case acts as a substitute alarm clock.

Alice in Wonderland

Dream: I was playing in my back yard when I saw this hole in the ground. I crawled through it and suddenly I was Alice in Wonderland. I ate some cookies and grew very tall and I pushed the queen and her men away like many cards.

Dreamer: A 7-year-old girl.

Association: The night before, she had been reading the book about Alice's adventures. Her mother had scolded her about reading with too little light.

Interpretation: The girl's mother was very strict, and her father and brothers tended to back up the mother. In the dream, she became tall Alice and was able to vanquish the evil queen (mother) and her men (father and brothers).

Aliens

Dream: I was visited by four aliens, tall men with green eyes. They surrounded my bed and said, "You've been put into bondage for twenty years."

Dreamer: A 32-year-old man with schizoid features and ego-dystonic homosexuality.

Association: He was feeling alienated from other people. His mother had called him the night before the dream.

Interpretation: This is a prophetic dream, predicting the dreamer's 20 years of exile (bondage). The aliens may represent externalized projections of his oedipal guilt. The bondage represents his self-imposed punishment, probably because he has committed emotional incest with his mother. The number four perhaps alludes to the four elements (earth, fire, water, wind) and the four corners of the earth: hence, it means "everyman." The aliens may also stand for his depersonalization and alienation from himself and others.

Dream: I was kidnapped by some aliens. They took me into their spaceship and proceeded to give me a physical examination.

Dreamer: A 38-year-old schizoid woman.

Association: She had watched a documentary about flying saucers and wished she could fly away on one.

Interpretation: The aliens represent magical figures that harken to the primitive fantasies of childhood. The spaceship is a womb. The dream is a wish to go back to the womb and be taken over by a fairy godmother/godfather, thereby evading the responsibilities of adulthood.

Alter Ego

Dream: I'm standing at the mirror. My reflection begins to speak to me. We get into a terrible argument. My alter ego tells me I'm no good. I promise to change.

Dreamer: A 27-year-old woman with a borderline personality.

Association: During a recent visit to her hometown, her mother rebuked her, saying, "You'll never change."

Interpretation: The alter ego represents the dreamer's mother. The fight between herself and her reflection symbolizes the conflict between her child self (id) and the part of herself that identifies strongly with her mother (superego). This split in her personality has long caused her to go through repetitive cycles of penitence and rebellion.

Amputation

Dream: I dreamed that I went on a hike and was able to walk several miles without getting tired.

Dreamer: A war veteran who had had both legs amputated.

Association: The day before the dream he watched a television show about a national park.

Interpretation: This is a simple wish-fulfillment dream of regaining something that has been taken away. Such dreams by handicapped individuals are common.

Angels

Dream (hallucination): The dreamer glanced up at a tree and found it was full of angels.

Dreamer: William Blake, eighteenth-century British romantic poet. Reported in Abrams (1962).

Association: Throughout his childhood Blake was said to have had many visions of a religious nature, such as the one above. Other visions included seeing God looking at him through his window and receiving a visit from Ezekiel. He viewed such visions as more real than the "Vegetable universe [which] is but a faint shadow" (p. 918). In a poem, "Infant Sorrow," he had written of the dangerous world into which a baby is born.

Interpretation: What Blake saw as visions more real than reality might well have been hallucinations. Angels in a tree might suggest a longing for protection in the dangerous world, and in Jungian terms it might suggest an archetypal struggle in the boy between good and evil that so pervaded the later "Songs of Experience."

Animals

Dream 1: I had two pets—a panther and a tiger. The tiger was always getting out of its cage, which was like a solarium, and I was worried that he would kill somebody. I thought, "I've really got to get rid of that tiger sooner or later, before it gets out of control." The panther, meanwhile, was lying around on the rug and wasn't dangerous.

Dream 2: A tiger and a panther were following me around. The panther would slide up to my leg in a friendly way. The tiger was crouched behind, as if ready to pounce. I was afraid of it.

Dreamer: A 37-year-old schizoid woman.

Association: When she was a little girl she had a stuffed panther.

Interpretation: The tiger probably represents aggression, while the panther likely stands for her sexuality and tender feelings. She is afraid of her own aggression and has not integrated this part of her personality. Thus in the first dream it is kept isolated in a solarium, and she wants to get rid of it (disown it), while in the second dream it is crouching in the distance. The panther, harking back to her first stuffed animal, which was a transitional object, signifies her positive feelings about her sexuality and tenderness, as well as the tender, safe bond with the symbiotic matter.

Dream: It was night and I was lying in my bed. Suddenly the window opened on its own and I was terrified to see that some white wolves were sitting on the big walnut tree in front of my window. There were six or seven of them. The wolves were quite white and looked more like foxes or sheepdogs, for they had big tails like foxes and they had their ears pricked like dogs when they are attending to something. In great terror of being eaten, I screamed and woke up.

Dreamer: The Wolf Man, one of Sigmund Freud's patients (1918), a man who suffered from a phobia of wolves. He had this dream when he was 4.

Associations: He remembered that his older sister had teased him by repeatedly showing him a book of wolves, which scared him; she also once masturbated him. His governess often threatened to cut off his penis. His parents were frequently absent.

Interpretation: Freud saw this dream as an indication that the Wolf Man as a boy had witnessed the primal scene—that is, had seen his parents having sex. The wolves in the dream are his parents (particularly his father) peeping at him through the window. This image represents a reversal of his peeping at his parents. Freud further interpreted the dream as a wish by the Wolf Man (and a fear) of being castrated by his father. However, the wolves might also represent the general feeling of abandonment the boy must have felt during the frequent separations from his family, when he was left in the hands of his teasing sister and sadistic nanny—as though he had been "thrown to the wolves." He made the wolves white so as to make them less frightening and more like sheep.

Dream: I was walking in a beautiful meadow and feeling happy. Suddenly many animals began to run out of the woods and attack me. There were all kinds of them—bulls, lions, dogs, raccoons—all of them surrounding me. I held my hands on my temples to shut out their noises and ran away.

Dreamer: A 23-year-old woman who had for years suffered from migraine headaches and agoraphobia. In her childhood she had been sexually and physically abused by her brothers.

Associations: The dreamer was being pressured by her boyfriend to marry him.

Interpretation: The hostile animals in the dream most likely symbolize the dreamer's oppressive thoughts. She holds her hands on her temples to drown out these thoughts, which, if they invade her consciousness, would threaten to destroy her sense of herself. These oppressive thoughts are probably connected with fear, guilt, and anger with respect to the sexual and physical abuse she suffered as a child. She now projects that her boyfriend (who is pressuring her to marry him)—and all men—will abuse her this way.

Anus

Dream: I was just fucking X, put in one finger, then two, three, then four, and then my whole hand was in his anus with Vaseline on it. I could see him wanting more. He was an absolute helpless mass in front of me. This aroused me.

Dreamer: A 30-year-old homosexual man with anal-retentive features, as reported by Socarides (1980).

Association: He had just visited his family the weekend before the dream. Everybody there was so successful and heterosexual; such meetings frequently produced depressive feelings and intensified the need for homosexual acts. In the presence of his mother, it was difficult for him to be a man: "I lose my power." If he could attach himself to a man, "I could find myself."

Interpretation: The dream is, according to Socarides, a reparative fantasy. Through such dramatization, as well as real-life acting out, "the pervert further stabilizes his sense of self, reinforces his object relations, overcomes destructive aggression and feelings of vulnerability, and brings pleasure to an internalized self-object" (p. 250). However, since no true object relatedness results from such symbolic acts, and no internalization takes place, there is "no true ego enhancement, and the perversion must be incessantly repeated" (p. 250).

Arms

Dream: I screwed off my arm and tossed it aside and felt very happy.

Dreamer: A young man who suffered from painful arthritis of his right arm.

Association: He often spoke of the torturous pain of his arm, which he could not cure and which inhibited his sleep.

Interpretation: This is a simple wish to screw off the diseased arm and be rid of the torture.

Dream: I was on the street and I saw a couple shouting at one another. Suddenly the man's arms fell off. He kept shouting and waving the stumps of his arms at her, as if he didn't notice. I was appalled.

Dreamer: A 30-year-old battered woman.

Associations: She thought of how her father used to beat her mother, and of her fear of her husband beating her when they had quarreled the night before the dream.

Interpretation: The couple who is fighting in the dream represents the dreamer's mother and father and probably also her husband and herself. The arms falling off may signify a wish that her husband's arms would fall off so that he could not batter her or, on another level, that he would be castrated. The fact that she is appalled may be evidence of her guilt at having this wish.

Ascent

Dream: I'm walking up a stairway, and the stairway keeps going higher and higher. I pass by many rooms, but I can't go inside of them to rest, because the stairway passes them by. In some of the rooms I see some children playing. After a while I'm getting tired and wondering where the stairway is going to lead. I wake up anxious.

Dreamer: A 29-year-old obsessive-compulsive man.

Association: The man talks about the endless demands of his father, for whom he works.

Interpretation: The stairway symbolizes the endless expectations placed upon the dreamer by his father, requiring him to shoulder responsibilities from his childhood on. The rooms he must pass by suggest the many opportunities he is required to bypass. The room of children perhaps denotes the childhood he has lost.

Asian

Dream: I was throwing a party, but I slept through it. At the end of the party I woke up and talked to some people. There was nobody I knew. Back in bed there was an Asian woman, a friend of my sister's. I had casual, passionless sex with her.

Dreamer: A 32-year-old obsessive-compulsive man with depressive features.

Associations: The Asian woman had dark skin and he was a bit disgusted with her. He had spoken to his sister the day before.

Interpretation: The Asian woman represents the dreamer's sister, toward whom he has incestuous impulses. She also represents his guilt about those impulses (he feels disgusted with her). Sleeping through the party signifies the depression that makes him feel that life is passing him by. The fact that he does not know anybody at his party shows his sense of isolation.

Awakening

Dream: I had been in a coma for a long time, and then I awoke. My mother was there and I said, "Good-bye, Mother."

Dreamer: A 34-year-old woman.

Association: She complained about her mother's "smothering" relationship with her.

Interpretation: The coma imparts the smothering by the dreamer's mother. Awakening means separating emotionally from her mother.

B

Baby

Dream: I'm holding a baby and I have to cross a bridge with the baby. The river is flooding over the bridge and I have to cross before the bridge collapses. I manage to run across. When I get home the baby poops and I clean him. He is a good baby.

Dreamer: A 30-year-old schizoid man whose father was absent and whose mother was a borderline psychotic who resented the nurturing role and was abusive and intrusive.

Association: He recalled that his mother would often remind him that his birth was a Caesarian by lifting her skirt and showing him her birth scars, screaming, "See what you did to me?"

Interpretation: This dream and a series of others by this man harks back to his oral fixation. It may be an indication of his wish that he could have taken care of the baby within him who had not gotten the nurturing he needed due to his mother's postpartum depression and resentment of being a mother without the help of the absent father. The bridge perhaps symbolizes his journey through childhood, and the flooding water his intrusive and abusive mother. He manages to nurture the baby as he himself would like to have been nurtured, and the baby is a good baby who poops and smiles and prospers from the dreamer's caring.

Dream: A baby was dying. It was buried under the ground. I was digging furiously to get to the baby before it died. But I couldn't reach it in time.

Dreamer: A 27-year-old depressed man whose mother had suffered from postpartum depression at the time of his birth, when her husband, the boy's father, had deserted them.

Association: He recalled that his mother had taught him to read when he was 2 years old, and always treated him like a young adult companion.

Interpretation: The baby represents the dreamer's self as an infant, the self who never became nurtured. In fact, he had to repress his baby needs and feelings (bury them). The ground may be seen as a symbol of mother (Mother Earth) - an enveloping and suffocating mother. Now, as an adult, he wants to dig up the baby (undo the repression), but the baby has died (the repression is too strong).

Basement

Dream: I'm sitting in back of my church. A beautiful woman walks in and sits in the pew in front of me. She's naked, but nobody seems to notice her but me. I hear loud rock and roll music coming from the basement. I can't concentrate on the sermon.

Dreamer: A 33-year-old engineer with an obsessive-compulsive personality.

Association: He spoke of a problem with retarded ejaculation in his sexual relationship with his girlfriend.

Interpretation: This dream contains what Freud called a displacement from below to above. The dreamer is attracted to the naked woman (his girlfriend), but there is a conflict between his superego (the church) and his id (the rock and roll music from the basement).

Dream: I discover a basement in my house that I didn't know was there. I go down the steps and find a sink with a lot of beer bottles in it. I take the bottles out so I can wash my hands.

Dreamer: A 40-year-old woman with an obsessive-compulsive personality.

Association: Her older brother, toward whom she had often expressed rivalrous feelings, is fond of drinking beer.

Interpretation: The basement probably represents the dreamer's unconscious envy of her brother. It contains her wish to have a penis (the sink, a vaginal symbol, is full of beer bottles, phallic symbols), like her beer-drinking brother.

Bath

Dream: I'm in bed with a woman who looks like my mother. I feel embarrassed and repulsed by her. Then a man breaks into the room and forcibly drags me into a bathroom where he proceeds to take off my clothes and give me a bath. I'm trying to stop him, afraid of getting a disease.

Dreamer: A 35-year-old paranoid male who still lived at home with his mother.

Association: The dreamer talked of his recurring fears of sleeping alone and of memories of sleeping with his mother after his parents divorced. She had allowed him to sleep in her bed (nonsexually) until he reached puberty, especially on nights when she had been drinking.

Interpretation: The dream expresses the dreamer's paranoia and latent homosexuality. His oedipal guilt about his incestuous relationship with his mother results in fears of punishment (rape, castration) by his father. The bath symbolizes not only rape and castration, but perhaps also a rite of initiation into manhood and a cleansing of his oedipal guilt. As such it is both feared and craved. The fear of disease may also symbolize his fear of the eruption if his latent homosexuality and also his fear of contamination by his father's masculinity, which his mother abhors.

Bathrooms

Dream: I was in a hotel suite with a strange woman. She told me I could use any bedroom I wanted. I went into a bedroom and then into the bathroom. I saw a door and found another bathroom, then another. One bathroom had a shower with four shower heads. Then my parents and brother were there. I showed them the suite with many bathrooms, but they seemed uninterested. I took them down a staircase and found another suite of rooms, and more bathrooms. I went into one of them to take a shower but somebody had hung some clothes in it and I couldn't.

Dreamer: A 37-year-old woman suffering from depression.

Associations: She had recently stayed in a hotel with her father. She could never have a serious conversation with her parents or her brothers.

Interpretation: The bathrooms may symbolize the family's intimate secrets. Finding more and more of them (and going down the staircase to find them) denotes a descent into the secrets and her unconscious. The shower with four shower heads perhaps alludes to her childhood fantasy of having a penis (or perhaps four penises). Her desire to take a shower represents a desire for emotional cleansing. However, the clothes hanging in the shower (perhaps the family's dirty laundry) prevent it.

Beach

Dream 1: Tricia and I were on the beach. We were going to go snorkeling, but she was very frightened. It was frustrating to me. I went in by myself.

Dream 2: Jim and I went to the beach to body surf. A big wave came in. We swam out as hard as we could, then started swimming with the wave. The wave closed out and I went straight to the bottom. I felt punchy. Didn't know which way was up.

Dreamer: A 39-year-old depressed man who had recently broken up with his girlfriend of several years.

Associations: About the first dream he said, "I felt sad when I woke up; Tricia had problems she refused to deal with." He related the second dream to memories of his father diving for conch shells when he was a boy. He saw the water in each instance as a symbol of his unconscious.

Interpretation: The dreams have two main layers of meaning. The uppermost represents his feelings about Tricia and Jim. Her refusal to go into the water denotes both her fear of her unconscious and her fear of sex (a frequent complaint of his). In the second dream, he and Jim do deal with their unconscious (go under water), but he becomes disoriented by the plunge. Body surfing is also a slang term for sex, and the second dream perhaps also signifies his turning away from women and seeking comfort and sexual union with a man (his association to his father diving for shells). On a deeper level, the two dreams symbolize his turning away from his frustrating mother (who had problems similar to Tricia's) and seeking union with his father.

Bear

Dream: We were at Jim's house in the woods. A bear came into the bedroom while we were sleeping, a mother bear, and she gave birth to a cub. We took care of the cub for her and many friends were there, his and mine, to give us support.

Dreamer: A 45-year-old woman.

Association: She had been dating Jim and going with him to his house in the country, and was feeling frustrated because she wanted to live with him and he was indecisive. Jim told her he had recently seen a mother bear with two cubs.

Interpretation: The dream is her wish to live with him, raise a child, and live happily surrounded by friends. She feels too old to have a child, so in the dream she has a bear give birth to the child. The bear thus serves as a substitute or alter ego.

Beard

Dream: I saw two Japanese and a Chinese woman, nude, sitting next to each other. I saw their pussies. Their pubic hair was like men's beards.

Dreamer: A 24-year-old woman who suffered from anorexia.

Associations: She hated Asian women. She said all her old boyfriends always ended up going out with Asian women.

Interpretation: In this dream she gave her hated rivals men's beards — the same beards worn by her ex-boyfriends — signifying perhaps that their genitals were possessed by these men.

Bed-Wetting

Dream: I was walking in the woods and I heard barking. Big, mean dogs were running after me. I woke up and the bed was wet.

Dreamer: A 4-year-old boy who suffered from nocturnal enuresis.

Associations: His father was very angry at him about wetting the bed, and often "barked" at him like a dog. His mother, on the other hand, was sympathetic, taking his side against the father.

Interpretation: Bed-wetting by children is usually preceded by anxiety dreams such as this one. The bed-wetting is a symptom of some unresolvable conflict. In this case, it is both an act of defiance against the father and a means of getting the mother's sympathy. The dream itself symbolizes his fear of his angry father (the dogs) and his being lost in the woods (in the confusion of his family environment). Woods might also represent phalluses.

Dream: The house was on fire and I had to use a waterspout to try to put it out. I woke up wetting the bed.

Dreamer: A 6-year-old boy.

Association: The boy's mother had just given birth to another baby, who freely wet his diapers. She had yelled at the dreamer, "I don't need two babies."

Interpretation: The fire probably represents both the boy's anger at his mother, and her anger at him. The dream is both a wish to burn out the house, and the guilty (or heroic) desire to save it.

Bees

Dream: I went into the cellar to get something and was attacked by a swarm of bees. I try to find whatever it is I'm looking for, but the bees keep buzzing in my ears. Maybe, I thought, if one of them stung me, the buzzing would stop.

Dreamer: A 29-year-old heroin addict.

Association: He had once been stung by bees while peeping through the window at his sister while she was taking a shower.

Interpretation: The swarm of bees is his guilt about his incestuous feelings about his sister. The cellar perhaps denotes his unconscious, where he goes to get something (his sexuality?). To stop the guilt (the buzzing) he must be stung (get an injection of heroin).

Bells

Dream: I was walking down the street and heard church bells. A white bird swooped down and winked at me.

Dreamer: A 27-year-old obsessive-compulsive man who is a religious fanatic.

Association: He had recently broken off an engagement.

Interpretation: The church bells symbolize the broken engagement and his feelings of guilt. The white bird represents his wish for a sign from God that he is absolved of the guilt.

Bird

Dream: Jane and another woman walked in and asked me humbly to join them. "No," I said, "I have something to do." They went into the bedroom. After a while I went to the door to check up on them. They were naked, making out on the bed. I didn't feel angry. I deserved it for telling them to get lost. She needed affection and I wasn't giving it to her. The other woman was going down on Jane and suddenly a bird flew out of Jane's pussy.

Dreamer: A 30-year-old man with suicidal impulses.

Associations: The bedroom reminded him of an uncle's bedroom. The uncle's wife, like his girlfriend, was named Jane. This uncle committed suicide.

Interpretation: The dream is a dramatization of one of the dreamer's obsessive fears: that his girlfriend might turn out to be a lesbian. In the dream he tells her to get lost and this results in the lesbianism. The bedroom is associated with an uncle who committed suicide, and his girlfriend is named Jane, like her aunt, who he thinks drove his uncle to suicide. The two women may also represent his two younger sisters, whom he used to tell to get lost, and who likewise then excluded him from their lives. Thus when he feels "I deserved it" he is alluding to this guilt toward his sisters. The bird flying out of Jane's vagina symbolizes birth, and harks back to both his sisters' births, which were traumatic for him because they took his mother's attention away. The aim of the dream thus may be to assuage his guilt and find entry back into the world of women.

Birth

Dream: I heard a noise under my bed and looked down and saw a cat give birth to kittens. The mother seemed to smile at me.

Dreamer: A 35-year-old woman.

Association: She and her husband had been trying hard to have a child.

Interpretation: The birth of the kittens under her bed is a symbolic wish for her own fertility. The smile of the mother cat is a smile of blessing.

Dream: I was with my mother somewhere. Then I was inside of her, crawling out of her vagina. Her legs were spread out, like she was giving birth to me, only I wasn't a baby, I was my present age, and I was wearing a suit.

Dreamer: A 37-year-old depressed man.

Association: He complained that he felt as though he was dying at his present job, due to lack of opportunity for advancement.

Interpretation: The birth scene of himself entering the world in a suit suggests the desire for a new beginning, particularly a new business beginning. It also suggests wanting to go back to the womb and be reborn and nurtured by his mother so that he could have more self-confidence.

Black Bird

Dream (poem): One dreary night, while he pondered, weak and weary, he heard a tapping on his chamber door. He had been mourning the loss of a beautiful young maiden named Lenore and then fallen asleep, when suddenly there was this tapping. He went to the window and opened it and a black bird—a raven—flew in and perched above his door. He asked what his name was and the raven replied, "Nevermore." Then he began to talk with him. He asked him if there was "balm in Gilead" and the bird replied, "Nevermore." Then he shouted, "Take your beak out of my heart and leave!" and the bird again replied, "Nevermore," and would not go away.

Dreamer (author): Edgar Allan Poe, who had been unusually close to his beautiful mother when she died at a young age. Paraphrased from "The Raven."

Association: Throughout his tragic life, Poe spoke regretfully about his mother's early death.

Interpretation: Poe's poem, "The Raven," was reportedly a reverie and can be interpreted as a dream. The raven is probably a symbol of death, and the raven's often-repeated exclamation, "Nevermore," represents Poe's inner voice of doom projected onto an external object. "Lenore" is his mother, whose death he never overcame. Hence, the raven was telling him that he would never be happy again, that he (death) would keep his beak in Poe's heart forever. This was both a prediction and a wish. His chronic mourning perhaps siginified a refusal to move forward as a way of holding on to a lost relationship and assuaging guilt.

Blank

Dream: I dreamed about blankness. It was as if I were looking at a blank screen.

Dreamer: A 28-year-old manic-depressive woman.

Association: She reported that on the day before she had read in the newspaper about a man who had suddenly died of a heart attack.

Interpretation: Blankness symbolizes a wish for death, and in manic-depressives such a dream generally occurs during a switch from a depressive to a manic mode. The manic episode following such a dream indicates an attempt to deny death and the depression surrounding it. The newspaper account of a man's death reminded the woman of a traumatic death (abandonment) from her childhood that she did not want to remember.

Blindness

Dream (Greek myth): An oracle told Laius, the King of Thebes, and his wife, Jocasta, that if they had a son he would grow up to kill his father and marry his mother. When Jocasta gave birth to Oedipus, she took the infant to a shepherd and instructed him to kill her son. Instead, the shepherd gave him to a man in the service of the King of Corinth. Oedipus was adopted by the king and grew up not knowing he was the prince of Thebes. Later, the same oracle told him that his fate was to kill his father and marry his mother. To avoid this fate, he left home. In his wanderings, he met an old man and killed him in an argument; it was his father. He then wandered to Thebes, where there was a plague. Heroically ending the plague by answering a riddle, he was rewarded by marrying Jocasta (who, unbeknownst to him, was his mother). Later, when he found out that the old man he had killed was his father and the woman he had married was his mother, he blinded himself, and Jocasta committed suicide.

Interpretation: Freud viewed the Oedipus myth as a universal statement about human neurosis, and he coined the term Oedipus complex as a label for what he believed to be the cornerstone of neurosis. According to him, the myth grows out of the phallic phase through which every male must pass, during which he wants to sexually possess his mother and get rid of his father. (For women, there is a similar phase and similar complex, sometimes called the Electra complex, in which they want to marry their fathers and get rid of their mothers.) If children are able to resolve these complexes, they develop normally. If not, they develop Oedipus complexes and Electra complexes as adults and harbor accompanying fears of castration. Oedipus's act of blinding himself is symbolic of self-castration. Unconsciously, people suffering from severe Oedipus complexes often psychologically castrate themselves (i.e., resolution of the Oedipus complex leads to superego formation).

Dream: I saw a little girl standing on a hill looking at the sun. I tried to warn her but it was too late. She went blind.

Dreamer: A 32-year-old woman suffering from hysterical blindness.

Association: Her husband had died in a car accident soon after finding her in bed with another man. She had this dream the night before she woke up blind.

Interpretation: The dreamer became blind soon after her husband's death. The little girl in the dream is herself. Looking at the sun stands for doing something forbidden (having the extramarital affair), and perhaps also symbolizes being exposed to the sun (her affair exposed to her husband). The blindness may also represent a punishment to fit the crime: her husband had *seen* her illicit act and died, so by blinding herself, she might not see her own guilt anymore.

Blonde

Dream 1: I was living in a hotel with my husband. There was another woman, a blonde, and I suspected that he was having an affair with her. Then his hair changed color, it turned blonde like hers, and I knew it was true.

Dream 2: I woke up and looked in the mirror and saw that my hair had turned blonde. My husband was amazed.

Dreamer: A 29-year-old hysterical woman.

Associations: She had been having marital difficulties with her husband and had sexually pushed him away angrily. The hotel reminded her of a residency for homeless children where she worked. Her mother had long blonde hair which she used to compare unfavorably with her daughter's dark brown hair.

Interpretation: The first dream symbolizes her fear that she has pushed her husband away (as she pushed her male boss away at the residency where she works) because of her anger at men. She anticipates losing him to another woman. At a more primitive level, the dream recreates a traumatic event of her oedipal phase when she "lost" her father to her mother (who had long blonde hair). The symbolism of her husband's hair turning blonde is an example of dream condensation; the change in hair color denotes his bond with the blonde woman (mother). The second dream is a wish that she could be blonde (powerful) like her mother and win back her husband (father).

Blood

Dream: I was at my friend Julie's house. George and I were taking a bath together in a big old-fashioned bathtub. I hit my hand on the side of the bathtub and George said, "Oh, there's a lot of blood." I looked at my hand and saw a slit from side to side. I went inside to get dressed. A younger woman was helping me to get dressed. I couldn't lift my hand. She said, "That dress isn't appropriate." Grandmother came in and I asked her to tape my hand but she said there was no tape. The blood changed color from light to dark red. George screamed, "For somebody who has to go to the hospital, you're sure taking a long time."

Dreamer: A 29-year-old hysterical woman who had been sexually abused as an infant and little girl.

Association: She had tried to have sexual intercourse with a man that weekend and had become too frightened to proceed.

Interpretation: The blood that turns from light to dark red is perhaps menstrual blood. (The dark color may also represent her guilt or her shadow [Jung].) The slit that goes from side to side may be a symbolic vagina. The bath with George connotes sexual intercourse, which for her is fraught with fears of abuse, harking back to her early childhood when she was sexually abused by an uncle. At the time of the abuse, she could get no help or support from anyone, just as in the dream nobody can help her dress or put on bandages. George yells at her for taking too much time (replicating perhaps the general hostility of her father). Her grandmother was the only one in her childhood to whom she could turn. Dreams that symbolically repeat traumas are attempts at mastering those traumas.

Bomb

Dream: I'm using a video camera to record a landscape. Burt doesn't want me to do it. I start hitting him, very violently. A woman approaches us and sees me pounding him. I think, "Now she knows the truth about me." She says she's going to call the police. I place a bomb in Burt's mouth and in my mouth, killing him and myself. As the bomb blows up, there are beautiful images like a Hollywood movie.

Dreamer: A 27-year-old borderline woman.

Associations: She had been quarreling with her husband, Burt, and wondered if she should separate from him. During her adolescence she attempted suicide several times. She often speaks of her rage at men.

Interpretation: The bomb represents her rage. The woman symbolizes her mother. Her mother behaved in a way that enraged the dreamer during her childhood, trying to control her every thought and action, and the dreamer reacted by attempting suicide (turning the rage against herself). In the dream she is externalizing this anger, displacing it onto her husband; the woman (her mother) threatens to call the police (her father), so she commits suicide (as in her adolescence) but takes Burt with her. Oral images (bombs in mouths) may allude to toxic nursing during the oral phase. The fact that she views the violent scene as if it were a movie is an indication of her dissociation. That she both internalizes and externalizes the rage may denote therapeutic progress.

Book

Dream: I found some old books in my closet but was afraid to look at them.

Dreamer: A 40-year-old woman.

Association: She had just begun therapy and expressed fear of what she might find out.

Interpretation: The old books represent her unconscious, which she is hesitant to explore.

Bookpacks

Dream 1: I was in a hotel and found three bookpacks in the corner of the room. I wanted to open them. Then my parents and brother arrived.

Dream 2: I went to a store to buy a cover for my bed. When I got there I saw some bookpacks. I looked through all of them. The clerk was nice enough to keep the store open so I could keep looking.

Dreamer: A 37-year-old woman suffering from depression.

Association: She and her brothers used to have bookpacks when they were growing up; hers was smaller than those of her brothers. Her father had always been a voracious reader, but he was secretive and bonded more with his sons than with her.

Interpretation: The bookpacks probably represent masculinity and masculine privilege. The dreamer grew up feeling excluded from the masculine world of her father and brothers. Her curiosity about the bookpacks alludes to her curiosity about her brothers and her father at the stage of the discovery of the difference in sexual anatomy (bookpacks being phallic symbols). The packs may also symbolize the "secrets" of the world of masculinity, and opening them her admittance into that world. Hence, it is a rite of passage. The niceness of the clerk in the second dream symbolizes her wish that her father would have supported this curiosity, rather than discourage it as he had done in real life. It also expresses her hope that her male therapist will now do so.

Box

Dream (Greek myth): Zeus had the first woman created as a revenge on mankind for having accepted the fire that Prometheus had stolen from heaven. The gods all gave her gifts to make her attractive and dangerous to men, along with a box in which they had collected all the ills of the world. She was told not to open the box, but her curiosity overcame her and she opened it. Out flew all the ills that now afflict humankind.

Interpretation: Myths are the dreams of primitive men, codified and systematized. In this dream fire symbolizes power and sexual potency. Power corrupts. When mankind steals fire, he becomes corrupted. Pandora is a symbol of that corruption.

Her box symbolizes her womb, out of which come the generations of corrupt human beings. In both the Greek and Judaeo-Christian stories of creation, woman plays the role of the corrupting influence. D. W. Winnicott (1964) wrote that both men and women have a fear of woman — that is, an unconscious fear of the mother on whom they were initially absolutely dependent. Such unconscious fears predominate in primitive thinking and contribute to making women the scapegoats for humankind's ills.

Brothers

Dream: I was in bed when I heard a noise, like people trying to open my front door. Then I thought I heard three guys rifling through my things. The noise stopped and I got out of bed and found everything was missing—my computer, my furniture, my music equipment. The apartment was almost bare. Only one piece of stereo equipment was left. I went to the door and found three doors instead of one. Then I heard somebody coming up the stairs. It was the downstairs neighbor. He looked sheepish. I took a piece of wood and hit it against the door, but he wasn't frightened. He looked East Indian, had long hair.

Dreamer: A 31-year-old man with narcissistic and paranoid features.

Associations: The three men looked like his three brothers. Long hair means homosexuality.

Interpretation: The three men represent the dreamer's three brothers, who teased him as he was growing up and often accused him of being homosexual. In the dream, the brothers steal everything he owns (rob him of his masculinity). The neighbor who comes up and smiles sheepishly symbolizes the dreamer's paranoid fear that he may indeed be homosexual, projected onto the neighbor. His computer was his most cherished possession—he spent most of his leisure time alone with it — and it had become a fetish. Hence the stealing of the computer may have also had the meaning of stealing his love object or, in Freudian terms, his mother's phallus.

Dream 1: I'm in a car and I almost run into a child.

Dream 2: I'm walking in the woods. I kick a mouse and it bleeds.

Dream 3: I'm riding a bicycle with my brother. We see two lions in a field. They eat a squirrel and it is very bloody.

Dream 4: My brother finds a kitten under the house. He says, "Don't kill it," but I hit it with a shovel.

Dream 5: I was in bed with a boy. It might have been my brother.

Dream 6: I was swimming with my brother.

Dream 7: I was having anal sex with my brother. Someone came up behind us.

They were inserting something in my rectum. I awoke with intestinal pains and diarrhea.

Dreamer: A 37-year-old man suffering from colitis.

Association: He recalled that when he was a boy he had engaged in anal intercourse with his younger brother and had made him bleed. He also recalled that his father had administered enemas to him, which he perceived as rapes. He had had spells of diarrhea and chronic colitis since his early twenties.

Interpretation: This series of dreams shows the dreamer's progress as he went through analysis. In the beginning, the dreams are more symbolic and distorted; a child, mouse, squirrel, and kitten stand for the younger brother and the (bloody) anal penetration. Eventually, the brother himself appears more directly. Finally, in the last dream, he connects his father's administration of enemas (rapes?) and his anal sex with his brother. The colitis (intestinal pain) and anal-expulsiveness (diarrhea) appear to serve a defensive function, the colitis being at one and the same time displaced sexual excitement (from genital to colon), the construction of that excitement, and the atonement for it (the pain). The diarrhea may be an attempt to expel forbidden impulses as well as to ward off latent homosexual desires. As in the dream, the dreamer tended to get diarrhea attacks whenever he had anal-erotic impulses.

Bugs

Dream: I was at Bill's apartment and there were bugs everywhere. Termites. I was afraid the house was going to fall down. Bill had inherited this house from Barnie H.

Dreamer: A 32-year-old man struggling with latent homosexual impulses.

Association: He had recently been forced to resign from his job. Bill was a coworker. Barnie was a vice president of the company. He suspected that both Bill and Barnie were homosexuals.

Interpretation: The bugs represent many levels of meaning. While he was working at the company, the dreamer often thought his computer and telephone were "bugged." The bugs also symbolize the dreamer's hope that the company is about to collapse because of its moral rot (termites). Finally, the bugs stand for his attitude about Bill and Barnie's homosexuality (bugs perhaps meaning anal penetration) and his own homophobia.

Dream: I woke up and saw a bug crawl under my blanket.

Dreamer: A young hysterical woman.

Association: She had a phobic fear of bugs. Her grandfather once put a moth on her skirt and it terrified her.

Interpretation: The bug is a phallic symbol. Her phobia has to do with repressed feelings about having been sexually abused by a grandfather whom she found repugnant. She used to tell him, "Get away from me, stop bugging me." The bug also denotes her guilt about his sexual abuse. Her memory of the grandfather's putting a bug on her is a screen memory, defending against the repressed memory and feelings connected to the sexual abuse.

Bums

Dream: Joan and I were in a house somewhere. In the basement were all these men, some of them bums, some not so bad off. I was furious and went down and threw them all out.

Dreamer: A 34-year-old hysterical man.

Association: The night of the dream he and his girlfriend, Joan, had talked about sex and AIDS. She told him about the many men she had previously been with. He felt jealous.

Interpretation: The bums signify the men his girlfriend had previously slept with. Deprecating them as bums makes him feel justified in being furious and contemptuous toward them. The basement where they are staying denotes the place where all the secrets, including sexual secrets are kept (the unconscious), and are liable to erupt into consciousness.

Dream: I saw a homeless man on the street. People passed by and felt sorry for him. A woman gave him some money.

Dreamer: A 35-year-old depressed man.

Association: His wife was pressuring him to make more money.

Interpretation: The bum is the dreamer. The woman who gives him money is his wife. The hope in the dream is that perhaps if he were a bum his wife would stop pressuring him and give him some sympathy.

Burial

Dream: I was walking on the beach and I saw a man who had been buried in the sand so that only his head stuck out. I tried to help him out but he said, "Fuck you."

Dreamer: A 38-year-old depressed man.

Association: For several days he had not been able to get out of bed. He felt emotionally paralyzed.

Interpretation: The dream conveys the dreamer's physical state of depression, a state in which he feels as though he is buried by his own sadness and anger.

Dream: I'm in a dark place, somewhere in the woods. Suddenly I step into quicksand. I sink into the quicksand until I am completely buried. Amazingly I can breathe. "This isn't so bad at all," I think. The quicksand is moist and soft and cool like an embrace. When I taste it, it tastes like shit.

Dreamer: A 40-year-old obsessive-compulsive man.

Association: He has recently taken on a project that he thinks is too difficult for him.

Interpretation: The burden of his project makes him feel that he is literally buried in shit. It also appears to allude to his toilet training, to the stage of anal-eroticism, when he enjoyed playing with his feces. The wish in the dream is to regress to a time before he had to take on social responsibility, when he could enjoy his own excrement.

Burning

Dream: A child came to the dreamer's bedside, touched his arm, and whispered reproachfully, "Father, don't you see that I am burning?"

Dreamer: The father of a boy who had taken sick and died. The father had sat by the boy's body, which was laid out and surrounded by candles. Reported by Freud (1900).

Association: He had this dream as his son's body caught fire. Upon waking, the father found that the old man had fallen asleep and a candle had overturned. He felt guilty.

Interpretation: The meaning of this dream seems apparent. The father, in his sleep, must have smelled or sensed the fire in the adjacent room. However, Freud also sees in this dream a wish: the wish for the boy to still be alive and be able thus to come into his room and warn him of something.

Dream: My mother brought in a covered dish. When she opened it up I saw a brain. It was all dark and burned. There were still some flames around it.

Dreamer: A 15-year-old boy.

Association: His mother had been pressuring him about studying for an important exam.

Interpretation: The burning brain that his mother brings in on a platter is his own.

Dream 1: I am turning into a beam of white intense burning light.

Dream 2: I am facing a young boy. . . . His eyes are brilliant. . . . They emit flashes of burning light. . . . I am paralyzed by the flash. . . . He comes close and puts his mouth over mine. . . . I am overcome by passion.

Dream 3: I am making love with my sister. . . . A feeling of pleasure is spreading in the dream. . . . I suddenly feel her mouth wide open against my throat. . . . Boiling saliva is pouring from her throat into my neck. . . . It's burning me!

Dreamer: A 23-year-old woman suffering from a traumatic neurosis, as reported by Levitan (1980).

Association: She recalled that at the age of 1½ she had been standing in a bathtub when suddenly the tube from the washing machine came unfastened and a jet of scalding water sprayed her. She remembered a flash of light before losing consciousness, suffering third degree burns that caused her to be hospitalized for several weeks.

Interpretation: The three dreams contain reenactments of this original trauma. In the last two, the memory of the trauma becomes an aspect of scenes of sexual passion. This indicates, according to Levitan, the sharp ambivalence which lay behind the dreamer's sexuality.

Bus

Dream: I'm riding a bus. The bus begins to speed wildly along. I'm shouting at the bus driver but he pays no attention to me.

Dreamer: An impulsive 24-year-old woman.

Association: She complained that on the night before the dream she had drunk too much alcohol and stayed out too late.

Interpretation: The bus that speeds wildly along is herself. The bus driver symbolizes her id impulses, which she externalizes. The person who shouts at the driver is her superego.

Butterfly

Dream: I dreamed I was a butterfly, a lovely butterfly flitting about with joy. The butterfly did not know it was me. Nor did I know whether I had been myself dreaming I was a butterfly or a butterfly dreaming I was a man.

Dreamer: Chuang Zi, ancient Chinese Taoist philosopher and a follower of Lao Zi.

Association: Is there a difference between a man and a butterfly? This is what we mean by the transformation of things.

Interpretation: Chuang Zi wanted to make the point that when we are at the highest state of awareness, we no longer make distinctions nor do we have self-consciousness; we just are. However, one could interpret that the dreamer's choice of the butterfly has a certain meaning (as opposed to a porcupine, for example)—the former symbolizing beauty, grace, lightness, flight, and temporality. This may indicate the dreamer's libidinal wish to fly from flower to flower and forget himself in passion (joy).

C

Cage

Dream: I walked into my room and opened the closet. There was a cage on the floor, one of those metal cages they have in pet stores. And inside the cage was a strange animal. It was a lizard with wings, and it was flying around in the cage, trying to get out, bumping into walls. It looked at me and its eyes were almost human. I felt sorry for it.

Dreamer: A 19-year-old female college student who lived at home with her overprotective parents.

Association: She wanted to move out from her parents' house and live in a college dormitory, but her parents were stubbornly against the idea.

Interpretation: The animal in the cage symbolizes herself and her feeling of being trapped in her parents' house by their overprotectiveness, which does not allow her to fly. The fact that the animal in the cage is a strange breed, a lizard with wings, also alludes to her feelings of being odd, not like others. The lizard may also be a phallic symbol, denoting her envy of males and their freedom of self-assertion.

Camera

Dream: I was traveling with Kent to exotic places, celebrating our relationship. We were at an airport and I had my camera with me. I put it on the counter to talk to the check-in clerk, and then I looked around and my camera was gone. Kent waited by the check-in counter while I went to talk to the police. The police were nice and took me around in their car, but we never found the thief. By the time I got back to the check-in counter, our plane had left.

Dreamer: A 27-year-old woman with paranoid features who had recently married a man of whom her mother disapproved.

Association: She took her camera with her everywhere; it was like an "appendage." She felt her camera helped her to understand and control life.

Interpretation: The theft of her camera represented castration. She is being castrated because she is too happy (celebrating her relationship). The invisible thief is probably her mother, who was controlling and competitive with the dreamer all during her childhood. The police represent her father, to whom she goes for help in standing up to her mother's interference (which in fact did happen in her childhood). Her mother's interference causes her to miss the plane (miss out on life).

Cancer

Dream 1: A monster was kicking me in the testicles. Afterwards, one of them turned green, as though it were cancerous.

Dream 2: A strange man stormed into my room while I was sleeping and pulled the blankets off me. I held my hands over my crotch.

Dream 3: My father broke into my room. He looked like a monster. I was terrified.

Dreamer: A 30-year old hysterical man who had developed cancer in his right testicle and had to have it surgically removed.

Association: He recalled that as a child he had been a bed-wetter. His father had become obsessed with stopping this habit, and would break into his room in the middle of the night and throw off his blankets to see if he had wet his bed. The boy had had recurring dreams about it ever since.

Interpretation: The recurring dreams reveal a contributing source of the man's cancer of the testicle: a castration fear rooted in his father's hostile (castrating) relationship with him during the traumatic period of enuresis. At first he distorts the traumatic memory by making his father a monster or a strange man. In the last dream, the father appears as himself. His bed wetting had been related to incestuous oedipal wishes about his mother and had the unconscious aim of eliciting her attention and bringing her to his bed. Hence, the father's castrating behavior represented an actualization of the talion principle (revenge of the oedipal father). In the dream and in real life, the dreamer connected his castration fear with the development of cancer in his right testicle, noting that he had felt a pain (of constriction) chronically throughout his childhood and young adulthood. This constriction — a tensing up of his testicles in anticipation of being attacked by his father or father-representatives in his life — may have led to a chronic cutting off of blood to the testicle and eventually to cancer.

Dream: Herb and I return from the hospital after an examination. He tells me they found more cancer. Says, "Look in my eyes and see if you can see the tumors."

Dreamer: A 35-year-old depressed salesman whose brother had died of cancer.

Association: He recalled how his brother kept refusing to have the moles on his skin checked out, and when he did, how he would deny the importance of the doctor's diagnoses.

Interpretation: The dream is a wish that he had been able to help his brother spot his tumors sooner and prevent his death.

Dream: I dreamed Ted's heart began to rot and then to develop cancer. I somehow feel relieved by this.

Dreamer: A 27-year-old woman.

Association: She had complained that her husband, Ted, was emotionally unavailable.

Interpretation: Cancer of the heart symbolizes the husband's deadness of feelings. The dreamer is glad (relieved) that his emotional unavailability is organic.

Candles

Dream: I was looking in this shoe box. It was a deep shoe box so I couldn't see the bottom. I felt these candles inside, in pairs. I took my hand and ran through the box. I found one candle without a pair, then I couldn't find it again.

Dreamer: A young woman with hysterical trends.

Association: She said she felt as though she had found a treasure and then could not find it again. For some reason she was angry at her mother upon waking.

Interpretation: The candle is a phallic symbol. The box may be her mother's womb (her mother, who gave birth to her, should have supplied a penis for her as well). The candles in pairs may denote a sense of belonging (her mother and father). The solitary candle has no pair, so it can be possessed. The dream perhaps alludes to pregenital fantasies of finding a penis (treasure), and then the reality of not being able to (the candle is disappearing).

Dream: I was walking down a dark hallway. I found a candle and lighted it. Now I could see where I was going.

Dreamer: A young man.

Association: He felt confused about his career and his life.

Interpretation: The lighted candle represents enlightenment in his attempt to find his way in life.

Cannibalism

Dream: My friend had us over for dinner. He served his own head on a platter. He told us it was his head and said, "Eat, drink, and be merry." I tried to eat the hair but had to spit it out. Then I took the hair home and showed it to my mother. She said it wasn't real hair at all. It was a wig. That made me feel better.

Dreamer: A young hysterical woman.

Association: She recalled that her mother was always concerned about her hair, wanting to cut it shorter. She was reminded of the biblical story of Salome.

Interpretation: The cannibalism symbolizes the dreamer's primitive rage, harking back to the kinds of fantasies of cannibalism common in young children and primitive people. It also alludes to the biblical story of Salome, who danced for her father and then asked for John the Baptist's head on a silver platter. In this case, the rage is actually harbored toward her mother, who has continually demanded that she cut her hair (so that she could not compete for her father's attention). It is displaced onto the man, just as in real life. Finding out that the hair is fake lessens her guilt about this primitive rage. It is likely also an allusion to the mother's derogation of the woman's father, whom she often chastised for being weak (hairless, powerless).

Car

Dream: I was in a car with my mother. The car was going downhill. There was a ditch at the bottom of the hill and the car was going so fast that it could not possibly stop. At the critical moment magic happened, good magic, and the car went over the ditch without falling into it.

Dreamer: Philip, a 9-year-old boy with kleptomaniacal tendencies. Reported by Winnicott (1953).

Associations: He recalled that the saddest time of his life was when he was 6 and his mother had left him and gone away to a hospital to give birth to his sister. After his younger sister was born, his mother had little time for him.

Interpretation: Being in the car with his mother, going downhill toward a ditch, symbolizes a wish to sexually possess his mother, and the car going out of control represents his fear of their relationship going out of control. It may also represent his wish to kill his mother and himself, and the fear of his aggression getting out of control. The magic represents an outside force (a father-figure) saving him from his unconscious sexual and aggressive urges. Winnicott told the boy: "You're frightened that in the dream you had to use good magic because this means you have to believe in magic, and if there's good magic there also has to be bad magic. You don't like to use magic but you have to when you are forced to deal with things that happen in your life" (1953, p. 110).

Castration

Dream: Kathy cut my dick with a knife. Not all the way off, just gashed it. Then it looked like a lobster, and all this black shit came out of it. I wanted to break up with her.

Dreamer: A 29-year-old borderline man who had had an emotionally incestuous relationship with his alcoholic mother.

Associations: Kathy and he had quarreled recently and she had grabbed a knife and brandished it at him. On another occasion she had found a jar of Vaseline and chided him for masturbating. It reminded him of his mother.

Interpretation: He fears Kathy wants to castrate him. His member turns into a lobster (something creepy) and emits black shit (indicating his guilt feelings about masturbation, incest, and about himself as a man, as well as perhaps his desire to defecate on women).

Dream: The dreamer's friend invites him to have sex with her. As soon as he comes she reaches for a pair of huge, rusty scissors. She is cutting the string that is attached to a condom inside her, a condom she has inserted herself. As she cuts the string he is in a sweat for fear she will cut his penis off; in fact, as she cuts away he feels it is his penis, as though the string attached to the condom were a fiber of his body, but it is a dull pain that only makes him nervous.

Dreamer: Henry Miller, American writer. The dream is paraphrased from his book *Nightmare Notebook* (1975), which he wrote when he was in his thirties.

Associations: He wrote of his symbiotic and incestuous tie with his mother. The friend in the dream is a childhood friend toward whom he had had sexual fantasies.

Interpretation: The string "attached to a condom," which is at the same time Miller's penis, "as though the string attached to the condom were a fiber of my body," probably represents the umbilical cord as well as his incestuous tie (the condom) with his mother. In the dream his childhood friend, toward whom he once had sexual fantasies, turns aggressive and castrating (cuts his penis); this is perhaps an allusion to his primitive fantasies about his mother, of which he has written. It may also represent his ambivalence toward all women and his general fear of their psychological power over him. The "dull pain" that "only makes him nervous" perhaps denotes his defense against his castration fears through numbing.

Cats

Dream: I went bicycle riding with my mother. I had a box on the back of my bicycle. There were five cats in the box, all females with long hair. Suddenly the cats got out and ran away. I wanted to chase after them but my mother wanted me to stay with her. She liked being with me. But I ran after the cats anyway and found them hiding in small caves in a cliff. A vicious dog was barking at them. I rescued them.

Dreamer: A 35-year-old narcissistic man with a mother complex.

Association: His mother called him constantly, asking about his relationships with women. He had met five women in the last week.

Interpretation: The cats represent women with long hair. He has to keep them hidden from his mother (in a box). They escape and she wants him to stay with her. As in real life, she tries to prevent him from separating from her and bonding with other women. The small caves (wombs?) harboring the cats symbolize his own stunted, unborn sexuality. The barking dog denotes both his anger at his mother, which is displaced onto the women in his life and his mother's jealous rage at the women in his life. By rescuing the cats from the dog, he is overcoming his own ambivalence. The dream is not only a wish-fulfillment, but also a dream of sexual and emotional healing.

Dream: I was French kissing my cat. The cat was inside a closet. I felt complete love for my cat, and didn't want to leave the closet even though I had appointments to go to.

Dreamer: A 28-year-old woman with latent lesbian tendencies.

Association: She had talked about having sexual attractions to other women, but had not yet acted on these attractions.

Interpretation: The cat represents the dreamer's sexuality — and in particular her homosexual impulses, which heretofore had been in the closet. She is not yet ready to leave the closet.

Dream: I was sitting in the backyard when I saw something like meteors in the sky near the moon. Then I looked more closely and I could see these cats jumping over the moon.

Dreamer: A 32-year-old depressed man.

Association: He spoke of feeling isolated and emotionally numb, with only his cat for companionship. He missed his mother, who had recently died.

Interpretation: The cats symbolize the dreamer's feelings, which he had repressed to the point of numbness. The cats jumping over the moon suggest joyful contact with a woman (moon being a feminine symbol), as well as an unconscious nostalgia for the joy of his early childhood merger with his mother.

Cave

Dream: I was hiding in a cave. It was like a prison, but it was also like a fantastic hideout. I locked Eddy in the cave and came out. There was a baseball field. Suddenly Eddy escaped and yelled at me like a little kid, "You forgot about me!" "I'm sorry," I said. I felt sorry for him.

Dreamer: A 30-year-old male social worker suffering from depression.

Association: Eddy is a lovable, goofy man, one of his clients whom he likes a lot. The baseball field was like one that was near his home.

Interpretation: The cave represents the womb. The fact that the dreamer views it as both a prison and a hideout spells his ambivalence toward his mother; he is in conflict about whether to escape from, or bury himself in, his mother's womb. The baseball field near his house is a clue that this is about his childhood; Eddy symbolizes the dreamer as a child (lovable, goofy) who was abandoned by his father and enmeshed by his mother. Locking Eddy in the cave is an act of identification with his mother. It also symbolizes how he cuts off his own real feelings (the child inside) and takes out aggression on himself, which is the source of his depression.

Chains

Dream: I was in the woods and I came upon a tiger. The tiger had its arms and legs chained to a wall and looked quite tame.

Dreamer: A 33-year-old passive man.

Association: He had lost his temper with his wife.

Interpretation: The tiger represents his animal nature — his aggressiveness — which he wished to control (keep chained).

Dream: I walked into the house and found my husband chained to the kitchen stove. I started to laugh and he pulled a wad of dough out of his pocket and threw it at me.

Dreamer: A 28-year-old hysterical woman with a masculinity complex.

Association: Her husband had complained about her cooking and she had screamed, "You'd like me chained to the stove."

Interpretation: The dreamer's wish, realized in the dream, is to reverse roles and have her husband chained to the stove. And while he is at it, he can give birth as well (taking the wad of dough from his pocket).

Dream: My typewriter was encircled by chains. I urinated on the chains and the acid from the urine melted them.

Dreamer: A young phallic-narcissistic man with writer's block.

Association: He had not been able to write for months. It felt like impotence.

Interpretation: The typewriter in chains denotes his writer's block. Breaking the chains through urination perhaps means freeing himself through actualizing his phallic powers (sexual conquest).

Chasm

Dream (poem): In Xanadu, Kubla Khan decreed that a stately pleasure dome be built along the Alph River, which ran through "caverns measureless to man" ending in "a sunless sea." The walled-in estate had ten miles of fertile ground and towers "girdled round" and gardens with "sinuous rills" and a "deep romantic chasm." But it was a savage place as any ever haunted "by woman wailing for her demon lover" with a "ceaseless turmoil seething" as if the earth "in fast thick pants were breathing." It also included a "mighty fountain" that emitted "huge fragments" like "rebounding hail." It was "a sunny pleasure dome with caves of ice" where ancestral voices could be heard prophesying war.

Dreamer: Samuel Taylor Coleridge, the eighteenth century British poet who was addicted to opium. Paraphrased and quoted from "Kubla Khan."

Associations: Coleridge wrote this poem after it had come to him during a dream while he was taking an afternoon nap. He had just read an account in the newspaper about Kubla Khan's decision to build a huge estate.

Interpretation: Coleridge's conflicted sexuality seems to permeate the imagery of the dream. The "pleasure dome with caves of ice" suggests this conflict; it probably relates to his own internal sexual ambivalence as well as to his feelings about women (caves of ice). From a Jungian standpoint, the mixture of female (deep romantic chasm) and male (mighty fountain) symbols may denote Coleridge's struggle with this anima, and the "ancestral voices" may allude to the collective unconscious.

In Freudian terms, the ancestral voices may allude to the oedipal father and the caves of ice to castration fears. Or, these discordant symbols may be seen as the dreamer's fears of the voices within the frozen caverns of his own mind (the unconscious, disowned parts of himself), which stymied his own sexuality and capacity for genuine intimacy.

Children

Dream 1: I was in a summer camp. There were many children and they looked happy.

Dream 2: I was in a hospital. There was a child there, a girl wearing a body suit. She looked like she was 12 or 13, but the body suit made her look younger. I asked her how old she was. "I'm 5," she said. "I'm here because I'm trying to go back to 5, and my doctor says I have to work at it on a cellular level." A nurse came in and wanted to take off her body suit. The child didn't want to take it off. The nurse took it off, and said, "Oh, your back is so red." The girl said, "It itches."

Dream 3: I was standing on a street. A small child was waiting for a bus. The bus ran over her, and nobody on the street noticed. "They'll find out when they count heads," I thought.

Dreamer: A 29-year-old schizoid woman who had been abused as a child.

Association: She had recently visited her ex-boyfriend and his daughter, whom she said reminded her of herself as a child. The nurse looked like her mother.

Interpretation: Dreams about children generally allude to the dreamer's childhood. In these dreams, she is a passive observer of other children, indicating her repression of, and dissociation from, her childhood traumas and her present schizoid withdrawal. The first dream is a simple wish that she had been happy as a child. The second connotes the regression ("I'm trying to go back to 5"). The nurse who forces her to take off the body suit is her mother, who was not nurturing. The red, itching back perhaps signifies the itching of an infant with diaper rash and the abuse she suffered as an infant; it may also be the itch to be embraced by the body suit, which may denote a wish to go back to the womb or to die. The third dream may contain a suicidal wish, as well as her feeling that she was murdered as a child and had been invisible since then.

Dream: I was at a café and I saw this child crying. His mother held him in her arms and the child cried some more and shouted at the mother, "I'm going to express my feelings!" The mother said it was all right.

Dreamer: A 27-year-old passive man.

Association: He had been to a party that weekend and had felt bored. Other people were talking uninhibitedly, but he felt inhibited, especially about approaching women.

Interpretation: The child in the dream represents the dreamer's emotional side, which he has kept repressed. The dream suggests his wish to be more assertive, and the associated wish that his mother had supported his assertiveness as does the mother in the dream. In that case, he would have been less inhibited at parties.

Circles

Dream: I had been shopping but I couldn't decide what to buy. Then I drove home but for some reason the street that led to my house kept circling around it. I kept going around and around and couldn't find the entrance to my driveway.

Dreamer: A young obsessive-compulsive woman.

Association: When she thought of holiday shopping she got a headache.

Interpretation: The dreamer feels that her life is going nowhere and she is "going in circles." The thought of Christmas and buying gifts for a husband and family for whom she is emotionally alienated exacerbates this feeling.

Cleanliness

Dream: Jane and I were making love in somebody's house. It was a mess. I said, "We've got to clean up the house." A couple came in and we were still in bed. We refused to get out of bed.

Dreamer: A 37-year-old obsessive-compulsive man.

Association: He noted that he was always cleaning his own apartment several times a day.

Interpretation: Cleanliness signifies purity. The dreamer feels guilty about his sexuality, and his need to "clean up the mess" means assuaging his guilt. The couple who comes in may be his parents.

Dream: The police come to my house and accuse me of being a kleptomaniac. They say I've stolen some jewelry, including the most precious jewel in the store. My mother appears and says it is not true. She says, "He's clean," and I have her trust and love completely.

Dreamer: A young man with kleptomaniacal tendencies.

Associations: He reported that many of his daydreams had to do with stealing jewelry. His mother treasured her collection of fine rings, necklaces, earrings, and bracelets.

Interpretation: Stealing jewelry symbolizes taking sexual possession of his mother. The police represent his superego. The conflict between his incestuous desires and his harsh superego are the source of his kleptomania, but his mother vouches for the fact that he is clean (nonincestuous).

Climbing

Dream: I've climbed to the top of a tree. I can see my friend Bill in another tree. He yells, "Be careful. You're too high." I'm sitting on the highest branch and I'm afraid it will break.

Dreamer: A 34-year-old narcissistic man.

Association: He recently got a raise at his job and did not know if he deserved it.

Interpretation: Climbing here means ambition. His friend in the other tree is a friend toward whom he feels competitive. He has beaten out this friend (his brother surrogate) and feels guilty. The dream is a warning that he may be too ambitious and too proud: "Pride goes before a fall."

Closet

Dream: A hill, on which there was something like an open-air closet. A very long seat with a large hole at the end. Its back edge was thickly covered with small heaps of feces of all sizes and degrees of freshness. There were bushes behind the seat. I urinated on the seat; a long stream of urine washed everything clean. The lumps of feces came away easily and fell into the opening. It was as though at the end there was still some left.

Dreamer: Sigmund Freud, founder of psychoanalysis. Reported in Grinstein (1980).

Associations: Freud wondered why he was not disgusted by the content of the dream. He then thought of the Augean stables of Greek mythology, which were cleaned by Hercules. He also refers to *Gulliver's Travels*, in which Gulliver puts out a fire by urinating on it. On the day before this dream he had delivered a lecture but had been displeased with it and felt "no trace of enjoyment in my difficult work." When he was about 5 years old he witnessed a primal scene and urinated on the floor, evoking his father's wrathful prediction, "The boy will come to nothing."

Interpretation: The closet not only symbolizes his parents' house, but also a place where things from his past are hidden (the unconscious). Urinating and washing away the feces denote his ambition to surpass his father and take his mother for himself - to be a powerful man like Hercules, who cleaned the Augean stables, or Gulliver, who doused the fire in the queen's bedroom and thereby symbolically took possession of her, an ambition he first felt at 5. Yet like Hercules, who unwittingly slew his wife and children, and Gulliver, who engendered the queen's anger, he fears punishment (as he had as a boy, after his father had made his wrathful prediction). He therefore feels no enjoyment in his present success (lecture).

Dream: My husband pushes me into a closet. I hear him turning the key into the keyhole. Then the door opens and my husband is standing there. Then I look more closely and he is my father. He shuts the door and I'm in the dark.

Dreamer: A 27-year-old hysterical woman who had a strong emotional attachment to her father.

Association: She recalled that as a child her father once punished her by locking her in a closet.

Interpretation: The memory of being locked in a closet symbolizes the father's possessive and emotionally incestuous relationship with the dreamer. Turning the key in the keyhole represents sexual intercourse. Her father complex causes her to remain attached to her father to an extent that she unconsciously confuses her husband with her father, as the dream indicates. The dream ends with her being "in the dark," expressing this lasting confusion.

Clowns

Dream: I went to work and saw people in clown costumes outside my building.

Dreamer: A young schizoid man.

Association: He said he did not feel connected with his work.

Interpretation: The clowns signify the dreamer's schizoid withdrawal from his predicament, forced to go to a job each day that he does not enjoy. In another sense, the dream may represent an externalization of his inner conflict, the clowns denoting the inner voice that mocks him and yearns for playfulness and the avoidance of responsibility.

Coat

Dream: A dog jumped on me. I had my green coat on. I tried to push the dog away but he began to hump me, and soon there was this huge pile of sperm on the floor. I looked at my coat and luckily no sperm got on it.

Dreamer: A 32-year-old anal-narcissist recovering from alcoholism and struggling with homosexual impulses.

Associations: The green coat was his favorite coat. The dog was a generic dog. His father committed suicide when he was 4. He wished his mother would leave him alone.

Interpretation: The "generic" dog who has anal sex with the dreamer and the pile of sperm on the floor represent his oedipal guilt. The dog may also stand for the dreamer's father, toward whom he feels much guilt (for being too close to his close-binding, emotionally incestuous mother and for wishing, as a child, to get rid of his father) and the dreamer's anger (because the father abandoned him and left him in the mother's clutches). The "pile" of sperm may also denote a pile of feces, harking back to the anal stage when his anal-erotic attachment to his mother was intensified. Having his father degrade him anally serves to dispel this guilt. The "green" coat probably signifies the dreamer's youth, and a wish that somehow he could salvage his innocence (keep the coat from becoming soiled). This dream is typical of those of anal narcissists (Schoenewolf 1996), containing elements of anal-eroticism and the grandiosity (green coat) that defends against forbidden anal impulses.

Color

Dream: I dreamed in bright colors. I was outside and the grass was bright green and the sky a bright blue and I was wearing a bright yellow dress. I walked along and felt happy. Then I was looking at the dream, wondering why I was dreaming in color.

Dreamer: A 32-year-old woman suffering from depression.

Association: She almost always dreamed in black and white.

Interpretation: The dream in color signified a breakthrough in her therapy. Some of her repression had cracked, releasing a formerly trapped emotionality and vitality. The "looking at the dream" might signify her development of an observing ego.

Dream: My sister colored my hair. She made it two shades, dark blue and burgundy. I was happy about it, trusting her. She said, "It will be fine." I was laughing but saying, "I want to take this off." I thought to myself that if I don't like it I could change it later.

Dreamer: A 25-year old woman with narcissistic features.

Association: She had always consulted her older sister about her hair. Her sister was a beautician. She felt ambivalence toward her.

Interpretation: The blue and burgundy perhaps symbolize the dreamer's ambivalence toward her sister, who has always pretended to care about the dreamer but does not really respect her feelings. In the dream, as in real life, the dreamer cannot express this ambivalence and instead laughs as if everything is fine. The dark colors may also represent dark aspects of herself that she does not want revealed, or her struggle with her animus (blue being masculinity and burgundy being femininity, i.e., menstrual blood).

Dream 1: I looked out of the window and it was a beautiful day. The colors were so bright, they hurt my eyes.

Dream 2: I was in a museum looking at the paintings of the primitive expressionists. I had never noticed before how luminous the colors were.

Dream 3: I walked into a meadow and saw multicolored flowers.

Dream 4: I saw a beautiful rainbow. The colors were glowing.

Dream 5: I saw a Christmas tree with the most beautiful lights I'd ever encountered.

Dreamer: A 37-year-old woman who had become blind due to a childhood illness at age 7.

Association: She continually regretted that she could no longer enjoy the wonderful sights of life.

Interpretation: The colorful dreams are fulfillments of the dreamer's wishes.

Dream: I was talking with Mary and her face began to change colors, one after the other. I suggested that she should see a doctor but she refused.

Dreamer: A 39-year-old passive male.

Association: He often complained to his wife that she was too moody and needed a therapist.

Interpretation: Mary's change of colors represents her changing moods. In the dream, as in real life, she refuses help.

Computer

Dream: I went to my office and somebody had stolen my computer disk and my mouse. Somebody had also stolen my monitor and replaced it with a smaller monitor, and at first I didn't notice. I had to tell my boss and couldn't adequately convey my anguish.

Dreamer: A 32-year-old masochistic male businessman who suffered from feelings of inadequacy and castration fears.

Associations: He had been promoted quickly by his company and did not feel worthy of it. His boss, a woman, seemed to favor him; yet when she found out he was engaged in outside literary activities, she had him return the notebook computer he had been using at home. Recently he had been assigned a new larger office. He waited two weeks to move into it.

Interpretation: Computers symbolize power; the bigger the computer and the more functions it has, the more power it symbolizes. The people stealing his computer disk (memory), mouse (hand), and monitor (eyes), were taking away his power — castrating him. One thief was his boss, who he was afraid was going to resent his promotion or any show of masculinity. The other thieves perhaps represented his two sisters and mother, who in his childhood had pampered him but made him feel guilty for being a male. His anguish about telling his boss about his stolen computer components related to his fear that she, like his mother and sisters, would envy his male power and try to steal it.

Conservatives

Dream: I walked into the kitchen and Stanley was talking to my wife. He was talking about politics and as he was talking, his face changed and he turned into Newt Gingrich. I began to argue with him. "You're a conservative bigot," I said. "Get out of my house." Jane was surprised.

Dreamer: A 32-year-old man who is obsessed with radical liberalism. He tends to politicize his feelings.

Associations: He recalled having political discussions with his father and brother, and feeling frustrated because he could not express his views. His brother looks like Newt Gingrich, the Speaker of the House in the United States Congress.

Interpretation: Newt Gingrich stands for his older brother and father, both of whom are more traditionally masculine than the dreamer. His father favored his older brother, and the dreamer always felt like a "sissy" compared to them. His obsession with radical liberalism in the dream, and in real life, is fueled by his antagonism toward his brother and father, who in real life and in the dream are conservatives. However, in real life he is not able to stand up to them; in the dream he tells them off and tosses them out of his house, to his wife's and his own amazement.

Corner

Dream: I am sitting in the corner of a huge room. I look around and I can't see the end of the room. I try to stand up to get a better look but find that I can't move.

Dreamer: A 17-year-old schizoid girl.

Associations: She had been caught in the middle of her parents' divorce, and felt trapped. She was confused about her life.

Interpretation: The corner represents her feeling of being cornered (trapped) by her parents, not knowing which one to support. The large room with no end probably symbolizes her fear of the future, with its unlimited expectations.

Counterclockwise

Dream: I woke up and looked at my clock and noticed that the hands were going backwards, counterclockwise. The photo of my husband on the end table was upside down.

Dreamer: A 32-year-old woman.

Association: She complained about the lack of vitality in her marriage.

Interpretation: The clock going backwards and the upside down picture of her husband both symbolize that the dreamer feels her life and marriage are on a wrong, or regressive, path.

Court

Dream: I was in a cafeteria. Robert Shapiro, the famous lawyer, was there with his client. I was involved in a court case with this client and I felt furious. They tried to taunt me, to get me to say something incriminating, but I kept quiet. As I left, I said, "I'll do my talking in court." As I walked out of the cafeteria, there was applause.

Dreamer: A 45-year-old masochistic professional man who had been involved in several court cases.

Association: He woke up thinking about a woman at whom he was currently angry over a business dispute. He felt the woman had abused him, and during his waking hours he sometimes fantasized about taking her to court.

Interpretation: The dream is an extension of his wishful fantasies. In the dream he has the woman nemesis represented by a famous attorney, whom he verbally defeats in the cafeteria, to the applause of the other diners. On a deeper level, the dream perhaps also represents vindication against his older brothers, who used to taunt him and try to get him to lose his temper. From his childhood on he had fantasized about becoming famous (getting applause) as a way of exonerating himself with regard to oedipal guilt.

Cows

Dream 1: "Pharaoh dreams; and behold he stood by the river. And behold, there came up out of the river seven well-favored cows and fat-fleshed; and they fed in a meadow. And, behold, seven other cows came up after them out of the river, ill-favored and lean-fleshed; and stood by the other cows upon the bank of the river. And the ill-favored and lean-fleshed cows did eat up the seven well-favored and fat kind."

Dream 2: "Behold, seven ears of corn came up upon one stalk, full and good. And, behold, seven thin ears and blasted with the east wind sprang up after them. And the seven thin ears devoured the seven good and full ears."

Dreamer: Ramses II, Pharaoh of Ancient Egypt. As reported in the *Bible* (Genesis).

Associations: Pharaoh was very disturbed by these dreams and called all the magicians and wise men to his side to explain the dreams. None could. Finally, Joseph, a Jewish slave, was able to do it.

Interpretation: Joseph's interpretation was that both dreams were saying the same thing: the seven fat cows and seven good ears of corn represented seven fertile years and the seven thin cows and ears of corn that devoured the seven fat cows and ears of corn were seven years of famine. However, another interpretation might view the fat cows like "fat cats" — symbolic of the king's overindulgence at the expense of others. The thin cows would represent the peoples whom Pharaoh had enslaved and who he feared might rise up against him. The fact that he was so tormented by these dreams points perhaps to the eruption of guilt.

Criticism

Dream: He dreamed of writing a critical review of a newspaper story about Ibsen, and the following sentence entered his mind: "It's written in a positively norekdal style."

Dreamer: Sigmund Freud. Reported in *The Interpretation of Dreams* (1900).

Associations: A colleague had recently sent him a paper to review — probably written by W. Fliess — which he thought was too emotional and subjective. He had also recently read an article about Ibsen.

Interpretation: Freud regarded this dream as one of the clearest examples of condensation in dreams, referring particularly to the word norekdal. The word is a combination of the names of the characters in two of Ibsen's plays — Nora, from *A Doll's House*, and Ekdal, from *The Wild Duck*. Both of these plays were concerned about whether truths should be kept hidden or revealed, and both were about emotional women. Hence the "norekdal" style in Freud's dream sentence means "Ibsenesque" or "emotional" and refers to Freud's unconscious concern as to whether he should reveal his criticism of his colleague's paper or spare Fliess from this truth. In addition, he may have been concerned about the truths he himself was revealing through his psychoanalytic research.

Crying

Dream: "The strange young man in the fez bursts into tears. . . . Swann tried to console him saying, 'why be so distressed.' . . .?"

Dreamer: Marcel Proust, the novelist, who suffered from severe asthma. Like most asthmatics, he had problems with separation. In *Swann's Way* (1928), his autobiographical novel about his youth, he cannot separate from his mother even for an evening, and has similar problems with his girlfriends.

Association: Swann (Proust) is thinking about separating from his beloved, Odette, when he has this dream.

Interpretation: This dream, like many dreams of asthmatics and other individuals suffering from psychosomatic illnesses, shows a denial of feelings and a displacement of those feelings onto another person in the dream. Hence, while Swann was feeling sad about the prospect of separating from Odette, in the dream it is another man who is crying, while Swann is consoling him. This dream also indicates a split between Proust's mind and body. Behind this denial and split may be a wish that he would not have to feel this sadness.

Dream: I had a disturbing dream. I dreamed that Father and Mother were very ill and were going to die. I woke up crying, and feeling guilty.

Dreamer: A depressed 23-year-old woman who still lived with her dominating and intrusive parents.

Associations: After the dream, while she was tossing in bed, she made up her mind to be a better daughter, helping her mother more around the house, assisting her father with his clerical work.

Interpretation: This dream is a wish for her parents to die. Unconsciously, she believes that only their death will free her of their domination. But her conscience won't allow her to own such thoughts, so she wakes up feeling guilty and crying, not about their death, but about her own wickedness. She makes up her mind to assuage her guilt by doing good works.

Dream: A young man sitting in front of me in biology class turned and poked his pencil in my eye, and it immediately began to swell. I was frightened and upset and ran crying to my mother.

Dreamer: A 22-year-old bride.

Association: She had this dream just after her wedding night.

Interpretation: This dream shows the young woman's feelings about sexual intercourse. The young man represents her husband, and the pencil is his penis. To her, intercourse was a violent, terrifying, and upsetting event. The swelling eye represents pregnancy, and indicates a fear of becoming immediately pregnant. She wants to return to mother and flee from the responsibilities of married life.

Dream: A neighbor is crying. I rush up to her. I say, "Why are you crying?" She says, "Because your daughter is going on an airplane." I say casually, "Why be frightened about that? She often travels."

Dreamer: A 59-year-old woman suffering from severe rheumatoid arthritis, as reported by Levitan (1980).

Associations: The dreamer's condition worsened sharply six years earlier, after her husband's suicide. At the time of the dream she was completely bedridden. The dream occurred the night after she had been given the news that her daughter was moving to a new city far away. She was quite shocked by the news.

Interpretation: Arthritic individuals tend not to feel their feelings, according to Levitan, but to somatize them instead. In this dream the dreamer projects her concern about her daughter's death, masked as a concern for her safety on the airplane: "Why be frightened about that? She often travels." This is an indication of the underlying anger that is attached to, and precludes, the feelings of any sadness or concern for her daughter.

D

Dancing

Dream: I'm at a dance. It looks like a ballroom, but it's actually the lobby of my company. I see many of my co-workers there, as well as my manager and boss. Everybody is dancing together in a circle and I join them.

Dreamer: A 31-year-old passive woman.

Association: She had been feeling bad because of all the politics on her job. In her family she was the child who was the "peacemaker" when conflicts developed between her parents or siblings.

Interpretation: The dancing in the lobby of her company represents her wish for cooperation and harmony among the staff at the company where she works.

Darkness

Dream: I was walking along in the woods, when suddenly the sun went down. I could see it moving down. Then it became too dark to walk. I looked around and there was still light behind me. I was afraid to go further into the dark, but I thought it would be weak of me to go back into the light.

Dreamer: A 22-year-old woman.

Association: She had fears about therapy.

Interpretation: The darkness denotes the unconscious. She wants to explore it but is afraid. But to turn back to the light (the conscious) feels like copping out.

Dawn

Dream: I was at my desk and there was a new window in my room behind the desk. I looked out and saw the pink light of dawn. I thought it was the most beautiful dawn I'd ever seen.

Dreamer: A 29-year-old student suffering from anxiety and insomnia.

Association: He was cramming for a math test and could not find the solution to a problem. Then he dozed off.

Interpretation: The dawn behind his desk symbolizes his wish for a solution (a fresh insight) to his mathematical problem.

Death

Dream: My husband has died and I called his daughter by his former wife and asked what we should do about his funeral. He had never said what he wanted me to do when he died.

Dreamer: A 40-year-old woman.

Association: The day before the dream her husband had had an anxiety attack, the symptoms of which were similar to a heart attack. She went to sleep worrying that he was going to die during his sleep.

Interpretation: This is a warning dream, letting the dreamer know of the depth of her concerns about her husband's health. There is also an apparent wish to bond with her stepdaughter. Historically, some people have mistakenly seen such dreams as prophetic, especially if it turned out that the subject actually did die. However, most such "prophetic" dreams, if traced to their sources, will show that there were clues that death might be imminent.

Dream: My fiancée had a car accident. She was killed instantly. Jim called me and told me the news. I was terribly upset.

Dreamer: A 29-year-old obsessive-compulsive man.

Association: She had pressured him to marry her for several years and had finally given him an ultimatum. Reluctantly, he had agreed to do so.

Interpretation: This dream represents a wish for his fiancée's death. The fact that he is upset upon hearing the news is an indication of his feelings of guilt.

Dream: I broke into my therapist's apartment and found her lying face down, naked, in the bathtub. She was dead.

Dreamer: A 25-year-old man with perverse, sadomasochistic trends.

Association: He remembers once going home to find his mother naked, face down on the bed. At first he thought she was dead, but then found she was drunk and had passed out.

Interpretation: This is a wish-fulfillment dream. His therapist is his mother in the transference. The dream is an indication of the rage the dreamer harbors toward his mother, who was a seductive alcoholic.

Dream: I died and then came back as a tall, beautiful evergreen tree. I felt very strong and safe and could watch children playing and provide shade for them but stay uninvolved.

Dreamer: A 48-year-old depressed man.

Association: He had been contemplating suicide.

Interpretation: This is about the wish to be reborn. In the next life he does not want to be involved with anybody, but be strong and evergreen (immortal) like a tree. This desire expresses his narcissistic drive. He also wants to provide his children with the shade (protection from the sun's fury, i.e., narcissistic injuries) that he could not find in his own childhood.

Dream (poem): "Since I could not stop for Death, he stopped for me; the carriage held but just ourselves and Immortality." As we drove slowly along, I traded my work and leisure for his civility. We passed a school where children "wrestled in a ring," fields of grain, the setting sun. We paused before a house "that seemed a swelling of the ground," the roof scarcely visible. It seems like centuries since the day "I first surmised the horses' heads/Were toward eternity."

Dreamer: Emily Dickinson, American poet, who suffered from lifelong depression. Paraphrased and quoted from her poem, "Because I Could Not Stop For Death."

Associations: This "dream" reflects her deep religious faith and is associated with her having been rejected by the one man she loved, after which time she lived the life of a recluse.

Interpretation: The symbols in this poem represent a death wish. Death here is not simply ceasing to exist, but uniting with her Christian God in heaven. The images of the school where children wrestled, fields of grain, the setting sun, represent her life flashing before her. The house that was "a swelling of the ground" with only the roof visible could signify both a burial mound and a return to the womb — the swelling of the ground being the mound of Venus and the house denoting the poet herself. The carriage being pulled by Death signifies the dreamer's having given up on life.

Dream: Richard is lying in bed, dead. I know he's dead but he's been lying there for days, starting to decay. Suddenly he starts to move. I reach out to touch him and he grabs me. I start to scream and he says, "I'm not going to scare you to death." My brother and sister come into the room and watch TV as if this is all natural. Then Richard's body starts to change into that of a teenage boy. He sits up and says, "How can I get any rest with all this noise?" I'm still trying to decide what to do with his body. Then he turns into a little girl and says, "Wouldn't this be a good revenge?" He gets off the bed and touches me on the cheek. "You have to let *me* go, too," I tell him.

Dreamer: A 40-year-old depressed woman whose husband, Richard, has recently died.

Association: She recalled a similar dream about her father's body decaying.

Interpretation: This is a mourning dream. In the beginning she knows her husband is dead, but lets him lie there. This expresses her wish that he were still alive.

The metamorphosis into a teenage boy is both her wish and her husband's (he often yearned to be a teenager again). However, the metamorphosis into a little girl who says, "Wouldn't this be a good revenge?" probably represents her revenge at her father. She had always felt her father hated her because she was a girl; having Richard (her symbolic father) turn into a girl would be a turn of the tables.

Democrats

Dream: I was at a party and it turned out that all the people there were Democrats. I recognized some prominent politicians and some movie stars. Then I was outside and the people at the party were all taking off their clothes and jumping into a swimming pool. The pool looked funny, though, because the water was brownish in color. When I went closer I saw that it was like a cesspool, and there were turds floating around in it.

Dreamer: A 37-year-old man who suffers from political narcissism (the narcissistic politicizing of his feelings).

Associations: He had read an article about a fund-raising party for the Democratic party attended by Hollywood stars. His own social life was nonexistent.

Interpretation: The dreamer views Democrats as swimming in a cesspool (being up to their necks in excrement). This symbolism hints at the source of the dreamer's obsessive and narcissistic hatred and fear of Democrats: his anal-retentiveness, traceable to his harsh toilet training and a fixation at the anal-sadistic stage. Because of this harsh socialization, he has repressed his own sexuality to a great degree and is envious of the freedom with which Democrats conduct themselves. In his dream, he reverses things, putting them in the excrement (on the potty) instead of himself.

Devil

Dream: Two devils were spinning around inside my head, one blue-eyed, one brown-eyed. Then they flew out of my mouth.

Dreamer: A 40-year-old paranoid schizophrenic.

Association: He had just begun psychotherapy and had spoken of voices inside his head, sometimes of his parents.

Interpretation: The two devils inside his head represent his split-off, internalized bad parent objects. He wants to get rid of them through therapy, perhaps make them magically fly out of his mouth.

Dream: I was screaming at my husband. As I was screaming, he smiled at me evilly, and two horns sprouted on the top of his head, like he was a devil. I began screaming even louder and hitting him on the face.

Dreamer: A 43-year-old hysterical woman.

Association: Her husband always acted like he was so innocent and she was a monster.

Interpretation: In the dream she reverses the real-life situation, making her husband into a devil and herself a victim. In fact, the dream alludes to the actuality of the husband's passive-aggression.

Dirt

Dream: My hands had gotten dirty. The dirt was thick and black and I couldn't wash it off. I kept going to the sink to wash it off, but nothing happened. I woke up feeling horrified.

Dreamer: A 37-year-old obsessive-compulsive woman.

Association: She noted that in her waking life she tended to wash her hands ten or fifteen times a day.

Interpretation: The frequent handwashing of an obsessive-compulsive is a ritual designed to ward off unconscious guilt or the fear of disapproval. The guilt may relate to an early sexual humiliation, and the fear of disapproval is often linked to a harsh toilet training experience in which a child felt humiliated. The dreamer fears that the guilt will emerge and result in further humiliation, which her ego could not bear.

Dream: I was on the street and women looked at me in disdain. I found a mirror and saw that my nose was dirty. It had a large smudge on it.

Dreamer: A 24-year-old man plagued by premature ejaculation.

Association: His wife had refused sex for three weeks.

Interpretation: The dirty nose symbolizes a dirty penis. The dreamer feels guilty about chronic masturbation, voyeurism, and other perverse activities. Behind such activities are feelings of insecurity about his masculinity and self-consciousness. His premature ejaculations stem from this insecurity.

Dissection

Dream: The dreamer saw himself dissecting his own pelvis. While he was doing it, he noted that he had none of the awe that he would have thought would accompany such a task.

Dreamer: Sigmund Freud, as reported by Gutheil (1951).

Association: Freud had this dream after writing his most famous book on dreams, *The Interpretation of Dreams.* It took him a year to overcome his resistance to publishing the material.

Interpretation: Freud interpreted the dream to represent the dissection involved in his own self-analysis. His wish to be less nervous about publishing such intimate details of his inner life manifested itself as a lack of awe about the dissection.

Distance

Dream: I was on a hill and I could see some people in the distance. I recognized Mary and Bobby. I waved at them but they didn't see me. I made out some people from my church and waved at them but they didn't see me either. I felt very lonely.

Dreamer: A schizoid man.

Association: He said he did not feel connected with anybody.

Interpretation: In the dream his wife, Mary, his son, Bobby, and the members of his congregation are all at a distance from him, denoting his emotional isolation. His narcissistic need to be superior to everybody (on the hill) creates this distance.

Diving

Dream: I was diving under water. I reached a sunken ship that looked like a hotel you would see in Western movies. Went down deeper and there was a ghost floating around in the water — a shrunken old man. I went down to another level, fearing I was going too deep. There was a room that had old stuff in it — hats, gloves, and umbrellas.

Dreamer: A 38-year-old depressed man who had been severely neglected as an only child.

Associations: He remembered that his father used to dive under the water and come up with conch shells. He had loved to go to Western movies as a child. The ghost reminds him of his father.

Interpretation: The dream represents a regression back to his early childhood. Diving into the depths symbolizes this regression, or a trip into the unconscious. It also represents an identification with his father. The Western movie hotel is a signpost of the age at which he went to Western movies, when movies and his own fantasy life were more important than any real contact with human beings. The ghost of his father denotes a period during which he wished for his father's death. The room in the deepest level may be his mother's womb or his parents' bedroom. The "old stuff" in it is his father's old hats, gloves, and umbrellas (signifying perhaps that his mother had possession of his father). There are no living people in the depths, just as in his early childhood he felt deprived of contact with his parents.

Dogs

Dream: I was waiting for a bus. For some reason the buses were on the wrong side of the street. When I crossed over I had the sense of something being wrong. Suddenly these vicious dogs began appearing. They looked like black poodles, but they were angry and showing their teeth. One chased me into the bus.

Dreamer: A young male with a passive, schizoid personality.

Association: He recalled having had many dreams in which ordinary scenes turned disastrous, and in which tame animals turned wild. He recalled that when his father drank, he turned mean, like an animal.

Interpretation: The vicious dogs represent externalized object representations of the dreamer's own rage, which he disavows and has split off and projected onto the dogs. His recurring dreams of animals turning wild are linked with his passivity and with his inability to own his own aggression. They may also denote his drunken father. As a child, whenever he expressed aggression to either parent, it was turned back to him and he was angrily rebuked. Thus he began to internalize aggression.

Dream: I was masturbating a dog. It was a dog's penis, but the animal was bigger than a dog, more like a horse.

Dreamer: A 37-year-old schizoid woman who was raised by her father.

Association: She remembered when she had first seen her father's penis when she was 5. She had been enlisted to bathe him when he was ill. She also remembered her pet dog.

Interpretation: The dog's (horse's) penis stands for her father's penis, which she had been curious about as a child and wanted to touch. However, guilt about her incestuous impulses distorts the dream image, turning her father into her pet dog, then a horse. Her fixation to this period keeps her from being able to relate to men in her present life.

Doubles

Dream: I was sitting in a restaurant when I saw another man who could have been my double. He was dressed just like me and was eating a meal identical to the one I was eating. I really couldn't believe it.

Dreamer: A 35-year-old man with a heart condition.

Association: He had been told by his physician that he did not have long to live.

Interpretation: The double of himself represents his wish that somehow he will continue living even if he dies of a heart attack.

Dream: I was arguing with myself. It seems there were two of me, myself and a double. The double was screaming, "Absolutely not. And I mean, absolutely not."

Dreamer: A 35-year-old man with an eating disorder.

Association: The man had had an eating binge the night of the dream.

Interpretation: The double denotes the dreamer's harsh superego introject of his overcontrolling father. This harsh introject and the need of his inner child (id) to rebel against it is the source of his eating disorder.

Dragon

Dream: I was living in a cave, and the entrance to the cave was guarded by a dragon. I found a spear and jabbed it into the dragon's eyes and killed it. Below the dragon was a beautiful forest. I walked down the hill to the forest.

Dreamer: A 28-year-old masochistic man with a mother complex.

Association: He was still living with his mother (his father had died when he was 7), and had been wanting to move out for several years.

Interpretation: On a Freudian level, the dragon is his devouring mother, the cave her vagina. He has to kill this dragon-mother in order to grow (go into the trees). On a Jungian level, the dragon may represent the dreamer's "wild" unconscious, which he must "slay" in order to achieve individuation.

Dream: A dragon was chasing me down a dark street.

Dreamer: A 32-year-old alcoholic man following an all-night drinking binge.

Association: His sister kept calling him to ask about his health. He wished she would stop bothering him.

Interpretation: The dragon represents his guilt, particularly his incestuous feelings about his sister. The dragon is also the addiction of alcoholism, which is devouring his soul, from which he cannot seem to escape.

Dream

Dream: I dreamed that I remembered a dream that I had when I was 16. In this dream I went on a ski trip and called home and found out that my father had died.

Dreamer: A 34-year-old writer with close ties to his parents.

Association: When he was 16 he wanted to go with friends on a skiing trip but his father opposed it. He was now planning another such trip.

Interpretation: The dream within the dream alludes to a real memory (the previous skiing trip). In the dream he actually goes on the trip, but discovers that his father is dead. This is indicative of guilt feelings about his present trip, resentment about not having been allowed to go on the previous one, and a wish for his father's death.

Dress

Dream: I'm walking along a sunny path with a girl who is wearing two dresses, one black and a white one underneath. We embrace.

Dreamer: A young man whose mother had just died.

Association: The girl's face alternately looks like both his mother and his fiancée. The two women did not get along.

Interpretation: This is an example of what Freud called *condensation*. The black and white dresses symbolize the dreamer's dead mother and fiancée united as one. It represents an attempt to integrate his feelings about them. It may also suggest that his girlfriend is in mourning on the surface but happy (white) underneath.

Drowning

Dream 1: I was in a river and the current was dragging me with it and I was afraid I was going to drown.

Dream 2: I was in a sea. My ship had gone down or something. I was clinging to a piece of wood, but the waves were going over my head and I knew I would drown.

Dream 3: I was swimming with all my might to get to the shore. I couldn't quite reach it.

Dream 4: I was in a cove and the tide suddenly came in and the water shot over my head. I kept flapping my arms to keep my head above the water, but I was running out of breath.

Dream 5: I was drowning, but then I saw a woman in the distance. She swam toward me and took my hand.

Dreamer: A 24-year-old obsessive-compulsive man.

Association: He had been a workaholic all his life. Recently he had met a woman.

Interpretation: This series of dreams, which occurred over the period of a year, shows the source of the man's obsessive-compulsive characterology — a fear of drowning (i.e., of being overwhelmed by depression). He swims mightily (works fiercely at his job) to escape this depression throughout the first four dreams. In the fifth, a woman reaches for him. The woman stands for his new girlfriend, whom has managed to lure him away from his work and is teaching him how to relax and enjoy life.

Drunkenness

Dream: Tommy and I were driving in his Thunderbird. I looked at the speedometer and it said 130 miles per hour. "Stop, I'm going to have a baby soon," I yelled. He had been drinking and he had a mean look in his eye. I couldn't get him to stop.

Dreamer: A 36-year-old recently married man whose wife was pregnant. He suffered from manic-depression.

Association: He recalled that when he was 16 he had had a car accident. Tommy had been driving the car and he was drunk. The car hit a tree. He injured his stomach and had had trouble with too much stomach acid ever since. He associated the look in Tommy's eye with the look his mother got in her eye when she drank. When he had told his mother that his wife was pregnant, she had replied, "That's nice."

Interpretation: The dream condenses the present, the past (when the dreamer was 16), and the distant past (when the dreamer was a child and his mother would stare angrily at him while in a drunken stupor). On one hand, the speeding car in the dream represents his feelings that life is going too fast. He is not really ready for his wife's pregnancy or the responsibility of having a baby. The fact that in reporting the dream *he* is going to have a baby may allude to a feminine identification. On the other hand, it alludes to traumatic fixations in his past, which arouse fears about the present. The driver is symbolic of both his friend, Tommy, and of his mother, who has not been supportive of his wife's pregnancy and who he fears wants to sabotage it.

Eagle

Dream: My girlfriend and I were driving in a car when we saw an eagle and a snake in the side of the road. The eagle had the snake in its claws and the snake was biting the eagle on the leg.

Dreamer: A 37-year-old man.

Association: He recalled seeing a mythological drawing of an eagle and a snake. "Battle of opposites, right?"

Interpretation: The eagle and the snake represented the dreamer and his girl-friend, who had lately been having frequent arguments as they traveled through life (in the car). For them it was truly a battle of opposites. In addition, the dreamer's superego and id may also have been in conflict, the eagle symbolizing morality and the snake the libido. From a Jungian standpoint, the battle may denote his own struggle with his anima.

Ear

Dream: I was lying on your couch and I looked around and suddenly noticed you didn't have any ears. I said, "Look, Doc, you don't have ears." "Is that right?" you answered. You didn't seem to think it was a big deal.

Dreamer: A 24-year-old narcissistic woman with low self-esteem.

Association: She had been feeling frustrated by her psychoanalyst in recent weeks.

Interpretation: The lack of ears indicated the dreamer's fear that her psychoanalyst was not listening to her. This alluded to her father, who had been emotionally unavailable and thought his daughter was oversensitive and made too much of things.

Earth

Dream: I was in some kind of spaceship and I was trying to land on earth. But I couldn't find a place to land. I kept flying back and forth but there were mountains and rocks and lakes everywhere I looked. No smooth ground.

Dreamer: A 27-year-old man with paranoid features.

Association: He wished he could meet the right woman for him, but something always seemed wrong with each woman he met.

Interpretation: Earth stands for woman. The spaceship imparts the dreamer's isolation and flight represents his ungroundedness. He cannot find a place to land (the right woman), so he must keep flying back and forth perpetually.

Earthquake

Dream: I felt my house shaking and realized there was an earthquake. I ran outside and saw that only my house was being shaken by the earthquake. Everything else was still.

Dreamer: A 30-year-old woman suffering from anxiety, multiple phobias, and migraines.

Association: Sometimes when she walked on the street she felt as though she was outside her body.

Interpretation: The earthquake stands for her internal conflicts, which trigger her anxiety, phobias, and headaches. Going outside her house to find peace is the symbolic equivalent of depersonalization.

East

Dream: I saw a blonde-haired woman walk by. Then I looked up at the weather vane on the top of the barn and it was pointing to the east.

Dreamer: A 38-year-old man.

Association: He said he hated blonde-haired women and liked Asian women because they were more spiritual.

Interpretation: The "East" in this dream denotes the dreamer's wish to find his own spirituality and to unite with a spiritual, Eastern woman.

Eating

Dream 1: I was at my parents' house. They were eating with my sister. When I tried to sit down at the table, my mother said, "No, we don't have enough."

Dream 2: I was eating bowls of Jello. No matter how much I ate, my stomach still felt empty.

Dream 3: My mother was feeding me, but the food kept spilling from the spoon and falling on the floor. I felt frustrated and lonely.

Dreamer: A 45-year-old man suffering from a peptic ulcer.

Association: His mother had abruptly weaned him as an infant and he was then fed by a cold, older sister. His mother had always favored this older sister.

Interpretation: The dreams show that the source of his peptic ulcer, as well as of the recurring themes of his dreams, is related to oral frustrations that began in his infancy. The dreamer had felt rejected by his mother all his life, and this frustration was converted into a somatic symptom (the ulcer). The Jello in the second dream is similar to the baby food that was fed to him by his sister and that was not fulfilling to him, particularly emotionally. Alexander and Wilson (1935) did pioneering studies about ulcer-prone personalities, showing how their unconscious need for nurture is linked to oral frustrations and leads to the excessive acidity in their stomachs, which oversecrete in anticipation of being fed whenever they experience stress.

Elephant

Dream: A white king elephant entered the dreamer's body, but without causing her any pain. The elephant gently impregnated her.

Dreamer: Mother of the Buddha Shakyamuni, a founder of the Buddhist religion. Reported in *The Buddhacarita.*

Association: She had this dream the night before becoming pregnant with her son, and saw this as an omen that her son would be the latest reincarnation of Buddha. While carrying the child, she remained free of any of the usual fatigues, depressions, or fancies that often accompany pregnancy. (See Joseph's dream about Jesus.)

Interpretation: The elephant is considered holy in the Buddhist religion, and the white king elephant is, as its name implies, the king of elephants. In addition, white here stands for purity, and thus the birth of Buddha Shakyamuni, like that of the birth of Jesus Christ, was considered an "immaculate conception," undefiled by sensual pleasure. Since the legend of the coming of Buddha, like the coming of Christ, was commonly known, one could conjecture that the Great Maya may have had a narcissistic wish to give birth to a god, and hence created a self-fulfilling prophecy.

Enema

Dream: I was having sex with a woman, when suddenly I felt a pain in my anus. She was sticking her finger in my rectum and it was painful and exciting. Then her finger changed into a plastic tube, as though she were giving me some kind of enema. I ejaculated and woke up.

Dreamer: A 22-year-old masochistic man who had suffered from constipation from an early age.

Association: He recalled that his mother had had an obsession with his bowel movements and used to give him frequent enemas, which sexually aroused him.

Interpretation: The dream portrays the fixation to the period in which his mother gave him enemas. The enemas symbolize forbidden sexual intercourse with his mother, as well as rape. His constipation defends against these forbidden feelings and the submission to rape.

Dream: My father was giving me an enema in my ear while I was sleeping. In the dream, I woke up and felt much smarter.

Dreamer: A 40-year-old man.

Association: His father had been obsessively preoccupied with his toilet training and later with his education.

Interpretation: The dream is a condensation of the father's two preoccupations.

Enlargement

Dream: I was with Kent and his brother. We were riding in a helicopter and taking photographs. Kent's brother had a camera and I had a camera, but I thought his camera was better and I asked where he got it. He said from his father. When we finished taking photographs we came to my apartment and he took his film out of his camera and it was already developed. Then the photos grew into poster-size enlargements. I asked him again where he got this camera and he said from his father.

Dreamer: A 31-year-old woman with hysterical and phobic features.

Association: She felt that the father in the dream was really her own father. Her father had always been depriving.

Interpretation: The cameras represent penises. Kent's brother has a more powerful penis, which he got from his father. The dreamer associates this father with her own; hence the meaning is that she did not get a penis of her own, she got a vagina, which she feels does not do as many things as a penis. The pictures from Kent's brother's camera come out already developed (ejaculation) as opposed to her pictures, which take time (nine months) to develop. And his pictures become immediate enlargements (have erections), while hers do not. The dream is an expression of her penis envy and her wish for a penis and perhaps to be a male, like Kent's brother, who could then have a closer bond with the father.

Epileptic Dreams

Dream 1: I was in school. The other students were teasing me. I wanted to fight back but somebody was holding my arms.

Dream 2: Somebody was smothering me. They had a pillow over my mouth. I wanted to cry out but couldn't.

Dream 3: I was in my room and a fire broke out. The fire was all around me. I couldn't escape.

Dream 4: I was driving on the freeway. A car cut me off and another ran into me from the side. I didn't know what to do.

Dream 5: I was swimming in a pool. Suddenly it became a whirlpool and I was about to drown. My throat was full of water and I couldn't scream.

Dream 6: I was suddenly paralyzed.

Dream 7: My mother asked me a question and I couldn't speak.

Dream 8: I couldn't think.

Dream 9: I saw my brother lying on the street. Apparently somebody had killed him. I looked around for help.

Dreamer: A 38-year-old woman suffering from epilepsy.

Associations: The woman had all of these dreams during a two-week period leading up to an epileptic seizure. During this period she encountered many frustrations on her job.

Interpretation: Each of the dreams show the dreamer helpless to express or cope with a dilemma. These dilemmas are symbolic of both the pressures in her present life, and the conflicts in her childhood, which left her with a murderous rage at her younger brother, who was favored by her parents. In the epileptic attack, according to Stekel (1911), the epileptic's criminal and sadistic urges, which are insufficiently repressed, break through. The seizure represents an act of aggression that must be muffled, so it is reduced to spasmodic jerks and punches and the biting of one's tongue. Recent writings on epileptic seizures have returned to the prepsychoanalytic view that such fits are organic in origin, a view with which this author disagrees.

Equipment

Dream: I went skiing with Mark. He wasn't able to get his equipment together. I felt held back by him.

Dreamer: A 33-year-old masochistic man with a severe castration complex.

Associations: Mark had been strongly advising him not to quit his job. He had recently gone skiing with Mark and Mark had been very competitive with him, always wanting to ski faster.

Interpretation: Skiing symbolizes, on one level, power and achievement (quitting his job and getting a better one). On another level it may represent sexual prowess. The dream is a reversal whereby the dreamer outdoes his antagonist, even though the antagonist tries to hold him back, because the antagonist cannot get his equipment (his genitals) together (erect).

Erection

Dream: As I looked out my bedroom window I could see construction workers on a building site nearby. It seemed that overnight they had erected an enormous building. It shot way into the sky. I was astonished.

Dreamer: A young man with sexual conflicts (partial impotence).

Association: For some time he had suffered from bouts of impotence with his wife.

Interpretation: The astounding overnight erection of the building outside his bedroom (where his impotence occurred) signified his wish for an overnight potency.

Dream: I am in a bathtub. I have an erection and touch it. I show it to my wife, who wants to take a picture of it. Then my penis is detached, floating around. But I tell myself it is nothing, as this always happens.

Dreamer: A 38-year-old phobic man who suffers from impotence. As reported by Rangell (1952).

Association: The dreamer has often spoken of his phobia about dolls. He tries to avoid seeing them.

Interpretation: Rangell interprets that the detached penis signifies castration. When his wife/mother sees his forbidden erection (photographs it), he is castrated. The castration fear underlies his impotence and his doll phobia. Seeing a doll is a reminder of his castration, apparently traceable to some incident in his childhood. His reassurance that "it is nothing" is his attempt to accept this castration.

Dream: I watched my mother put the bread into the oven and could see it rising through the oven window. I woke up with an erection and didn't know why.

Dreamer: A 32-year-old alcoholic man with a mother fixation.

Associations: He recalled occasions when his mother had walked around the house in various states of undress.

Interpretation: The rising of the bread symbolizes erection. The fact that the dreamer did not know why he was excited when he woke up indicates his denial of his incestuous feelings toward his mother. The metaphor of bread rising in an oven may also represent pregnancy and the dreamer's wish to make his mother pregnant and partake in the birthing and nurturing process (something he was not allowed to do as a boy—his mother kept him at a distance when she gave birth to and nurtured his younger sister). It may also denote his womb envy.

Evidence

Dream: I had to keep an eye on a child in a wading pool. Then I had to steal something, some papers or evidence, about the headmaster of a school, to prove he was corrupt. While searching in a cabinet I found art supplies. Someone caught me and I hit him and ran out.

Dreamer: A 40-year-old obsessive-compulsive male artist.

Association: When he was a child, his mother had several mysterious (to him) miscarriages or abortions. His father was a self-righteous, aloof man.

Interpretation: This dream condenses many levels of meaning. The evidence he seeks of corruption of the headmaster probably refers to his psychoanalytic search to understand and expose the emotional abuse of his parents (the cabinet being his father). The person whom he hits is his father, who opposes his therapy. The child in the pond (a fetus in the womb) is perhaps both himself and the babies his mother lost when he was a child. The mysterious disappearances of babies made him fear for his own life.

Dream: My parents were on trial, but they made me eat the evidence. Afterwards, I started acting guilty.

Dreamer: A 56-year-old man.

Association: Whenever he visited his parents, he felt guilty.

Interpretation: The dream has a "sins of the fathers" motif. The guilty parents transfer that guilt to their son, thereby making him into a criminal (neurotic).

Examination

Dream: I'm back in my high school trying to take an examination. To my horror, I can't think of a single answer. I stare at the test questions and my mind goes blank.

Dreamer: A 32-year-old man with an addictive personality.

Association: He had gone to a high school reunion recently and was surprised at how much some people had changed. "People who were nerds in high school were now doctors."

Interpretation: Examination dreams are common and sometimes tend to be recurring. Most of them are metaphors about being put to the test in one's life. However, this recurring dream represents the dreamer's unconscious sense of failure in life since high school. It signifies his sense of not having lived up to his and his father's expectations and coming up short in comparison to his schoolmates.

Dream: I walked into a large examination room to take an examination in genetics. I suddenly realized that I hadn't studied for the test. I went up to the teacher and began to argue with him. Why do I need to know about genetics? That's not my major.

Dreamer: A 49-year-old psychoanalyst.

Association: He was going to have to give a lecture on the etiology of schizophrenia the next day.

Interpretation: The dream is warning him that he does not know enough about, or put enough stress on, the genetics of schizophrenia. It expresses his fear that someone in the audience might expose his ignorance if he does not adequately prepare himself.

Dream: We were given a pop quiz in biology. I sat looking at the paper and felt very frightened. I started to shake and then I was afraid I might even faint. I thought I had been well prepared, but now I felt so paralyzed and couldn't even lift my pen.

Dreamer: A 24-year-old man suffering from generalized anxiety who was about to get married.

Association: He recalled that he had felt afraid of his last two exams, even to the point of fainting like in the dream, but had gone on and done quite well. He wondered if he'd faint at his wedding.

Interpretation: Freud viewed examination dreams of this sort as reassurances; such dreams allude to a past experience when the dreamer felt afraid of an exam, yet passed it despite his fears. In this case, the dreamer's fear seems to be about performing sexually on his wedding night. He is afraid he will be paralyzed (impotent), and will not be able to lift his pen (not get an erection).

Excrement

Dream: The dreamer saw his analyst's daughter in front of him and where her eyes should have been, there were two patches of excrement.

Dreamer: The Rat Man, a young man suffering from obsessive-compulsive disorder. Reported by Freud (1909b).

Associations: The patient had previously seen a girl sitting on the stairway of Freud's office and assumed she was Freud's daughter. He claimed that Freud was trying to get him to marry his daughter.

Interpretation: Freud's interpretation of this dream was, "You want to marry my daughter not for her beautiful eyes but for her money." In classical psychoanalysis, excrement is seen as symbolic of money, since the first act of giving that an infant must make is to give up his feces to his mother. Hence, feces is the original barter arrangement: I give my feces, you give your approval. The Rat Man was diagnosed as "anal retentive" — as are most obsessive-compulsives. He did not want to give up his feces, and resented having to pay for his sessions. However, the dung that he saw as Freud's daughter's eyes might have had other meanings as well; it may have alluded to his unconscious feeling that if he married a woman he would have to give up his feces to her, or to urges of wanting to defile women.

Explosion

Dream: I'm in a war zone and a bomb is exploding. I run to my house and rush inside just as another explosion occurs. Inside I see people walking around naked. I go upstairs and my friend Tom and his sister are in my bedroom. I have sex with her and come all over her body.

Dreamer: A 44-year-old bachelor with an emotionally incestuous attachment to his sister.

Associations: In the dream, his bedroom looks more like his sister's bedroom. Upon waking, he felt that his friend's sister looked very much like his own sister.

Interpretation: This is about the dreamer's incestuous impulses about his younger sister. Intercourse with his sister first appears in disguise—as being in a war zone and as explosions. Similarly, the sexual partner is also at first seen in disguise—as naked people and then as Tom's sister. The forebiddenness of the incest causes this symbolization of the sexual union and of ejaculation (explosion). The explosion may also refer to the dreamer's violently conflicting feelings about these incestuous wishes and to ambivalence toward all women (dating being like going into a war zone). Finally, through secondary elaboration, he recognizes that the girl in the dream is his sister.

Dream: I was going into an apartment building. I passed a woman and a little girl. I saw a stuffed doll and wanted to pick it up, but the little girl wanted it too. I tried to reach it but couldn't. Then I tried to go up the stairs but the stairs had disappeared. Outside I saw the super and he was angry. He said the building had exploded. I looked up and saw that the top three floors, including the one my apartment was on, had collapsed. I realized my cat had died and felt horrible pain.

Dreamer: A 25-year-old woman who suffered from hysteria.

Associations: The woman and girl reminded her of herself and her mother. The stuffed doll was like one she had had as a child.

Interpretation: The explosion connotes the dreamer's rage at her mother, which, through identification with the aggressor, gets taken out on herself. The building is herself, the top representing her head or brain. Not being able to reach the stuffed doll harks back to her deprivation as a child. Her cat represents her strongest libidinal bond, but may also symbolize her innocence and will have to live. This is a parable: in trying to hurt others, you end up hurting yourself.

Dream: The dreamer was crossing the Tagliamento and could hear the explosions of the Australian bombardment. He cried out, "We are undone!"

Dreamer: Napolean, Emperor of France. Reported in Freud (1900).

Association: He was awakened by a bomb explosion while he was asleep in his carriage, and remembered having just had this dream.

Interpretation: Hearing the explosion in his sleep was the direct stimulus of the dream. However, it revived the memory of one of his previous battles, at Atole, where he had suffered a loss. The dream was rooted in fear of repeating that experience.

Dream: I'm flying an airplane very low, just a few feet from the ground. I see a house and there is a naked woman near the window. I drop a bomb on the house and see it explode, and I feel very guilty.

Dreamer: A 23-year-old man with borderline features.

Association: He lived at home with his mother, and spoke of how his mother was always embracing him since his father had died.

Interpretation: The airplane flying low symbolizes the dreamer's sexual feelings about his mother, which are becoming dangerously aroused. The earth and the naked woman symbolize his mother, and the house perhaps symbolizes her engulfing vagina. The explosion represents the violence of incestuous intercourse as well as his rage at her.

Eye

Dream: A man with strange eyes was looking at me. I went around the corner to the hospital.

Dreamer: A 27-year-old hysterical woman.

Association: She had a phobia about getting pregnant.

Interpretation: In her unconscious, a man's eyes are symbolic of aggressive phalluses that can get her pregnant. Hence, she goes to the hospital (for an abortion).

Dream: A man was bothering my mother. I looked at him and he started to bleed.

Dreamer: A 33-year-old psychotic.

Association: The man might have been his father.

Interpretation: In the magical thinking of many psychotics, the eyes have murderous powers.

Dream: I saw a man with an eye in the middle of his forehead.

Dreamer: A 45-year-old Asian woman.

Association: She felt anxious about being in a new country.

Interpretation: According to Eastern philosophical (Buddhist) writing, an eye in the middle of the forehead denotes inner peace.

Dream: I saw eyes looking at me from all over my ceiling.

Dreamer: An alcoholic man going through withdrawal.

Association: He felt as though he was quite disgusting.

Interpretation: The eyes are the dreamer's guilt projected externally.

Eyelid

Dream: I lost an eyelid and because of this my career is in jeopardy.

Dreamer: A young man with a "Jewish complex." Reported by Stekel (1911).

Association: He had recently applied for a job and feared he would be turned down because he was Jewish.

Interpretation: The loss of an eyelid symbolizes circumcision. The dream expresses his "Jewish complex."

Eyesight

Dream: She was pushing her baby in a stroller when she lost her grip and the stroller ran into traffic out of her eyesight.

Dreamer: A young woman patient of Fritz Perls, as reported by Faraday (1974).

Association: None given.

Interpretation: Perls asked the woman, "When did you have your miscarriage?"

Face

Dream 1: I looked in the mirror but I couldn't see my face. I could see my eyes staring back at me, as if disapprovingly, but there was no face.

Dream 2: I was walking along and my hat kept sliding down onto my chest, because I had no face.

Dreamer: A young schizophrenic man.

Association: He had always felt invisible.

Interpretation: The invisible faces in these dreams allude to the dreamer's delusion that he does not, in fact, have a face. The face has been deprived of a normal cathexis, and so it ceases to exist in his own mind. He had developed this form of withdrawal and depersonalization as the result of his having suffered from a continuous series of humiliations in his early childhood, which he perceived of as a chronic "loss of face."

Dream: A man threw a vial of blood on my face. I was horrified.

Dreamer: A 39-year-old woman with hysterical features.

Association: She spoke about her anger at men and her regret about having to be a second-class citizen.

Interpretation: The vial of blood is menstrual blood. She feels cursed to be a woman, as though it were a "slap in the face" by men, as well as a "loss of face."

Fairy

Dream: A tiny woman with transparent wings, no bigger than a hummingbird, was hovering about mkept swatting at her , thinking she was a bug, but then I looked up and saw the woman's face and body. She was naked and had a tiny tuft of golden pubic hair that matched her long strands of golden hair. She smiled at me and said in a high voice, "It's all right, I'm on your side."

Dreamer: A 33-year-old male poet with manic-depressive and narcissistic features.

Association: He had been going through a depressive cycle and felt very alone.

Interpretation: The little woman is his good fairy, come to protect him from his bad objects, external and internal. She represents his introjected (and then projected) good mother of childhood primitive idealization.

Falling

Dream: I am falling out of the sky and into a dark pit somewhere in the middle of the earth.

Dreamer: A young teenage girl who had been raised in a strict Catholic household. She had just had sex for the first time the day before the dream.

Association: She had a feeling the sky was heaven and the pit was hell.

Interpretation: Dreams of falling are among the most common type of dream. This dream reflects her guilt about her fall from grace and virtue in the eyes of the Catholic church and in the eyes of her parents. The pit might be seen not only as hell but as her own womb, with its sexual desires that were devouring her. The dream may also represent her need to punish herself and expiate guilt.

Dream: The dreamer fell off the balcony of her sixth-story apartment.

Dreamer: Ann Faraday, British psychologist. Reported in her book *The Dream Game* (1974).

Association: When she had been standing on the balcony the day before, she wondered if the railing was safe. (It turned out that the railing was indeed rickety.)

Interpretation: This dream is a simple warning. The unconscious mind has become aware of something that the conscious mind was perhaps too distracted to notice.

Dream 1: I saw myself coming down the elevated stairs. Suddenly I dropped dead and fell down the stairs.

Dream 2: I was on the Woolworth tower looking down. Suddenly I slipped and fell to the ground. My body made a hole in the ground as it was smashed to pieces.

Dream 3: I was shot at and was hit right through the head. I fell to the ground.

Dreamer: A male patient, as reported by Kardiner (1941).

Association: The patient suffered from post-traumatic stress syndrome from incidents during his involvement eight years earlier in World War I.

Interpretation: The dreams of people suffering from post-traumatic stress, epilepsy, and severe abuse serve to discharge emotion through repeated recreations of such traumas in symbolic form. The dreamer envisions varied forms of torture or death and then, upon awakening, feels a sense of triumph over them. The aim is to master the traumatic situations that once overwhelmed the ego and threatened to destroy it. Horror movies serve much the same purpose for people in general, and those most attracted to horror movies are perhaps those who have suffered the most horrible traumas.

Dream: I was in my bedroom and my mother came in the room to wake me for school. I rolled over on my bed and as I did so I slid off the bed and out of the window. I began falling and I became more and more frightened because I thought the end was near. But when I landed, I discovered that the grass was unusually long and soft, and I was fine.

Dreamer: A narcissistic businessman of about 35 years of age who had left home when he was 17 years old.

Associations: He recalled how old-fashioned both his mother and father were, and how he had always resented their strictness and his mother's doting on him. He thought their overprotectiveness had hampered him. His mother still called him several times a week and had called him the day before the dream.

Interpretation: The immediate stimulus of the dream is the mother's phone call the day before. It awakens unconscious memories of the mother's pampering and his annoyance with it. The mother's caretaking in the dream (waking him up to go to school) only serves to cause him to roll off the bed and out the window. The fall may represent both his wish to escape her doting and his guilt feelings (fear that the end is near) about hating her — how can he hate somebody who is so good to him? The dream also pertains to his present conflict about how close he should be to his parents. However, in the end, he falls on soft grass as if to console himself that the closeness is not too much. Narcissistic grandiosity is perhaps apparent in his miraculous landing.

Dream: The dreamer fell from the top of the Empire State Building onto a beautiful soft bed of pine needles.

Dreamer: Peggy Cass, American entertainer. Reported by Faraday (1974).

Association: She said the falling sensation was quite pleasurable.

Interpretation: Faraday, noting that the dreamer described the fall as pleasurable, and the landing as a bed, suggested that she saw herself as a "fallen woman." The dreamer replied, "Not anymore . . ."

Dream: The dreamer was holding onto a turret on the pinnacle of the building. There was a large spike at the top. She had her fingers around it. There was something in her other hand that she did not want to let fall. In attempting to rearrange it, she lost her grasp and fell.

Dreamer: A 35-year-old single woman brought up in an extremely religious family. Reported by Gutheil (1951).

Association: The patient recalled a section from the *Bible* about Jesus' temptation by the devil on the pinnacle of the temple.

Interpretation: The dream portrays the conflict between her sexual longings and religious conditioning. The long spike is a phallic symbol, which she holds onto precariously. The object in her other hand is probably the *Bible*. In trying to balance between the two forces, she wavers and falls.

Dream: I'm standing on top of a high building with my husband. He embraces me and tickles me to make me laugh. A woman nearby says, "Watch out." Suddenly I lose my footing and fall from the building, tumbling and screaming. My body hits the pavement and shatters into a thousand pieces.

Dreamer: A 30-year-old woman suffering from acrophobia.

Association: Recently she had had an argument with her husband in which he had hit her. When she was a baby, her father used to throw her high into the air and then catch her. Once, he missed and she fell to the floor. (She did not remember this incident, but her mother had told her about it.)

Interpretation: Falling and splattering alludes not only to the fear of annihilation by her husband, but also harks back to the trauma of her father's dropping her, the memory of which lingers in her body ego. It is this original trauma that remains as the source of her acrophobia, recreated in this traumatic dream. The woman who shouts, "Watch out," is her mother, who she wishes had protected her from this trauma.

Dream: I'm falling in space, but it's great. I'm not afraid.

Dreamer: A 39-year-old woman suffering from sexual frigidity.

Association: She had been expressing frustration about her inability to have orgasms.

Interpretation: The dream is a wish to let go, let herself fall, so that she can experience the ecstasy of orgasm.

Fame

Dream: I was in the subway, going down the stairs, when I saw a famous person. It was Woody Allen. I recognized him immediately, and I asked myself, "Do I want to talk to him? He's a child molester." He used to be somebody I respected, but now I felt disillusioned. Then he bumped into me twice and didn't say excuse me. He was quite rude. I tried to say something but decided against it.

Dreamer: A 32-year-old passive male.

Association: A few days earlier he had wanted to say something to his boss but had stopped himself because the boss was having marital difficulties.

Interpretation: Dreams of meeting famous people often represent the dreamer's narcissistic wish to be acknowledged by a famous person and hence to enhance his or her own feelings of self-importance. In this case, the dream goes a step further. Upon meeting the famous person, the dreamer feels superior to him and discovers that he is rude. The dream also represents a symbolic recreation of the dreamer's passivity (his inability to say anything when Woody Allen is rude to him), a passivity that can be traced back to his relationship with his narcissistic, domineering father.

Fashion Show

Dream: I was living with my parents on the bottom floor of an apartment building. On the top floor was a fashion show. We went up to this floor and sat in a compartment near where the models were. My father and I looked around. Then the show started and a woman came out in a satin gown, waving her hair. She flirted with me with her eyes. Later I took the elevator down and there were two men in the elevator. Then one of the men turned into a woman. I felt attracted to her. We kissed passionately while my mother looked on.

Dreamer: A 32-year-old woman struggling with ego-dystonic lesbian urges.

Association: Her parents had recently visited her from a foreign country. Her mother is always competing with her, and doesn't ever let her be alone with her father.

Interpretation: The fashion show on the top floor of the building probably represents sexual liberation (rising up the elevator). The models represent the dreamer's mother, who was a beautiful woman, and projections of the dreamer's own sexuality and exhibitionism. The wish in the dream is that she could actualize her sexuality and have it accepted. The man on the elevator who turns into a woman stands for the dreamer's wish to integrate her masculine and feminine sides and suggests her bisexual orientation. The lesbianism is also an attempt to win her mother's approval and acceptance of her sexuality and avoid competing with her mother for men (her father).

Father

Dream 1: I was in Father's Mission Hall. Fairbairn was on the platform but he had Mother's hard face. I lay passive on a couch on the floor of the Hall, with the couch head to the front of the platform. He came down and said, "Do you know the door is open?" I said, "I didn't leave it open," and was pleased I had stood up to him. He went back to the platform.

Dream 2: I was being besieged and was sitting in a room discussing it with Father. It was Mother who was besieging me and I said to him, "You know I'll never give in to her. It doesn't matter what happens. I'll never surrender." He said, "Yes, I know that. I'll go and tell her," and he went and said to her, "You'd better give it up. You'll never make him submit," and she did give up.

Dreamer: Harry Guntrip, British psychoanalyst. Reported in his paper, "My Experience of Analysis with Fairbairn and Winnicott" (1975).

Associations: He had the first dream a few weeks after beginning treatment with Fairbairn. His father was a Methodist minister, whom Guntrip resented for not standing up to his abusive mother. The second dream came a year later.

Interpretation: The locale of the first dream is an amalgamation of Fairbairn's consulting room and the dreamer's father's church. To Guntrip, the dream shows a clear negative transference of his "severe dominating mother" onto Fairbairn ("he had Mother's hard face"). The open door signifies the dreamer's need to escape the events that happened in childhood. His wish that he could stand up to his mother is represented in the dream by his standing up to Fairbairn as a symbolic mother. In the second dream, he gets his father to protect him from his mother. This dream shows the progress he has made in therapy, indicating that he has traced the deepest source of his anger to his earlier, preoedipal deprivation and abuse by his mother.

Dream: I was in my therapist's office and he came over to the chair and leaned over me in a sexual way, as if to kiss me. Then he changed into my father. I felt very upset.

Dreamer: A 24-year-old woman who suffered from depression and suicidal tendencies.

Associations: She recalled that her mother had gotten angry at her for being too affectionate toward her father when she was about 7 years old. She thought her mother had meant she was being too sexual with her father. From that time on, she had acted emotionally distant toward him.

Interpretation: Her therapist in the dream is a current transference symbol of her father (he changes to her father). In the dream she makes her father the sexual aggressor, whereas in real life her mother had accused her of being sexually aggressive toward her father. In the dream, as in real life, she again rejects him. It is a repeating pattern in her life.

Dream: The dreamer's father was standing with her on a hill that was covered with wheat fields. She was quite tiny beside him, and he seemed to her like a giant. He lifted her up from the ground and held her in his arms like a little child. The wind swept over the wheat fields, and as the wheat fields swayed in the wind, he rocked her in his arms.

Dreamer: The Philosophy Student, a young, intellectual woman. Reported by Jung in "The Relations between the Ego and the Unconscious" (see *The Portable Jung* 1971).

Associations: The patient had developed an erotic transference toward Jung, in which she idealized him — as she had done her own father — viewing him as her savior and god. The psychoanalysis had been at a standstill when she had the dream.

Interpretation: Jung's interpretation was that her dreams were a message from her collective unconscious. She was making him into a doctor of superhuman proportions, a gigantic primordial father, a god who is at the same time the wind, and in whose protecting arms she was resting like an infant. He said her dream description of her father was like the mythical nature demon/god Wotan. Another likely interpretation is that she had regressed in therapy to an early infantile age, at which she had sought protection from an idealized father (who in reality had not given her such protection). She now sought it from Jung.

Dream: I was in a house, at the inner side of a door which was a crack open. Outside was my father, loaded with gift-wrapped packages, wanting to enter. I was intensely frightened and attempted to close the door in order to keep him out.

Dreamer: Mr. Z, a shy, narcissistic professional. Reported by Kohut (1979).

Associations: Mr. Z was an only child, and his parents separated for a year when he was 4. His father had an affair with a younger woman, then returned to his mother when Mr. Z was 5. He had the above dream when the father returned.

Interpretation: Kohut interpreted this dream twice, first using classical psychoanalytic, and then *self psychology* (the name he gave his school of analysis) terminology. Initially he saw the dream as referring to the boy's ambivalent attitude toward the returning father, his castration fear, and his tendency to retreat from competitiveness and male assertion and regress to a preoedipal (before the third year) attachment to his mother. In the second interpretation, made some years later, he saw the dream as indicative of the mental state of a boy who had been all too long deprived of his father. This second interpretation stressed the positive needs of the boy. Probably both interpretations have merit.

Dream: I'm sitting in an outdoor cafe. A couple walks up. Turns out they run the boarding house where my father is staying. I ask if they know him. The man says he does. I ask what he is like. "He's a very difficult man. Always critical." His wife, a beautiful woman, imitates my father, saying, "If your rooms are so dreadful you must be pigs."

Dreamer: A 30-year-old schizoid man whose father has been distant and hostile all his life.

Association: He wrote to his father that he was coming to visit in a month. His father replied that he was too busy to see him.

Interpretation: The dream is an acknowledgment that his father is indeed a difficult man. The dreamer does not trust his own judgment, however, so he has a beautiful woman of the kind he admires make this judgment. The beautiful woman may also be his mother, who often mocked his father.

Dream: My father and I are staying in a motel together. He comes out of the bathroom naked and lies on the bed. I begin to masturbate. He looks over and then begins to masturbate too.

Dreamer: A 27-year-old man with bisexual tendencies.

Association: He recalled an incident when he and his father stayed at a motel together. His father had lain in bed naked but "he would never do anything like jerking off."

Interpretation: His wish is that his father would masturbate with him, which would be a sign to him that his father accepts his sexuality and welcomes him to the world of men.

Fear

Dream 1: I arrived at my office at 2 P.M. and was afraid my boss would be disappointed. Then I realized I wasn't at the office, I was at my parents' house. But people from the office were there, at my parents' house. It was confusing. I woke up feeling scared.

Dream 2: I was in a suburban neighborhood like the one where my parents live. There had been a fire. I looked down the street and saw some people having a prayer meeting on the lawn. I saw my cousin, a naive kid, running out of his house. I had the feeling that he started the fire. I chased after him but couldn't catch him. I woke up feeling scared.

Dreamer: A 33-year-old man with obsessive features.

Association: My cousin in the second dream is me. It's me who's running from the fire. The people praying are my family.

Interpretation: The fear in both dreams is the fear he felt toward his parents. The impossible expectations they placed upon him caused him to feel that he was always disappointing them, which caused him to be angry at them. He projected that they were angry at him, which caused him to fear them. In the first dream, through condensation, his boss and the office become his parents' house. This indicates the parental transference toward his boss. In the second dream, the fire in a suburban neighborhood represents his wish to burn down his parents' house. The fear he feels upon waking is the fear of his parents' retaliation for his hatred of them. Unable to own this anger, he projectively identifies his cousin as the angry pyromaniac.

Dream: I was with my son and he kept rushing up to men on the street and French kissing them. I was appalled. "Stop that," I told him. I was so afraid he was going to be homosexual.

Dreamer: A 48-year-old hysterical woman.

Association: She said this was a recurring dream and that she had been preoccupied with the fear that he would be homosexual since he had been an adolescent.

Interpretation: The fear in this dream, and in the dreamer's real life, masks a wish for her son to be homosexual. At the age of 17, her son still slept with her when they went on trips together. She had clung to him and unconsciously did not want him to separate from her and bond with another woman. Since she did not want to acknowledge this wish to herself, she had developed a reaction formation of over-concern about his becoming homosexual. Although she was in conflict about his being homosexual, she preferred that possibility to his going to another woman.

Dream: I was alone with Larry, and I kept looking at the buttons on his shirt. I was suddenly terrified of his buttons. I didn't know why. I couldn't look at them.

Dreamer: A 40-year-old epileptic woman.

Association: She recalled that she had been molested as a little girl by a man who wore long underwear with buttons.

Interpretation: The buttons symbolize the penis of the older man who had molested her. Through this displacement of her fear of penises to buttons, she warded off the traumatic memory while retaining a button phobia.

Feces

Dream: A fully grown man finds himself in the large public bathroom in the basement of the primary school he attended as a boy. He feels an urgent need to defecate and is glad as he enters a small toilet booth that no one else is around. He discovers, at first with alarm and disgust, that the walls of the cubicle he's chosen are covered with feces. It is mostly dry and hard, but some of it is fresh and oozing. It is not only foul, but poisonous — dangerous, as if it contains a malodorous corrosive. But then it occurs to him that the odor seems familiar, and his anxiety lessens with the realization that it's actually his own excrement. He's used to it and doesn't mind it. Now he feels safe and comfortable and can defecate and urinate in peace.

Dreamer: Patient X, a young single man with an anal-retentive personality, as reported by Shengold (1989).

Association: After telling his analyst the dream, the young man remembered almost crashing his automobile the day before, and said he might be angry because the analyst raised his fee.

Interpretation: The metaphor of the isolated toilet that was walled-in feces represented a place of sanctity. Shengold notes that this symbolized his anus and rectum as a place of defensive retreat where he could control dangerous anal-sadistic, murderous feelings and impulses. The excrement-lined room also represented the bathroom to which he retreated all during his adolescence, usually in response to situations of psychic danger; it had been his site for restorative masturbation.

Dream: I went to the bathroom to get ready to go out. The bathroom was dirty. The toilet and bidet was full of feces. I flushed the toilet, but the feces didn't go away; instead the toilet overflowed. A yellow piece fell out and stuck to the rim.

Dreamer: A 29-year-old obsessive-compulsive woman.

Association: She had been physically abused as a child. Her parents had told her she was a monster. She tended to clean and scrub the bathroom several times a day. The yellow piece reminded her of a fetus.

Interpretation: The image of the dirty bathroom with the toilet and bidet overflowing with feces is a symbol of the dreamer's past, which is overflowing with repulsive and toxic memories that threaten to invade her present life. It may allude to toilet training, which is a time when the infant must submit to authority for the first time, a time when the dreamer was first made to feel like a monster by her parents, who did not want her. The yellow fetus suggests her childhood fear that her parents would flush her down the toilet.

Feet

Dream: I dreamed that my right foot grew to a foot long. The left one remained normal. I wondered how I could walk.

Dreamer: A 25-year-old woman.

Association: Her older brother was going to visit her.

Interpretation: The foot may be a symbol of the penis; she wishes she could have a penis like the older brother she admires.

Feminists

Dream: I was at a political rally and I was shouting my disagreement with what was being said up on the platform. Then this group of women surrounded me, wearing buttons saying something about women. They were apparently feminists. Next we were in this bedroom that was on the side of the auditorium (you could still hear the cheering) and they were holding me down and I was naked. One of the feminists had this large bread knife and she cut just the head of my penis off. I still had a stump and felt thankful for that.

Dreamer: A 27-year-old man suffering from gynophobia.

Association: His mother had a bread knife like the one in the dream.

Interpretation: The dreamer's morbid fear of woman stems from unresolved fears of re-engulfment and castration by his mother, a borderline. It gets transferred onto feminists in this dream. The feminists symbolize his fear and loathing of his mother, which he has largely repressed. The dream also conveys his fear of self-assertion (speaking out at the rally) and its consequences, also traceable to his mother's domination.

Fetus

Dream: I see something crawling in and out of a dark, narrow passage. I seems like a tiny red animal, like a fetus. I watch it closely to make sure it does not suffocate.

Dreamer: A young man suffering from bronchial asthma, as reported by Alexander and Wilson (1935).

Association: None given.

Interpretation: Alexander claims to have examined almost 6,000 dreams of forty-five asthmatics and found that the main themes of their dreams were intrauterine fantasies and depictions of pregnancy, abortion, and birth. The dream above shows an identification with the fetus and a longing to regress back to the mother's womb.

Dream: I was looking in the closet for my coat when I saw something on the floor. It was covered with fetuses, still alive, slithering here and there. I was aghast.

Dreamer: A young obsessive-compulsive woman.

Association: She recalled the three abortions she had had while she was in her teens.

Interpretation: The fetuses are the abortions she had, which have now become "skeletons in the closet."

Fever

Dream: I saw a snake writhing on the ground as if it had a fever. I felt disgusted.

Dreamer: A 39-year-old hysterical woman.

Association: She had a fear of men.

Interpretation: The dreamer's fear of sexual passion (fever) is generated by an underlying envy and disgust of penises (snakes).

Files

Dream: I was in a dark room. I saw a filing cabinet in the corner. I pulled out some files and a rat jumped out.

Dreamer: An obsessive-compulsive young man.

Association: Upon waking, he wasn't sure if a rat or some feces had jumped out of the drawer.

Interpretation: The dream is about the fear of losing control due to what may lurk in his unconscious. The rat/feces alludes to the anal phase and the fear of soiling, that is, of losing sphincter control and bringing shame on himself. ("I smell a rat.") The files are memories. The waking confusion is an example of what Freud called *secondary elaboration.*

Filicide

Dream: All the members of my family were dead. I had somehow killed them. I buried them in a mass grave, a hole in the ground. After I covered them with dirt I could see through it and there were rats eating them.

Dreamer: A 39-year-old woman suffering from chronic depression.

Association: She expressed the thought, "I can't live until they're dead." She had this dream after a lover had stolen a great amount of money from her and run off with it.

Interpretation: This is a wish-fulfillment dream without much dream censorship. During times of great distress a dream like this will break through the censorship as repression and other defenses momentarily lapse. The dreamer had had a horrible childhood in which she had been emotionally abandoned and abused, but generally the memories and feelings were repressed and her dreams were more distorted.

Fingernails

Dream 1: I was at my parents' house, sitting on the living room floor, doing my fingernails. My brother was complaining about me and I moved away from him. He said my fingernails were bothering him. I said, "How can my fingernails be bothering you? I know I'm not welcome here, but this is too much!"

Dream 2: I was at my grandmother's country house. My friend Eve was there with me. We walked to the back where there was a stream, took off our clothes and got into the water. Eve had the same kind of fingernail polish as I did, bright red. She said, "This feels so good." "Yeah," I said.

Dream 3: Back at my parents' house. I felt deep emotional pain. We were getting ready to go somewhere and my father was arguing with my mother, complaining about the color of my nail polish. I was sobbing.

Dreamer: A 24-year-old woman with borderline features.

Associations: She had always felt safe at her grandmother's house. Her father had been physically abusive when she was a child and she had escaped to grandmother.

Interpretation: The red fingernails symbolize the dreamer's sexuality, with which her father and brother are uncomfortable. Because of their rejection of her, she is driven into a lesbian relationship with her friend Eve, depicted in the dream. However, the bond with Eve occurs in her grandmother's backyard, where it is safe, and has more of a meaning of adolescent bonding than of adult sexuality. Since Eve can accept her sexuality (red nails) the dreamer can better accept her own.

Fire

Dream: I saw the upper part of my body becoming first fire, then water. My face became watery, then fiery, then watery. As I saw this, I tried to censor the dream as I was dreaming it. I didn't like seeing it

Dreamer: A 24-year-old woman who suffered from depression and suicidal impulses.

Associations: She spoke of her conflicts with her mother, who wanted to keep her dependent on her. She had been studying Jungian dream theory, and noted that fire and water were two of the four primitive elements.

Interpretation: She interpreted that the dream signaled a conflict between her spiritual (water) and her sensual (fire) sides. Two other sides, earth and air, were missing. On another level, the dream signals the conflict between the part of her personality that identifies with her mother (water), and the part that is angry at her (her real self), a part she has had to suppress all her life. The third part of her, which looks on at the conflict and wants to censor it, represents her superego (that is, her ego-ideal), which despises both extremes. This third part also shows how much she has dissociated from the other two parts, which are themselves fragmented.

Dream: A house was on fire. My father was standing beside my bed and woke me up. I quickly dressed. Mother wanted to stop and save her jewel case, but Father said, "I refuse to let myself and my two children be burned for the sake of your jewel case." We hurried downstairs and as soon as I was outside I awoke.

Dreamer: Dora, one of Freud's patients, an 18-year-old hysteric (Freud 1905).

Associations: She had this dream the night after an older man who was a friend of her father's tried to kiss her and she slapped him. The next day, as she was taking a nap, the man who had kissed her came into her bedroom and woke her, saying he was looking for something. She then demanded a key to the room and was told there was none.

Interpretation: The fire symbolizes the fire of passion, the older man's as well as her own, both of which frighten and disgust her. The jewel case represents, according to Freud, Dora's virginity. Dora's wish is that her father would rescue her from the fire (passion). Hence, in the dream it is her father, not his friend, who wakes her; however in the dream, as in real life, he does not protect her virginity and it must be sacrificed for the good of the family. The dream also alludes to a time in Dora's childhood when she used to wet her bed and her father would wake her, rescuing her from the wet bed, and perhaps from the fire of her infantile masturbation.

Fish

Dream: I'm in an auditorium full of people. The host of a show is going around the audience with a microphone. He comes to me and introduces me to the audience. "This is L. He's from Norway but grew up in Australia. He's learned a lot in his life and crossed many boundaries to get here." "Yes," I say, "I've crossed many boundaries to get here, and I'll be crossing many more." "Well, tell me a little about Norway," the host says. "Vel," I say in a Norwegian accent, "Norway ist a country vith a lot of fish, eh, ja, and a lot of bondage. Fish and bondage. Those are the two tings about Norway, ja." I notice a youngish, dark-haired girl sitting next to me, and ask if she has anything to say. The interviewer has now moved away.

Dreamer: A 31-year-old man with narcissistic features and an ego-dystonic homosexual orientation.

Associations: The host reminded him of his new therapist. Fish reminded him of a woman's vagina, which smelled to him like fish, or the smell of his mother's bed. The young girl seemed like his mother. He feels that his mother put him into bondage.

Interpretation: Fish is symbolic of his mother's vagina; bondage represents the emotional tie with his mother. The host of the show, standing for the dreamer's male therapist, signifies the dreamer's hopes of meeting a good father who will introduce him to the world and give him the fatherly support he craves in order to talk about his past, actualize his potential, and separate from the fish and bondage of his mother.

Five

Dream: I went back to the furniture store where I used to work as a salesman. Somehow, I was working there again. Larry, the manager, smiled and said,

"Congratulations, you were number five last month." I could sense the president of the company somewhere in the background, looking at me cautiously.

Dreamer: A 33-year-old recovering alcoholic.

Associations: The president's name was Harold, the same as my father's. I was the fifth member of my family [father, mother, brother, sister, himself].

Interpretation: The five, symbolic of his position in his family, is here made into a fortunate number, signifying achievement and assertiveness (good sales). The president of his company stands for his father, who committed suicide when the dreamer was a little boy. The dream is perhaps his wish that his father was still around to help him learn to be assertive and build his self-worth.

Fleeing

Dream 1: I was surfboarding on the water.

Dream 2: I was skateboarding through the air.

Dream 3: I was running along a winding road.

Dream 4: I was on a motorcycle, fleeing from a crazy killer. I had to ride over a bumpy trail, so I had to go slowly. The killer was right behind. I saw this body of water, accelerated, and jumped across it, landing on a prepuce — I mean precipice. The killer didn't see me.

Dreamer: A 35-year-old obsessive-compulsive man.

Association: He spoke of how his boss had been pressuring him for several weeks.

Interpretation: Each of the dreams, all of which the dreamer had on the same night, represents an aspect of escaping from an intolerable situation. The killer is his boss and perhaps his father, who, like his boss, was overbearing. The slip in which the dreamer confused "prepuce" with "precipice" indicates that his motorcycle (his phallus) landed on a prepuce (the skin that covers the penis and the clitoris). It also brings to mind the mound of Venus. Hence, at the deepest level, the dream may be about castration fear and about escaping his father's wrath by jumping into the lap of his mother.

Flying

Dream: The dreamer was flying through the air and performing acrobatics as he did so.

Dreamer: Johnny Carson, noted American entertainer. Reported by Faraday (1974).

Association: He related that he had this recurrent dream on nights after he had given a good performance.

Interpretation: Flying themes are among the most common of dream themes. Faraday interprets this dream to indicate that Carson really "gets a lift" out of showing off his verbal acrobatic skills. However, the dream could also relate to the phallic narcissistic stage of childhood, when boys discover their penises can perform feats of "magic."

Dream: The dreamer was flying along near to the ground. He tried to fly higher but it made him feel anxious, so he stayed at a medium height.

Dreamer: Jimmy Dean, American entertainer. Reported by Faraday (1974).

Association: When asked how he felt about "flying high" in his life, he replied, "Funny you should ask that. I've just been offered my own show on Broadway but turned it down because I didn't feel quite *up* to it."

Interpretation: Faraday views this dream as pertaining to a conflict about ambition. It may also pertain to feelings of low self-esteem or fear of competition.

Dream: I found I could fly if I flapped my arms with all my might. I flew out of my bed and along the ceiling of my house. Then I flew out of a window and I was above my yard. I flew over the field in back of my house and a cow chased after me. I was just above him out of reach and managed to fly away.

Dreamer: A young boy.

Association: He had this recurring dream during his childhood.

Interpretation: Flying represents his wish to escape from the abuse of his family, particularly his hostile, alcoholic father. The cow symbolizes his father.

Dream: I was flying in an airplane with a strange woman, telling her about my boyfriend. I tried to cover up the problems we've been having. She seemed understanding.

Dreamer: A young woman with latent homosexual impulses.

Association: She had been having arguments with her boyfriend and was curious about sexual intimacy with another woman.

Interpretation: Flying represents sexual intimacy, in this case of a homosexual variety. The wish is that such intimacy with another woman would be more gratifying, and she would find such a woman more understanding than her boyfriend.

Fog

Dream: I was driving on a foggy road and couldn't see where I was going. Suddenly I crashed into a tree.

Dreamer: A 44-year-old woman.

Association: She had felt confused since her mother died.

Interpretation: The fog stands for her confusion and depression. She fears that it will cause her to lose control.

Food

Dream 1: I was dining with three men. There was lots of food. The men were enjoying it and it seemed fine for them. But I thought something was wrong with it.

Dream 2: My mother brought some food to my bed. I was sick. I had the feeling that the food was poisoned and that's why I was sick.

Dream 3: A mother was feeding her baby. I sensed the milk was bad and wanted to stop her. But it was none of my business.

Dream 4: I was at a wedding. At the banquet, they brought out silver platters with breasts on them. A woman next to me said they were human breasts and that they were a delicacy. I declined to try one.

Dreamer: A 27-year-old woman suffering from anorexia nervosa.

Association: Her mother had no breast milk when she was born. She recalled their fighting over food; she did not want to eat and her mother would force her.

Interpretation: These recurring dreams about food represent the leitmotif of the dreamer's life. From birth onward, food became an issue between her mother and herself. It became a control war, the mother forcing food and the daughter stubbornly refusing it. Food symbolizes love, or rather, her mother's withholding of love. The daughter's refusal to eat represents her withholding of love in response. The recurring dreams show variations of the theme of her refusing food. In these dreams she is still trying to master and discharge the early trauma.

Dream 1: War breaks out and I walk into a field, joyful that I will soon die, glad that I can now eat any kind of food I want.

Dream 2: I order goulash at a restaurant but can only eat a small portion. I complain to my old nursemaid that people are torturing me and that I want to set myself on fire in the forest.

Dreamer: Ellen West, a woman suffering from depression, anorexia, bulimia, paranoia, and suicidal impulses. Reported by Binswanger (1958).

Associations: She had these dreams while locked up in a mental hospital. A few days after she was released, she took a lethal dose of poison.

Interpretation: Food symbolizes freedom and self-soothing. Death also represents freedom—freedom from the torture of living. The immediate torturers were the staff of the mental hospital where she was staying. The original torturers were her parents. Her father was intrusive to a psychotic degree, demanding complete obedience while forbidding the expression of any anger. Hence all her anger was displaced and somatized — taken out on the people around her and on herself (the desire to kill herself). The only way she had ever been able to get her father to let up was to be ill; then she would get a modicum of sympathy. The war in the field and fire in the forest may stand for her rage, which she externalizes onto her environment.

Forest

Dream (fairy tale): Hansel was a woodcutter's son. Gretel was a little girl he found one day in the forest. When the woodcutter and his wife couldn't find enough food to eat, his wife urged him to take the children into the forest and abandon them. The children laid a trail and managed to find their way back home, but were set adrift again. Then they found a gingerbread house in which a witch lived. The witch lured them inside and tried to push them inside her oven. They managed to escape and Hansel turned into a fawn. They were taken to the king's castle, where Hansel was restored to human form and enabled to marry Gretel.

Interpretation: This story — based on the original German version of "Hansel and Gretel" — is basically a cautionary tale for children. The forest represents the dangers of life. These dangers include negligent parents and witches (bad mothers, women). The relationship between Hansel and Gretel represents a common fantasy of the only child, who wishes he had a sister or brother and sometimes makes up an imaginary playmate whom he finds in the forest or somewhere and brings home. Such fantasies often end up with marriage and a happy ending as this one does. Turning into a fawn and then back into human form is an aspect of the magical thinking of children, and suggests the adaptation to circumstances that any healthy being must master.

Freeway

Dream: Tess and I were in my old neighborhood. We had just murdered somebody, and had stolen a Volkswagen. An Asian man came along and stood on the runningboard as we drove along on the freeway. He looked like you (the therapist). As we drove, Tess changed into a man. We escaped by climbing over the mountains surrounding the city.

Dreamer: A 35-year-old man suffering from depression.

Association: He had recently stopped speaking to his mother, but she still called him and expressed dismay at his not wanting to speak to her.

Interpretation: The freeway denotes the journey back to the dreamer's childhood and unconscious. The therapist is riding along (on the runningboard) for support.

The therapist in real life has published a book on Asian philosophy, so the dreamer makes him into an Asian. The person murdered is the dreamer's mother, at whom he is in a rage. She had been disappointed in the dreamer as a boy, wishing she had had a girl instead. In the dream, the dreamer kills off his mother and turns his girlfriend into a man, reversing this wish. The mountains over which they escape perhaps denote masculinity (phalluses) or breasts (escaping them). Hence the dream may be a wish to kill his mother (and her deprecation of his manhood) and affirm his masculinity.

Frog

Dream (fairy tale): A young woman was visited on three consecutive nights by a frog. On the first and second nights she was horrified by him and sent him away. On the third, she relented and allowed the frog to come into her bed. The moment she kissed him, the frog turned into a handsome prince.

Interpretation: "The Frog Prince" is an allegorical story of a young woman's overcoming her fear of sex or of penises. It is also about not judging by appearances.

Dream: I was in a strange house and I found a hidden doorway. I went down a dark hall and found another room. I heard something in the dark and turned on a light. There was a trunk in the corner. I opened it and a frog jumped out.

Dreamer: A 28-year-old woman who has obsessive-compulsive features.

Association: She was afraid of dark rooms. She was also afraid of what she'd find out in therapy.

Interpretation: The frog represents the horrifying or disgusting things (such as memories of childhood sexual humiliations) the dreamer fears are lying in her unconscious.

Funeral

Dream 1: We were at my mother's funeral. My husband was crying profusely. I was trying to comfort him.

Dream 2: A woman on the street was crying. I rushed up to her and asked what was the matter. She said my husband's funeral was that afternoon. I said, "Don't worry, it'll be all right."

Dream 3: I saw a funeral procession coming down the street and remembered I had to buy paper towels.

Dream 4: We were at Father's funeral. There were a lot of people there, all of them crying so hard. I felt sorry for them.

Dream 5: I was walking along when I heard crying. It was somebody's funeral. I walked on.

Dream 6: The way people were carrying on, you would have thought we were going to a funeral.

Dreamer: A 43-year-old woman suffering from rheumatoid arthritis.

Association: She had developed symptoms of arthritis after she had been jilted and robbed of her savings by a con man lover.

Interpretation: Individuals who fail to experience their own feelings often develop somatic symptoms. The recurring dreams about funerals show how, even in her dreams, an arthritic patient does not experience her feelings but projects them onto others. The preoccupation with funerals indicates the underlying murderous wishes that the dreamer represses in waking life and that then become displaced onto herself (the arthritis).

Furniture

Dream 1: I was at an exhibition of my own drawings. Each drawing contained either two matching body parts or two matching pieces of furniture — that is, two faces, two tables, two right arms, two beds. I had reproduced them from a catalog and thought they were good, but another person said they were not good.

Dream 2: I was going back to my home country. My husband and I found an apartment in an old part of the city. When I got there I saw that it was full of antique furniture. It was so full of furniture we couldn't move. The bed was blocking the bathroom door. We decided to go back to New York.

Dreamer: A 24-year-old woman suffering from depression.

Associations: She had these dreams the same night, after she had found out that her visa was running out and she could not renew it. She would have to return to her country, which she did not want to do because of bad relations with her family. The bed in the second dream was her mother's.

Interpretation: The matching furniture and body parts denote a split and fragmentation in the dreamer's personality, and the fact that animate and inanimate objects are combined in this exhibition perhaps alludes to present and past splits. Moreover, reproducing these drawings from a catalog signifies a creative block — a lack of spontaneity. The second dream clarifies this theme. She fears that if she goes back to her home country, she will be confronted with a room full of antique furniture (old repressed memories will overwhelm her). The bed (her mother's old bed) may signify her mother's interference with her sexual relationship with her husband. On a more archaic level, it may also allude to the primal scene.

Gangsters

Dream: I went down to the basement and found some gangsters hiding out down there. They chased after me with guns and knives but I managed to run up the stairs and lock the door behind me. I wondered how I could go down there again, since that was where the wood for the fire was located.

Dreamer: A 33-year-old woman with paranoid features.

Association: The basement reminded her of the basement of the house where she had grown up, which actually did have wood in it for the fireplace. She had always felt afraid of that basement.

Interpretation: The gangsters in the basement denote the dreamer's own unconscious aggression, which she projected onto the external world. The basement also represents the horrors of her childhood, symbolic of her authoritarian father, of her fears of her incestuous feelings about him, and of his toward her. Her recurring fears of her father makes her reluctant to "go down there" where the "wood for the fire" (her sexuality) is located.

Garden

Dream: It was the 1800s. I was wearing one of those old-fashioned long dresses. My parents were dead and I was raised by other parents. They were trying to arrange a marriage for me, but the guy I was supposed to marry didn't like me. I tried to win him over but was not successful. Anyway, I wanted to marry the gardener, who thought of me as a little girl. I went out to the garden to talk to him about raising roses, but nothing ever happened.

Dreamer: A 37-year-old depressed woman who had had very abusive parents.

Associations: She had just read a Jane Austen novel. She recalled how difficult it had been to win her husband.

Interpretation: This dream is a romantic novel, expressing the dreamer's wish to romanticize (revise) her life. In her wished-for life, her real parents are dead and she is raised by more kindly parents who try to match her up with somebody. However, just as in her real life she had little confidence in winning her husband, she has no confidence in winning her dream mate over. (This also alludes to her relationship with her real father, who was rejecting of her.) The garden and the gardener who thinks of her as a child are other references to her father, and her wish that he would have loved her and nurtured her (turned her into a rose).

Gender

Dream: I was making love with Donna and then I changed into a woman. Then I changed back into a man. I kept changing genders and she didn't even notice. At one point I was a little boy making love to an older woman. The next morning my aunt called and asked us over for breakfast.

Dreamer: A 29-year-old man suffering from gender confusion and multiple perverse symptoms.

Associations: He had been raised by his aunt, who had dressed him in women's dresses.

Interpretation: The switching of gender in the dream is an expression of the dreamer's gender confusion. The little boy making love to an older woman is a regression to his boyhood, emotionally incestuous relationship with his aunt. His aunt transmitted her own gender confusion (her masculinity complex and resentment of men and male sexuality) onto the boy by belittling his masculinity and encouraging feminine behavior. Hence he grew up as a "girl" with a penis.

Dream: I was kidnapped by aliens and taken to their planet. The people were all female. I was relieved. When it was time to return to Earth, I asked to stay.

Dreamer: A 24-year-old hysterical woman with homosexual and misandristic tendencies.

Association: She tried to avoid men in every sphere of her life.

Interpretation: The dream fulfills her aversion to men.

Ghosts

Dream (fictional): A ghost appeared as the dreamer stood with the guards. Finally he began to speak: "I am thy father's spirit, doom'd for a certain term to walk the night. . . ." He said that he had been poisoned by the dreamer's uncle, now stepfather, Claudius, so that he could marry the dreamer's mother, Gertrude, the Queen of Denmark, and become king. He said Claudius had seduced the mother and they had conspired together against him.

Dreamer: Shakespeare (1610), speaking through his character, Hamlet. He is a young man suffering from depression, full of feelings of jealousy and rage at his mother and uncle/stepfather, who have recently married only two months after his father has died.

Associations: He had guessed as much. "Oh my prophetic soul!" he said upon seeing the ghost. "It is an honest ghost, that let me tell you ...." He was bitter about his mother, even before seeing the ghost, musing on how speedily she had married and rushed to "incestuous sheets," moaning, "Frailty, thy name is woman!"

Interpretation: Hamlet appears to be Shakespeare's most autobiographical character. Like Hamlet, he suffered from lifelong depression, apparent in the brooding quality of his plays. The ghost, a projection of his guilt, tells him what he already has suspected. Full of oedipal guilt and jealousy, he wants to kill his stepfather and possess his mother. The bitterness at women—"Frailty, thy name is woman," is perhaps an indication that he himself may have also felt teased and spurned by his mother, just as his father was, and he may also have wanted to kill his real father. Hence his anger at Claudius is doubly intense because Claudius has done what he himself once wished to do, which touches his own oedipal guilt. We are always harshest toward those who do what we secretly wish to do—and condemn—deep in our unconscious selves.

Dream: My girlfriend was visiting me and I was showing her our new house. We passed by a room upstairs where the door was open and we heard a growl. "The family ghost," I said. "I don't know who opened this door." I laughed nervously, latched the door, and we walked on.

Dreamer: A 42-year-old man whose girlfriend was pressuring him to marry her.

Associations: He recalled that his girlfriend had again brought up the subject of marriage, and he had again said that he did not know how to tell his mother.

Interpretation: The family ghost is the man's mother, who has clung to her son ever since her husband died when the boy was a teenager. At the same time, the family ghost is the dead father, whose death still weighs on the mother. Finally, this ghost (as do most ghosts in dreams) represents the dreamer's unconscious guilt projected and transformed into anger directed at him (by the ghost). Locking the ghost into the room is the dreamer's wish to be rid of the ghost so that he can marry his girlfriend and go on with his life.

Dream: I dreamed I was in my bathroom. I felt a ghost inside the bathtub behind the shower curtain. I was drawn to go inside. Once there, a dark man handed me a doll. I took the doll and left the shower, thinking that the doll was evil.

Dreamer: A 30-year-old hysterical woman who had become pregnant by a man she was no longer seeing, and whom she now feared and despised. She was planning to give the baby up for adoption.

Associations: She had talked to her ex-boyfriend over the phone and was angry at him because he was insisting that he had a right to make a decision about the baby. She was adamant about giving the baby up, remembering how she had abused her pet cats.

Interpretation: The ghost represents her ex-boyfriend, and the doll represents the baby he gave her. Her sense that the doll is evil stems from her guilt feelings about her relationship with a man she now feels is disgusting, but also from a deeper unconscious rage, which she tends to disown and project onto the external world. The dream is a warning that she must get rid of this evil baby she is about to give birth to, lest it and its father contaminate her life.

Giants

Dream (fictional): I landed on the shore of a country called Brobdingnag where all of the people were giants and I was no bigger than a thumb. While I was there, the Maids of Honor would sometimes invite me to their apartments so that they could have the pleasure of seeing and touching me. They would often strip me completely naked and place me full length on their bosoms; they made me feel disgusted.

Dreamer: Jonathan Swift, in the voice of his character Gulliver, as paraphrased from *Gulliver's Travels* (1726).

Association: Swift never married, and his writing is full of oral and anal imagery.

Interpretation: Freud (1900) and Grinstein (1980) compared the fantasies of Swift to dreams in which patients saw people as enlarged and belittled. They attribute these distortions to the dreamer's desire to express infantile visions and fantasies, making people very large (harking back to early childhood), or very small (compensatory wish fulfillments of small children). The scene in Brobdingnag in which the Maids of Honor put him on their huge breasts alludes to the suckling stage of childhood in which a mother's breast does seem huge. Some theorists (Klein 1932) believe that in the beginning the infant relates only to the mother's breast, and not to the mother herself. If the breast is a bad one (depriving), it is viewed as an offending breast. Swift's fantasy seems to indicate that his own breast-feeding was less than satisfactory (his disgust with the scent of the breast). The pre-genital images of defecation and urination that permeate his writings are indications of severe fixations at that level.

Girl

Dream 1: A little girl of 4 was playing outside, wearing a pink dress. She was with her father. His wife wasn't there.

Dream 2: I went into a building with a little girl.

Dream 3: I had to pick up a little girl at the airport. We are in a stretch limousine. We pick up an old woman and she says, "Look at that child; she doesn't have socks on."

Dream 4: A criminal is at our house. Mother is making dinner. The criminal, a man, and I go outside and swim in the river. There is a little girl with us, wearing a pretty dress. She swims with us in the dress.

Dreamer: A 27-year-old hysterical woman who had been sexually abused.

Association: She had these recurring dreams about little girls, and sometimes she thought they were her. They were always 3 or 4 years old. This was how old she had been when her father had sexually abused her.

Interpretation: The little girls represent the dreamer at the stage at which she was sexually abused and unprotected (without socks). In these dreams she herself is there, as an adult, taking care of herself as a child; this is an expression of her childhood wish to have an older sister to protect her from her father. The first dream is an oedipal dream of wanting her father to herself. In another dream the father is a criminal. This condensation shows her ambivalence about her father. The pretty dresses in two of the dreams perhaps represent a wish to recapture the innocence she lost back then.

God

Dream (Hebrew myth): Adam and Eve, the first human beings, lived in the Garden of Eden. God warned them not to eat of the tree of knowledge of good and evil, lest they die. But a snake told Eve it was all right to eat from the tree, so she did, and gave Adam some fruit from it also. After they had eaten, they realized they were naked and were ashamed. God found out and cursed them both to a life of hardship. "Cursed is the ground for thy sake; in sorrow shalt thou eat of it all the days of thy life. . . . for out of it wast thou taken: for dust thou art, and unto dust shalt thou return."

Interpretation: The story of the creation from the *Bible* is similar to other ancient myths of creation. The tree of the knowledge of good and evil symbolizes adulthood and taking responsibility for one's own behavior. The Hebrew God is represented as a vindictive, guilt-inducing parent who does not want his children to grow up and separate from him. Like the Greek myth of Pandora, the first woman is made responsible for bringing about evil and hardship upon men and women, although the snake, which may symbolize a phallus, could represent the man's unconscious complicity. Eating of the fruit may also symbolize intercourse for pleasure rather than for procreation, and the shame afterwards having to do with this forbidden activity, which results in their being sentenced to death (mortality).

Dream 1: I had a glorious vision. I was kneeling down, praying, when suddenly I see this blaze of light before me. Then I make out the figure of a face, then a body.

It's a naked figure of an incredibly beautiful youth (like Apollo or like some sun-god). He looked at me with strong, calm eyes. Then he sat very close to me and I saw he had a huge erection. He kissed my left ear and his tongue inserted a red-hot ruby into my brain.

Dream 2: I dreamed that Jesus Christ was making love to me. He kissed me, caressed me, and then screwed me. It was incredible.

Dreamer: A 25-year-old man suffering from an acute episode of schizophrenia. His mother had alternatively abused and exalted him, making him believe he was either the vilest of the vile or a noble genius. His father demeaned him as a "Mama's boy."

Associations: He had these dreams while staying at a monastery. He recalled a biblical story about a prophet who had a vision that an angel appeared and put a hot coal in his mouth, giving him the ability to foretell the future.

Interpretation: The two dreams indicate a narcissistic need to be "blessed" by a phallic god. This need stems both from his parents' degrading him (which made him want to prove them wrong), and from the pressure of his mother's defying him (he wanted to live up to her billing). The red-hot ruby denotes that his brain will be valuable, referring to the biblical story to which he associated: he will be a prophet. The sexual nature of these visions of being blessed (being seduced by a phallic god figure)—a theme prevalent in homosexual literature—psychodynamically represents a way of appeasing the hostile father figure (the oedipal loser) and being thus pardoned for "marrying" his mother and usurping his father's role. At the same time, it represents being initiated into and accepted by the world of men.

Dream: I was walking through a crowded street and felt that I was in some kind of danger. Then I thought about God and imagined His warm, magnificent face, and I knew He was protecting me. I gradually relaxed.

Dreamer: A 24-year-old devout Christian woman.

Association: The night before, she had been reading from the *Bible*—Psalms 23: "The Lord is my shepherd, I shall not want..."

Interpretation: Many religious people feel protected by their belief in an omniscient, omnipotent God who watches over them. This phenomenon may also represent a "divine transference"—attributing to a god figure the feelings they once had about their parents when they were very small children. It is typical of infants to view their caretakers as omnipotent and omniscient and to feel protected by them.

Dream: While Muhammad was engaged in solitary contemplation on the mountain of Hira, God appeared in the form of the angel Gabriel, and called for him to preach the gospel of the Lord.

Dreamer: Muhammad, founder of Islam. Reported in the *Koran*, the holy scripture of Islam.

Association: He claimed to have had many such revelations from God, telling him what and where to preach.

Interpretation: This mythological dream by Muhammad is similar to those of other religious figures, such as Jesus and Buddha, who also believed they were "called." Visions of God and angels signify divine affirmation. Psychoanalytically, such a vision might be regarded as a schizophrenic hallucination.

Dream: I'm walking up the stairway of an ancient monument. On top is a statue of a man with a long beard. It seems I'm to be sacrificed to this ancient God. I think it's all silly, but there's nothing I can do about it.

Dreamer: A 42-year-old man who was raised in a devoutly religious family.

Association: A few days before the dream his father had rebuked him for not going to church regularly.

Interpretation: The statue of God symbolizes his father, and his feeling of having to be sacrificed to this God parallels his ambivalence toward his father and the latter's fanatic beliefs.

Gold

Dream (fairy tale): A king offered to marry any girl who could spin straw into gold. He enjoined a miller's daughter to do so, and she was about to despair when an ugly dwarf appeared and said he could do it for her. However, he had one condition—that she would give him her first child. The maiden married the king, but then grieved so bitterly when her first child was born that the dwarf decided to teasingly give her one chance; she could keep the child if she could guess his name in three days. Two days were spent making vain guesses. On the third day one of her servants heard a strange voice rasping, "Little knows my dainty dame, Rumpelstiltskin is my name!" She kept the child and he killed himself with rage.

Interpretation: The metaphor in this story "Rumpelstiltskin"—spinning straw into gold—stands for giving birth to a superior child. The king wants a woman of good breeding who will produce a golden heir. However, Rumpelstiltskin, the ugly dwarf (a symbol for lecherous men or incestuous brothers), demands her first child. That is, he wants to sleep with her first. When she grieves, he plays with her by giving her a riddle he knows she can never guess. However, his own power goes to his head and he spills out the name while giddily singing a song. This story, like "Little Red Riding Hood," is a cautionary tale for little girls to be wary of men.

Golf

Dream 1: I was in my brother's apartment. All his golf things were hanging up on the wall—his tees, his scorecards, his gloves. They were all still there.

Dream 2: For some reason I was standing outside my old house with a guy I used to be on the high school golf team with but wasn't that friendly with. "Why are we hanging out now," I ask him, "when we never hung out in high school?"

Dreamer: A 35-year-old depressed man whose older brother had recently died of cancer.

Association: The friend in the dream had been on the golf team, but the dreamer did not particularly like him because he had been a "hot shot." He felt angry at his brother for dying.

Interpretation: Both dreams are about the dreamer's brother. The first is a wish for his brother to still be alive (his golf equipment still hanging in his apartment). The second is a coded message to the effect that in actuality his brother had never been that friendly toward him, and had acted like a "hot shot." Always seeking his brother's approval, he had developed a reaction formation toward him by hero worshipping him, and had not acknowledged this negative aspect of their relationship. In the dream he does. Golf in this dream represents masculine bonding.

Grapes

Dream: An alligator was sitting in a tree, happily eating a bunch of Concord grapes.

Dreamer: A regressed therapist in training analysis, as reported by Gedo (1980). He had this dream while experiencing extreme separation anxiety when his analyst took a vacation.

Association: The dream reminded him of Aesop's fable about the fox and the grapes, and of a story about a tiny dog that opens his mouth and swallows a much bigger opponent. The dog had been an alligator before his father cut off its tail. He recalls Freud's book about the "Wolf Man" and his dream of wolves sitting in a tree. But alligators could only get up a tree by magic, and grapes do not grow on trees. He feels sorry for one of his own female patients.

Interpretation: Gedo interprets the dream as an archaic wish for the attainment of omnipotence (magic), and self-reliance (doing without the analyst). At the same time the grapes symbolize the dreamer's female patient—she is the victim he is swallowing like an alligator. The act of swallowing the grapes is at the same time a sexual acting out of the transference. The various threatening emotions (murderous hostility toward his own analyst) are successfully warded off.

Grave

Dream: Somebody was digging up earth from a grave. I felt trapped and couldn't breathe. I saw a woman, but then she changed into a man. I refused her.

Dreamer: A 48-year-old schizophrenic woman.

Association: She recalled a poem: "Our August dignity must come to dust/ Oh keep in mind our origin is lust."

Interpretation: The grave (earth mother) is the womb, where the dreamer feels trapped and can't breathe. The woman who turns into a man symbolizes the dreamer's projected confusion about sexual identity and orientation. Her refusal of the man perhaps also signifies her sexual guilt (our "origin is lust").

Dream: I was walking on the street and I kept thinking, "This is a very grave matter."

Dreamer: A 42-year-old woman.

Association: She recalled a play she had seen the night before, in which one of the characters had said, "This is a very grave matter." The character reminded her of her sister, who had died. The dreamer had not cried at her sister's funeral and felt guilty about it.

Interpretation: The dream is an allusion to the guilt she still carries about her sister. It was a grave matter that her sister had died, and it was a grave matter that she had not been able to cry at her funeral because of her sibling rivalry.

Group Therapy

Dream: I was in the group, trying to figure out what was going on. I looked at Marion and wondered why she didn't like me. I couldn't understand why she would hate me so much. I had no such feelings about her at all.

Dreamer: A 35-year-old schizoid woman.

Association: She had recently quit a therapy group because she felt disturbed by her interaction with one of the people in the group.

Interpretation: It is quite common for people in group therapy to have dreams about the people in their groups, just as patients have dreams about their therapists. The therapy group stands both for itself and for the dreamer's family. In the group she could not understand why a woman hated her and attacked her. In her family, she couldn't understand why her stepmother had hated her so much. This lack of understanding indicates her defense mechanism of splitting, whereby she cut herself off from her own aggression and projected it onto others. Disavowing her own aggression, she could never understand why others hated her (thought she was aggressive). She saw herself as a nice person who only wanted to be liked and do the right thing.

Guitar

Dream: I was asleep. I woke up and heard a noise. I went down the hallway naked. There were a bunch of teenagers sitting on the fire escape outside the living room window. I jumped like a frog away from the window, but they saw me. They began to threaten me. I said to Patricia, "We have to call the police." I couldn't find the number. We went out to a pay phone but still couldn't get them. When we got back to the house, it was trashed, and they had broken my guitar. I heard something and saw this little boy. He ran away. I said, "You come back here."

Dreamer: A 34-year-old man who has suffered from depression.

Associations: For several months he had been complaining to authorities about a dance club in the basement of his apartment building that kept him up all night with its loud music. He recalled that when he was a teenager his parents used to complain that he played his guitar too loudly.

Interpretation: The guitar represents his main creative outlet; breaking it symbolizes taking away this outlet. It might also be seen as a phallic symbol that has been destroyed (castration). He is naked in the apartment, and finding it trashed perhaps also indicates a rape. On one level, then, the dream is a fear of retaliation by the people in the dance club about whom he has been complaining (to no avail) to the police. On another level, the dream alludes to his own unhappiness as a teenager (when his parents complained about his guitar and he felt similarly castrated), and to his childhood, when he was a lonely boy with no one (police) to turn to.

Dream: Pete and I are in a cabin. I give him my guitar and he says he's going to fix it. The band will play soon and I hope to play with it. But he gives me back a different guitar. "What happened to my red guitar?" I ask. He says this one's better. I try to play on it but it's no good. It makes fire engine noises.

Dreamer: A 33-year-old passive man.

Association: The red guitar in the dream was the favorite guitar that his ex-girlfriend had made him sell. She had complained that he preferred his rock band to her. Eventually, she had left him.

Interpretation: The guitar is his masculinity. It is also a transitional object, harking back to a red fire engine that his mother took away from him when he was a toddler, replacing it with a stuffed animal. The dream condenses three layers: it shows a distrust of his friend Pete in the present, alludes to his ex-girlfriend in the immediate past, and recreates the trauma of losing his transitional object as a toddler.

Gun

Dream: I took a gun out of my pocket and shot my sister. She fell to the ground and began meowing like a cat.

Dreamer: A 34-year-old man.

Association: His older sister teased him a lot as a child.

Interpretation: He wants to rape his sister (bring her to orgasm) with his powerful penis (gun), making her moan with passion (meow like a cat).

Hair

Dream: I was in the bathtub and my pubic hair began to grow. It grew like long vines of ivy, until it enveloped the entire tub and began to climb up and around the sides of the tub. I sat there in amazement and then called Bill. "Look what happened," I said. "Very nice," he said.

Dreamer: A 27-year-old woman with hysterical features.

Association: Her husband had been complaining about how inhibited she was sexually. She recalled the English ivy that grew up the walls of her family's house. Her father had chopped it down and she had felt very sad.

Interpretation: The dream is a wish for sexual freedom. The pubic hair growing and climbing the tub like vines denotes this liberation. The image also refers to her father's religious fear and suppression of her sexual feelings and his interference in her dating during adolescence.

Dream: I was sitting in a chair, dressed in white clothes. My mother was cutting my hair. I looked in the mirror and my hair was completely cut off, in a butch style, like a dyke. I felt horrified. I couldn't believe she had done this to me. I had asked her to trim it. I thought about my friend who's a lesbian, and thought, "Maybe people will think I'm her lover." Then I wondered what I would tell my therapist.

Dreamer: A 27-year-old woman with hysterical features.

Association: She said her mother was planning to visit her soon. Her mother was always trying to get her to cut her hair. Sometimes the dreamer had even cut it her-self. She also discussed having erotic thoughts about her male therapist.

Interpretation: The cutting of hair symbolizes a form of castration, since long hair for a woman is equivalent to a long penis in a man. However, in this dream it means in particular the loss of heterosexual attractiveness. The dreamer has developed erotic thoughts about her male therapist. When she was a child, she had such thoughts about her father and was quite close to him. One day her mother, who was competitive and controlling, severely rebuked her about it and she quickly dis-tanced herself from her father from then on. Subsequently any sexual feelings for a man felt taboo. This dream is a replica of that early episode. The white clothes denote sexual innocence.

Dream (Hebrew Bible story): After Samson had killed 1,000 Philistines with the jawbone of a donkey, the lords of the Philistines went to Delilah and said, "Entice him, and see wherein his great strength lieth, and see by what means we may pre-vail against him." He was the strongest man of Israel, but he had a weakness for the ladies. The lords offered his latest passion, a Philistine, 1,100 pieces of silver to deliver him. Four times she asked him the secret of his strength; four times he teased her and told her a lie. "And it came to pass, when she pressed him daily with her words, and urged him, so that his soul was vexed unto death, that he told her all his heart." His power, he said, was in his hair, which had never been cut. That night, as he slept in her lap, she had his hair cut. The next morning the Philistines came to get him and he had no power to fight. They put out his eyes.

Interpretation: Hair in this story of Samson and Delilah symbolizes power—specifically, masculine power, and long hair means a long phallus. Hence cutting the hair means castration. Having his eyes put out is an additional form of castra-tion. Like Oedipus, Samson has to pay for his indiscretion. Both slept with forbid-den women: Oedipus with his mother, Samson with a Philistine, who perhaps also represents the oedipal mother.

Dream: Suddenly long tufts of hair sprouted on my legs. I decided not to shave them.

Dreamer: A young woman with a masculinity complex.

Association: She recalled that her father always wanted her to be clean and neat (a lady).

Interpretation: This dream is a wish to be man (to have long hair on her legs like a man). The tufts of hair may also denote penises. As a child, her father wanted her to always be a lady, but he favored his two sons over her. In her dream, she was more like her brothers.

Dream: I was combing my hair in a restroom. My hair was falling out. Pieces of hair were all over the sink. I was really scared.

Dreamer: A young woman with a hysterical personality.

Association: Her mother was always telling her to cut her hair.

Interpretation: As in the famous biblical story of Samson, hair here symbolizes power—in this case, feminine power. The dreamer's mother was an attractive woman who, due to her own narcissism, discouraged her daughter from looking attractive and feminine. In the dream, the dreamer loses her hair (feminine power) and is afraid—of her own unconscious anger at her mother and of her mother's anticipated retaliation to this anger.

Ham

Dream: I was eating ham and eggs, and I noticed that the ham began to grow on the plate, as if it were alive. The thin slices puffed up like two balloons.

Dreamer: A 28-year-old actor with narcissistic features.

Association: He was in a production and other actors were accusing him of upstaging them.

Interpretation: The dream was telling him the same thing as his colleagues: that he was being a "ham."

Hamlet

Dream: I was in a play. The play was *Hamlet.* I was playing Hamlet and I was actually turning into him. After the play I went out on the street and I had become Hamlet.

Dreamer: A 43-year-old man with narcissistic features.

Association: His mother, like Hamlet's mother, had recently remarried. His father had died of cancer.

Interpretation: The dreamer's identification with Hamlet points to his oedipal feelings about his mother and his suspicion that somehow his mother caused his father's death. Like Hamlet, the dreamer feels jealous and angry about his mother's marriage, and regards the new husband as a usurper.

Hat

Dream: I went to an antique store and found an old hat and a pair of gloves. Then I was in a cab with a group of friends. Bill was there, and I showed him the hat and gloves I had found. They were Bill's hat and gloves from his childhood. He couldn't understand my fascination with these things.

Dreamer: A 37-year-old depressed woman who likes to dress in men's clothes.

Association: Bill never understood her, just like her father. The gloves and hat reminded her of her father.

Interpretation: The hat and gloves are in reality her father's, and symbolize her father's genitals. During the phase of sexual discovery, when she expressed curiosity about penises, including her father's, her father did not understand what she was talking about. He was embarrassed by such discussions. The dream alludes to this period of her childhood and is a wish to get validation of her childhood sexuality by her father (Bill).

Dream: I was sitting in front of a mirror trying on different hats. They were hats of completely different styles and each made me look completely different. It was funny.

Dreamer: A 39-year-old woman.

Association: She said she felt confused about her career.

Interpretation: Trying on different hats meant she was pondering different roles, lifestyles, and careers.

Hawk

Dream: When the dreamer was still in the cradle, a hawk came down to him, opened his mouth with his tail, and struck him many times against his lips with his tail.

Dreamer: Leonardo da Vinci, Italian Renaissance painter and sculptor. Reported by Freud (1910). Da Vinci was born out of wedlock and raised by his poor, single mother until he was 4 or 5; then he went to live with his father and stepmother.

Association: Da Vinci had a lifelong fascination with vultures, which he explained by tracing it to the above memory, which Freud decided was actually a fantasy or dream.

Interpretation: Freud saw the fantasy/memory as an allusion to being nursed by an intrusive, phallic mother. The hawk represents his mother, and the vulture's tail her phallus. Hence the nursing experience for da Vinci would have been a passive one, in which his mother and her nipple–penis were the aggressors. Da Vinci never married and was fond of boys, always having numerous apprentices around him. Freud traced his latent homosexuality to this early childhood experience of the intrusive mother and absent father, and notes that his ambivalence toward women was evident in paintings such as that of the Mona Lisa, who may either be smiling or smirking, or both.

Heaven

Dream: "And straightway coming up out of the water, he saw the heavens opened, and the Spirit like a dove descending upon him: And there came a voice from heaven, saying, Thou art my beloved Son, in whom I am well pleased."

Dreamer: Jesus of Nazareth, whose teachings are the foundation of the Christian religion. Reported in the *Bible* (Mark).

Association: He has this vision immediately after being blessed by John the Baptist.

Interpretation: According to Hebrew mythology, a messiah was to come, preceded by a messenger who would prepare the way. The above vision of being blessed by a deity, common throughout mythological literature, represents a divine affirmation of Jesus' status (the dove symbolizes God). Psychoanalytically, such a vision is similar to hallucinations typical of patients in mental hospitals suffering from schizophrenia.

Dream: I was sleeping and I saw myself floating upwards out of the window and into the sky toward heaven. John was there, smiling and waiting for me.

Dreamer: An 82-year-old woman.

Association: Her husband had recently died of a heart attack.

Interpretation: The woman, heartbroken by her husband's death, wishes to join him in heaven.

Hell

Dream (Greek myth): He was very much in love with his wife. Then a snake bit her and she died. Grief-stricken, he went down to hell to plead for her life and played such sweet music that Hades began to cry. He granted Orpheus his request that his wife follow him out of hell, but only on the condition that he not look back until they had completely entered the sunlight. However, just as he was about to step into the outer world, he looked back and his wife vanished. Later, his prolonged grief over his ex-wife so enraged the other women in the city that, during a festival, they tore his body to pieces and threw it into the river.

Interpretation: The Greek myth of Orpheus is similar to the dreams of depressed patients. The dreamer cannot accept the death of his beloved so he dreams of getting her back—in this case going to hell. Yet, even in his dream, he loses her again and she vanishes. (Compare this story to the Judaeo-Christian myth of Adam and Eve, where a snake corrupts Eve and she and Adam lose their immortality.) Orpheus is shown to be suffering from chronic grief, and the willfulness of such grief has a tendency to annoy others (as it does the women in this myth). The most strik-ing aspect of this dream/myth is the fact that Orpheus could not resist looking back. This seems to point to a universal tendency to rebel against authority. In Jungian terms, the dream may be seen as an archetypical tale of an individual's struggle toward individuation; the rings of hell parallel stages of that struggle.

Hercules

Dream: He saw Hercules upon the walls, reaching out his hands, calling to him.

Dreamer: Alexander the Great. Reported by Plutarch (110a).

Association: During the siege of Tyre, which lasted seven months, Alexander often dreamed of help from powerful figures.

Interpretation: In Greek mythology, Hercules was the strongest man alive. Alexander's dream was simply a wish to be strong against his enemy.

Hermaphrodite

Dream (Greek myth): Hermaphrodite was the handsome son of Hermes and Aphrodite. The nymph Salmacis became enamored of him and prayed that she might be so closely united that the two might become one flesh. Her prayers were answered and the nymph and boy became one body.

Interpretation: This myth can be seen, in Freudian terms, as a depiction of the woman with a masculinity complex who wishes not just to have sexual intercourse with a man, but to merge with him and possess his penis and his masculinity. In Jungian terms it might represent a woman's attempt to integrate her anima.

Dream: I was in the bathtub washing myself when I suddenly felt something at the top of my vagina. My clitoris had grown about two inches long and was erect. It was like a little penis.

Dreamer: A young woman with hysterical features.

Association: She remembered the first time she had seen her younger brother's penis.

Interpretation: The two-inch penis is about the length her brother's penis had been. The dream is a wish that harks back to the first discovery of her brother's penis, which engendered envy.

Hero

Dream: I heard a huge roar in my back yard and when I went out to investigate I saw this monster, like a dragon. I got my father's rifle and shot it. I heard applause and turned to see a naked woman sitting on the roof.

Dreamer: A 42-year-old man.

Association: He recalled that his father and mother had often had heated arguments in which the father threatened to shoot the mother with his rifle.

Interpretation: This is a simple oedipal dream and also coincides with the plots of fairy tales. The monster represents the father, and the naked maiden on the roof is the mother. The son slays the dragon and rescues the damsel—that is, saves the mother from the monster father and has her to himself.

High School

Dream: I was traveling on a steamboat when I saw a kid I had known in high school. Now he was an older man, but I thought, "He's still cute." I talked with him and we looked at the river together. He was paying a lot of attention to me.

Dreamer: A 40-year-old woman.

Association: She had had a crush on this man when they were both 15, but he was in the popular group and she was not. He had once rescued her from some boys who were bothering her. The day before the dream she had read a news article about steamboat trips up the Mississippi River.

Interpretation: Dreams of high school represent wishes to be young again. In this dream the wish is to reunite with the boy she had had a crush on.

Dream: I broke into my high school building, through the skylight, and stole some files. I had to find some proof of something. A shadowy figure saw me and shook his head.

Dreamer: A 42-year-old man.

Association: He recalled that right before graduation from high school, he had been expelled for drinking alcohol on a school trip.

Interpretation: The proof that he is looking for is that of his innocence. The shadowy figure is his high school principal. In this recurring dream, he wished to undo the high school trauma.

Highway

Dream: Ruth and I were in a house somewhere. An older couple rang our doorbell and asked us directions. We got out some maps and tried to tell them where to go. They pointed at the highway, which strangely went up into the sky. At the top of the highway was a platform held by ropes that, it seemed, had to be cut.

Dreamer: A 34-year-old man trying to separate from his parents.

Associations: He was about to move in with his girlfriend, and he suspected that his parents would disapprove of it. He did not know how to break the news to them.

Interpretation: The highway represents a path of life. The old couple wanting directions are his parents. (In reality, it is they who want to give him directions on what path to take in life.) The oblique wish in the dream is for his parents to die and go to heaven (the highway to heaven). The platform on the top of the highway, held by rope that had to be cut, represents, perhaps, the final judgment and "cutting of the cord."

Dream: I was in a car and the car kept going off the road. I was turning the wheel and nothing happened.

Dreamer: A 19-year-old impulsive student.

Association: He was about to fail out of college for the second time because he could not concentrate on his studies.

Interpretation: The road symbolizes mature goals, which the student cannot work toward, no matter how hard he tries.

Hitler

Dream: I sat with Hitler and we had a pleasant and interesting conversation. I found him charming and was very proud that he listened with great attention to what I had to say.

Dreamer: A young man suffering from mild borderline features, as reported by Fromm (1951).

Association: A German-American, he had spoken passionately against Hitler during many therapy sessions. His father, though not like Hitler, was an irrational authority.

Interpretation: In general, Hitler has come to symbolize evil. In this dream Hitler stands for the dreamer's father. The dreamer is apparently prone to splitting. In real life he oscillated between admiring and despising his father—at times seeing him as an ideal father (as the father wanted to be seen), and at times seeing him as a monster. He felt guilty about seeing his father as a monster. In the dream, he overcomes this guilt by seeing Hitler as an ideal leader.

Hole

Dream: I am at the bottom of a deep hole or pit. I try to climb up and have already reached the top, which I hold with my hands, when someone comes and stomps on my hands. I have to let go and fall back to the bottom of the pit.

Dreamer: A 15-year-old battered daughter of an alcoholic, as reported by Fromm (1951).

Association: This was a recurring dream. Her father beat her, her mother ran away with other men periodically, and she grew up in poverty and dirt, attempting suicide six times from ages 10 to 15.

Interpretation: The hole represents the girl's circumstance while growing up. The person stomping on her hands may be either parent or life in general. Fromm refers to such recurring dreams as the leitmotif of a person's life.

Dream (Taoist parable): The King of the North was rash and the King of the South was overbearing. They used to visit the Central King's palace and the King of the Center would treat them quite well and they were happy there. However, they were disturbed because the King of the Center did not have the seven holes in his head that all humans have—to see, to hear, to breathe, and to eat. So one day, wanting to repay him for his kindness, they decided to do the Central King a favor. They dug the seven holes in his head. The next morning he was dead.

Dreamer: Chuang Zi, in his ancient Chinese parable about the Central King.

Association: Chuang Zi was a follower of Lao Zi, who often wrote of human folly.

Interpretation: The Central King, who has no holes in his head, symbolizes the human being who is different from the rest, who goes his own way. The Kings of the North and South represent extremes of behavior—the person who is impulsive and the person who is moralistic. Hence, the parable is about how people distrust those who are different, and in trying to make them like themselves, kill their spirit.

Dream: There was a hole in the ground with a stairway made of stone leading down to an archway covered with green brocade. Beyond the archway was a rectangular room with walls of stone and a red carpet that led to a golden throne. At first the dreamer thought he saw a tree trunk that reached to the ceiling, and then he saw naked flesh. "On the very top of the head was a single eye, gazing motionlessly upwards." He stood paralyzed, afraid it would crawl toward him like a giant worm, and then his mother cried out in the dream: "Yes, just look at him. This is the man-eater."

Dreamer: Carl Jung, Swiss psychoanalyst, when he was a 3- or 4-year-old boy. Reported in Donn (1988).

Associations: During this period of his youth, Jung remembered that his mother went away to a hospital in Basel for several months, and Jung became feverish, developed eczema, and had insomnia. When his mother returned from the hospital Jung recalled that, "all sorts of things were happening at night, things incomprehensible and alarming. My parents were sleeping apart." Jung became sick again and had bouts of choking.

Interpretation: The hole in the earth perhaps symbolizes his mother's vagina. The rectangular room represents the womb. The green brocade is probably associated with the type of gown his mother wore, then popular in Vienna. The totem-like figure with one eye looking upward which might crawl to him like a worm is a phallic symbol—his father and his father's penis. His mother's scream, "This is a man-eater!" suggests that his mother may have disparaged Jung's father, or perhaps male sexuality (the worm). His own oedipal feelings might also have come into play, causing him to fear that his murderous feelings toward his father might be retaliated. However, Jung himself interpreted this dream as a message from the collective unconscious. In Eastern philosophy, one eye in the middle of the forehead looking upwards signifies enlightenment, which would then denote that Jung was looking for enlightenment from a father figure.

Home

Dream: I was on a road that seemed never to end. It would go left and right and back and forth. I kept thinking I wanted to go home, but I didn't know exactly what that meant or where it was.

Dreamer: A 30-year-old schizoid woman.

Association: She had recently lost her job and subsequently had to give up her apartment and move in with a relative.

Interpretation: Home symbolizes not only getting back her lost apartment and lost job, but also finding her lost self. The woman had not really felt relaxed with— "at home with"—herself since early childhood, at which time she was abandoned by her mother, with whom she had strongly identified. Losing her mother was like losing her self—and her home.

Dream: I was running around trying to find my home. I went down one street and then another street. Each street looked like my street, but my house wasn't there. I felt very forlorn.

Dreamer: A young boy, aged 9, whose parents had recently divorced.

Association: The day before the dream his mother had become angry at him and yelled, "If you don't be good, I'll send you to an orphanage."

Interpretation: The boy avoids going to an orphanage by running through the streets. But his home has disappeared. Loss of home may also represent loss of identity or the feeling of belonging, and loss of mother. Also, since the father departed, the home no longer feels familiar, no longer feels like home.

Homosexuals

Dream: Ted and I were staying at a bed and breakfast and were in a communal bathroom. Two women, suburban types with puffed up hair and too much make-up, passed by the hallway and saw us through the door. One of them said, "I didn't know they let gays stay in this hotel." I was furious at them, feeling especially protective of Ted. I worked up a big wad of saliva and spat it all over them.

Dreamer: A 35-year-old man with ego-dystonic homosexuality.

Association: His boyfriend was always on the phone with his sisters. He had not told them yet that he was gay.

Interpretation: The suburban women are Ted's sisters. The dreamer is furious at them for holding onto Ted, and for devaluing homosexuality (mirroring his own self negation). In his fury, he works up a wad of saliva (masturbates) and spits it all over them (ejaculates on them). The wish is to soil and contaminate them. The dream also alludes to his relationship with his mother, whom he blamed for his homosexuality.

Dream: I saw two homosexuals kissing on the corner. One of them was my brother. I shook my head and walked on.

Dreamer: A young man with latent homosexual impulses.

Association: His older brother always teased him about being a "sissy" and a "fairy."

Interpretation: In the dream, he displaces his homosexuality onto his brother, who is one of the men kissing.

Horse

Dream (fictional): I was walking with my father on the street in the small town where I was born. I was seven years old. As we passed by a tavern some drunken men came spilling out and one of the men told the others to get into his wagon and he would give them all a ride. The wagon was attached to an old sorrel. The sorrel couldn't pull all of them, so the owner of the sorrel began to whip the horse and then beat it with a shaft. His friends were laughing and urging the owner on. Meanwhile, I cried out to my father, "Daddy, Daddy, what are they doing? Daddy, they're beating the poor horse to death!" The owner of the horse continued to lash out, furiously, until the horse fell to the ground and died. He kept beating it even then. I rushed over to him and kissed the horse and then jumped on the owner and hit him with my little fists. My father grabbed me and carried me away. "They're drunk," my father says. I woke up drenched with sweat.

Dreamer: Fyodor Dostoyevsky, Russian novelist, through his character Raskolnikov in *Crime and Punishment* (1868). Paraphrased from the book.

Associations: The character of Raskolnikov probably represents Dostoyevsky as a young man, and the dream may well be one he himself had as a child. His father, a doctor, used to beat his serfs as well as his children, and he was so despised that he was murdered by his serfs when Dostoyevsky was in military school.

Interpretation: This is perhaps an allusion to Dostoyevsky's own childhood. The horse symbolizes Dostoyevsky himself, who was often beaten by his father. The image of "beating a dead horse" may represent the idea that Dostoyevsky could not comprehend his father's irrational beatings. The fact that the father in the dream is benign indicates his need to protect his father. In the dream the father's cruelty is displaced onto the drunken driver. This displacement represents the wish that his father had been benign and that somebody else had been cruel instead. It is normal during traumatic events to dissociate ourselves from the scene and imagine, "This is not happening to me, this is not my father who is doing this!"

Dream: I saw a beautiful white horse as I was walking in the meadow. I went up to the horse and he squatted down so I could ride him. He galloped through the meadow and I held onto his neck and it felt wonderful. The ride went on and on, through forests and over mountains. I was disappointed when I woke up.

Dreamer: A 23-year-old woman.

Associations: The night of the dream her husband had frustrated her again by pre-maturely ejaculating. As she was dozing off, she recalled the white horses owned by her neighbor when she was a child, and how she derived comfort by talking with them.

Interpretation: The white horse symbolizes a strong, gallant, heroic lover, who would take her for a long ride (sexually gratify her), as her husband could not.

House

Dream: My wife and I were living in an old, familiar house. She didn't want the house and wanted me to get rid of it. I wanted to keep it. At one point she tried to kill me, but a man stepped in and killed her instead.

Dreamer: A 47-year-old man.

Association: The old, familiar house was the one in which he had grown up as his mother's only son.

Interpretation: The house represents his mother, to whom the dreamer is still attached. The dreamer's wife resents this attachment and on many occasions he and his wife have almost come to blows over it. In the dream, he displaces his violent impulses onto another man. The amalgamation of the "old, familiar house" and his mother is an example of what Freud called *dream condensation.*

Dream: My house collapsed. I came home and it was in shambles. Then I walked down a country road and found a cabin. There was a woman inside and we made love. She had a cow in her barn.

Dreamer: A 39-year-old man with oral-addictive features.

Association: He said he was getting tired of living in the city with all its irritations.

Interpretation: The house represents a part of himself that he wishes to shed, like a snake sheds its skin, and then return to a simpler life—the paradise of early infancy in which he suckled at his mother's breast (woman = mother, cow = milk).

Dream: Somehow I own a huge mansion. It's not my kind of house, cold, full of statues, columns, marble halls. A crowd of people come in. My older brother is there, bantering monologues. My sister arrives unannounced, then leaves and I never know if I'll see her again. Mother is there but never says anything. I feel tired with so many people around, and they won't let me feel good about anything and I always have to be on guard.

Dreamer: A 39-year-old schizoid woman.

Associations: Her sister recently visited her unannounced and left suddenly. Her mother generally talks constantly and won't let her get a word in. She didn't know if she would invite them to her house again.

Interpretation. The dream reflects the quality of life in her own family as she was growing up. Her family always made her feel that she had to be "on guard" because they would not let her feel good about anything. The house perhaps symbolizes both her present house (which did not seem like hers when her relatives visited) and her depersonalized self. However, in the dream there is a reversal, in that her mother says nothing, whereas in real life she talks constantly. This reversal is what Freud referred to as *dream inversion.*

Dream: Rose and I were making love in somebody's house. It was a mess. I said, "We've got to clean up this house." People came into the house and we were still in bed. We never got around to cleaning the house.

Dreamer: A 38-year-old man who had just started a new relationship with a woman. He had an obsessive-compulsive characterology and would sometimes clean his own apartment several times a day.

Associations: The night before this dream they had had a discussion about sex and relationships, wondering whether they should be examined for AIDS. She had told him about past men in her life. The house reminded him of his mother's house in Long Island.

Interpretation: The house represents the dreamer's new relationship, which he feels is dirty. He wants to clean up the mess (the V.D.) and avoid contamination by her and by the men she has slept with, of whom he feels jealous. On another level, the dream may be an oedipal tale about having incestuous (dirty) intercourse with his mother and being ambivalent about whether he wants his father and brother (the people who come in) to catch them in bed.

Dream 1: I was in a dark house playing with cats. I went to get one of the cats and a rat jumped out.

Dream 2: I was living in a dilapidated house. I had a feeling of déjà vu. I didn't want to be there. It might fall down.

Dream 3: I was in the cellar of a strange house. I heard a noise and rushed back upstairs.

Dream 4: I ran away from my house. There were termites.

Dreamer: A 32-year-old ego-dystonic homosexual man.

Association: The cellar in the third dream reminded him of the basement where he had slept during his adolescence.

Interpretation: This series of dreams, which came on two successive nights, relates to the dreamer's homosexuality, about which he has a conflict. The houses denote the house where he grew up, in which he engaged in masturbatory practices about which he feels guilty (rats, termites). The déjà vu feeling is a clue that it is a memory from childhood. The dilapidated house may signify that his repression is "caving in."

Hubcaps

Dream: My car was dragging. I checked the wheels and saw that there were no hubcaps.

Dreamer: A 17-year-old girl with homosexual impulses.

Association: She had run away from her strict parents. She felt confused about her sexual orientation.

Interpretation: She cannot run far from home because she does not feel centered (no hubcaps on her wheels).

I

Ice

Dream: I was in a laboratory. I saw a large freezer in a corner and opened it. Inside was a large block of ice. I looked closer and saw something inside of it. It was what looked like some kind of heart. It was bigger than a human heart and I thought it might belong to some kind of experimental animal, like a gorilla or an elephant.

Dreamer: A 47-year-old man.

Association: He had recently visited a physician and found out that he had a blockage in an artery and was going to need bypass surgery.

Interpretation: The heart in a block of ice denotes both his state of frozen emotions and his wish that somehow his heart could be frozen until such time as scientists develop (in the laboratory) a new procedure or can transplant a new, bigger, stronger heart into his body, perhaps that of a gorilla or an elephant, that will not be susceptible to wear.

Dream: People were ice skating on a pond in June. I was afraid because the ice was so thin. Then a guy fell through the ice and continued skating under the ice like some fish. Everybody was quite amazed.

Dreamer: A 37-year-old woman with hysterical features.

Associations: She remembered seeing a Portuguese man-of-war underwater in Florida. She felt her life was out of control and confused since her recent divorce.

Interpretation: The man, who represents her, is "skating on thin ice" (she feels unsafe and vulnerable since her divorce). However, she hopes that if the ice breaks she'll be able to carry on, like a fish underwater.

Dream: I went to my husband and put a cube of ice in his hand. The ice melted immediately and turned into a white liquid.

Dreamer: A 23-year-old woman suffering from sexual frigidity.

Association: The day before the dream, her husband asked her what it would take to melt her cold heart.

Interpretation: The ice stands for the dreamer's sexual frigidity. The white liquid is perhaps sperm. The wish is that he will melt her coldness and they will enjoy sexual bliss.

Impotence

Dream 1: I'm swimming in a stream with Mary. I dive under water and swim up to her and notice that she has taken off her bathing suit. I get an erection and am about to make love to her, then I sense that somebody else is swimming in the stream. I come up and see my sister swimming nearby. I lose my erection.

Dream 2: My mother comes into my room. I'm talking on the phone with some-body—a woman. My mother turns into my sister, and grabs the phone away from me. I try to pull it back but she wins. She smiles triumphantly and hangs it up.

Dreamer: A 37-year-old man suffering from chronic impotence.

Associations: He lived with his mother and sister and did not think he should be having a sexual relationship if they weren't likewise involved. He found himself feeling jealous if a man showed interest in his sister.

Interpretation: The dream indicates the sources of his impotence (symbolized by the hung-up phone in the second dream): his sister, toward whom he has an unre-solved erotic attachment, and, to a lesser extent, his mother, toward whom he feels dependent. Unconsciously, he believes that if he remains virtuous, so will his sister. At the same time, any erotic urges toward other women arouse incestuous (hence taboo) thoughts about his sister. This fact also contributes to his impotence.

Incest

Dream: I'm lying on a huge web, unable to get away. A large black widow spider comes toward me. I think it's going to eat me, but instead it goes toward my geni-tals and begins sucking on them. It seems like incest. I'm excited and horrified and wake up upset.

Dreamer: A 39-year-old man suffering from impotence.

Association: He thought about his mother.

Interpretation: The black widow spider represents his mother. The dream shows his ambivalence toward his mother's smothering (her web). She is a frightening bug, yet sexually exciting. Insects, in general, often symbolize a guilty conscience. The dream also reveals the source of his impotence, his mother fixation.

Dream: I find a little girl on the street, a waif, all dirty and soiled. She has been molested by her brother. She tells me of this incest and I cringe. I rescue her and take her to my apartment and give her a bath. I buy her a new dress and give her a soda and a back massage. I'm very nice and loving to her, protecting her from her brother.

Dreamer: A 33-year-old pedophile.

Association: He recalled how his half-sister, 14 years older than he, had sexually molested him when he was a little boy.

Interpretation: The dream expresses the wish that someone had protected him from his half-sister, and the concurrent wish that someone would protect little girls from him.

Insect

Dream (fictional): "As Gregor Samsa awoke one morning from uneasy dreams he found himself transformed in his bed into a gigantic insect." In fact, he had become a cockroach. His family at first tried to take care of him, but his father insisted that he be kept locked in his room. Eventually, forsaken by the family and wounded by an apple that his father had thrown at him, he was left to die.

Dreamer: Franz Kafka, Austrian writer, who suffered from depression and poor health. Summarized from "Metamorphosis" (1912).

Association: Kafka often wrote of inferiority feelings toward his father. In the above story, the protagonist son has become the main provider for the family after his father's business falls to ruin, before he metamorphosizes.

Interpretation: This story can be seen as a nightmare of oedipal guilt. The cockroach is considered the lowest of insects, and on an unconscious level Kafka must have felt this way about himself. He is an insect because of his repulsive, incestuous wishes to take sexual possession of his mother, and particularly his sister, and get rid of the father. The fact that in the dream he has done so (succeeding in business when his father has failed), causes his guilt to be even more severe. He retreats to his room and hides there. His father's health improves as his deteriorates, and his father throws an apple at him. This apple perhaps signifies the biblical fruit of forbidden knowledge—incestuous thoughts—and seems to kill the insect at last and put him out of his misery. The story is a bizarre suicidal death wish, suggestive of major depression.

Insomnia

Dream 1: I had insomnia and then before I knew it I fell asleep and I saw someone in the dark coming toward me. He touched me sexually. I woke up with a start.

Dream 2: I had insomnia. Finally I dozed off and felt a snake in bed beside me. I woke up with a start.

Dream 3: I was in a public restroom, sitting in a booth. Suddenly I saw a hand come under the divider.

Dream 4: Two arms came toward me as I was sleeping on a beach.

Dream 5: I was studying for an exam, sitting at my desk, when I felt someone was under the desk about to touch me.

Dream 6: A bug was crawling up my thigh.

Dream 7: A bird flew out from under my skirt. I was horrified and woke up.

Dream 8: My uncle was trying to kiss me.

Dreamer: A 33-year-old woman with a history of insomnia.

Association: She had been molested by her uncle from the ages of 9 to 12.

Interpretation: The dream reveals the source of the dreamer's lifelong insomnia. She was afraid to go to sleep because she was terrified of her conflicting rage against, and erotic desires for, the uncle who had molested her while she was sleeping. She was only able to identify the source after a lengthy period of dream interpretation, culminating in Dream 8.

Intimacy

Dream: I was with a group of people. We were at somebody's house, and there were three women who were all interested in me. I spent most of the time with one of them. Then we got into a car and a male friend was going to drive us all home. Some of the women lived in Long Island, a long drive. I sat in the front seat surrounded by the two other women. One leaned her head on my shoulder and spoke to me in an intimate way, kissing my ear. I was afraid the other two would see her. I seemed to be dating all three at the same time, but didn't want them to know. I was quite worried.

Dreamer: A 45-year-old professional man.

Associations: He had been dating several women at the same time and all were putting pressure on him with respect to marriage. He recalled that his mother used to play him and his three brothers against one another.

Interpretation: This is a warning dream. It is telling the dreamer that he is playing a risky and agonizing game and that he had better make up his mind. The key word in the dream is "intimate." One of the women is acting intimately and he does not want the other women to know. In fact, he is afraid of intimacy, afraid of allowing any one woman to have control over him. So he plays women against one another as his mother once did with him and his brothers. The "long drive" itself may represent intercourse and "Long Island" may denote a long phallus.

Itch

Dream: I had an itch on my back. I took my shirt off and looked in the mirror and saw that between my shoulder blades I had about five or six tufts of hair. But the hair was about five inches long and was thick and hard, like spikes. Peggy looked at my back and was horrified. I said, "That's how it's always been."

Dreamer: A 32-year-old man with multiple perverse symptoms.

Associations: Peggy, his wife, had always said she hated hairy backs. His mother used to become furious at him when he was a boy if he failed to lift the toilet seat when he urinated.

Interpretation: The itch on his back is symbolic of his sexual guilt. The long tufts of kinky hair stand for phalluses—in this case dirty, unacceptable phalluses. The image is related to his guilt feelings about his perverse activities (chronic masturbation, frequenting pornography shops, voyeuristic and exhibitionistic practices in men's restrooms) and his fear that his wife will find out and rebuke him as his mother did about urinating on the toilet seat. There is also a wish that she *will* find out, even though she may be disgusted, and eventually accept his masculinity.

Dream: I had an itch in my nose.

Dreamer: A 23-year-old woman suffering from anxiety.

Association: Her husband was sexually frustrating.

Interpretation: The itchy nose perhaps stands for the sexual hunger of her vagina.

Jail

Dream: I was in jail for something I didn't do. I had been framed. I tried to talk to the guard, but he just waved me away, as though he knew I was guilty and didn't want to hear any excuses. Nobody would listen to me. Finally they let me use a telephone and I called my mother. Even she thought I'd done something. "This is your mother speaking. I know you," she said.

Dreamer: A 35-year-old man with paranoid and masochistic features.

Association: Whenever he visited his family, he always felt they treated him as if he had some kind of evil intentions.

Interpretation: Jail symbolizes the dreamer's situation in his dysfunctional family. He has been made the scapegoat of this family and they will not listen to anything he says. The family, in effect, gaslights him, making him doubt his own perceptions. In the dream, as in his waking life, his mother will not rescue him.

Jesus

Dream: I'm walking along, lost, trying to find my home. I meet a man with a Jeep. He asks if I want to go for a ride. We go to the beach, sleep in his Jeep. He looks like Jesus, with long hair and a beard. It turns out he *is* Jesus, but I don't like him. He's too nice, not smart enough. I find him irritating.

Dreamer: A 37-year-old woman suffering from schizoid characterology.

Association: Her father was a minister who preached to her of right and wrong, but she found him deceitful.

Interpretation: Jesus symbolizes her father. The dream is her oedipal wish to find a father figure who will take her home (help her find herself). She seeks an ideal- ized father (Jesus), harking back to her primitive idealization of her father, and has sex with him (sleeps in his Jeep). However, just as she became disillusioned with her real father, she also becomes disillusioned with Jesus (he's too nice, not smart enough). This is a "state of the self" dream.

Dream: My family was about to be burned by a fire. Suddenly Jesus came down from the sky and carried them out to safety. I was Jesus. My family was very grateful.

Dreamer: A 32-year-old paranoid man.

Association: He only felt real if he could serve people.

Interpretation: The dream is both a death wish and a rescue wish, symbolizing his ambivalence. It also shows his narcissistic delusion of grandeur (he is Jesus) and his hope to gain some love from his family by saving them.

Dream: "An angel of the Lord appeared unto him in a dream, saying, Joseph, thou son of David, fear not to take unto thee Mary thy wife: for that which is con- ceived in her is of the Holy Ghost. And she shall bring forth a son, and thou shalt call his name Jesus: for he shall save his people from their sins. Now all this was done, that it might be fulfilled which was spoken of the Lord by the prophet, say- ing, Behold a virgin shall be with child, and shall bring forth a son, and they shall call his name Emanuel, which being interpreted is, God with us."

Dreamer: Joseph, husband of Mary, mother of Jesus Christ. Reported in the *Bible* (Matthew).

Associations: Joseph had this dream after finding out that the woman he was going to marry had become pregnant, but not by him. The dream refers to an ear- lier Hebrew prophecy of the coming of the Messiah (to be conceived by a virgin) who would save Israel from its enemies.

Interpretation: The dream represents a wish by Joseph that his fiancée has been impregnated by God (the Holy Ghost) rather than by another man, which would be a scandal. Through this dream, he and Mary can both save face. The wish also ties in with the Hebrew prophecy of the coming of the Messiah. (It was not uncommon in those days—as now—for people to claim their child was the Messiah.)

Journey

Dream: I am going on a journey. I am going to Budapest.

Dreamer: Robert S., an obsessive-compulsive patient, as reported by Namrow (1980).

Associations: He thought it strange to have such a short dream when usually they were so detailed. He thought the journey meant the journey of analysis.

Interpretation: Namrow asked the dreamer what his thoughts about Budapest were. He replied that he was planning a trip to Europe, but not in the vicinity of Budapest. "You mean more in my vicinity," the analyst replied, "whom you *pester* with your hostility and envy while wearing a *Buddha*-like mask." The patient replied that the therapist was probably right, and recalled getting a headache in a previous session when the analyst would not answer his questions.

Dream: I was on a journey to outer space. I could see planets, suns, moons, and black holes drift by. It was dark and cold, but I didn't mind. I didn't know where I was going and didn't care.

Dreamer: A 24-year-old suicidal man.

Association: He had just been fired from a job. He wanted to tell the whole world to "go fuck itself."

Interpretation: The dream expresses a suicidal wish to leave the earth, with all its problems, and venture into outer space. It is also a death wish and perhaps a hope for some kind of life after death, albeit "dark and cold."

Judge

Dream: I was standing before this stern judge. He said to me, "I'll let you go this time. But you know it's your fault, and if you do it again, I won't be so lenient." I didn't say anything back to him, because I knew it wouldn't do any good. I shook hands with the clerk and left.

Dreamer: A 29-year-old female alcoholic.

Association: She was feeling guilty about having gone on a drinking binge.

Interpretation: The judge represents her superego (her internal censor), as well as her disapproving father, to whom she could never talk back. The bad thing she did was to drink and to thereby act out antisocial feelings.

Jungle

Dream: I was lost in a jungle. I heard strange animals and was frightened. A large black panther chased me. I woke up.

Dreamer: A 23-year-old woman suffering from anxiety and various phobias.

Association: She had not left her apartment for days. Her boyfriend called her "Miss Prim and Proper."

Interpretation: The jungle symbolizes the dreamer's repressed "wild" sexuality and aggression, which she projects onto the external world and then fears.

Key

Dream: I was digging up some dirt in my flower garden and I discovered an old key. I rubbed off the dirt and found that it was made of gold. I was so happy I ran into the house and showed it to my father. He shook my hand in a very manly way.

Dreamer: A 28-year-old woman with a masculinity complex.

Associations: Her father was generally cold and disapproving. She felt he preferred his sons over her and spent more time with them.

Interpretation: The golden key is probably the key to her father's heart, to the world of masculinity and all the privileges the dreamer associates with that world. It is that world from which she feels she has been excluded and to which she seeks admittance. The key is also a phallic symbol denoting her possession of a treasured organ that she once, at the age of 3, regretted so much not having, and which still looms large in her unconscious.

King

Dream: I heard a voice, as though from a loudspeaker, saying, "You are the new king of the underworld." I was expected to decapitate some people. I called my father to let him know.

Dreamer: A 32-year-old paranoid schizophrenic man.

Association: His father was a convicted murderer, who had been hostile toward him because of his close relationship with his mother. The father had an obsessional hatred of homosexuals.

Interpretation: King of the underworld signifies coming out of the closet as a homosexual. Decapitation means castration. The dreamer fears that his father will castrate him if he finds out about his latent homosexuality. Underneath the homosexual urges are even more unconscious homicidal urges toward his father and fears of retaliation.

Dream: I was in a former time, maybe in a former life. I was the favorite mistress of the king. He loved me better than his wife, the queen, but he couldn't leave her.

Dreamer: A 23-year-old woman.

Association: She had seen a historical movie. The countryside in the movie reminded her of the countryside near the home where she grew up.

Interpretation: The "former time" and "former life" refer to the oedipal period of childhood, when she was the favorite of her father (the king), but he couldn't leave his queen (mother) for her.

Kiss

Dream: The girl who is going to teach me how to use my computer came to my house. She was explaining the computer to me and then she started kissing me. I was disturbed.

Dreamer: A 41-year-old man.

Association: He had this dream the night before he was to meet with the woman friend who had volunteered to teach him.

Interpretation: This is a warning dream. He was married and did not want to jeopardize his marriage. The dream allowed him to get in touch with the erotic nature of his friendship, of which he had previously been unaware.

Dream: I was driving in a car with a strange man. The man seemed angry with me. Suddenly he leaned over and kissed me. I lost control of the wheel and the car crashed.

Dreamer: A 27-year-old man.

Association: The man feared that he was going to be fired from his job because his boss did not like him.

Interpretation: This kiss here is a "kiss of death." The strange man is both his boss and a male co-worker with whom he did not get along; on a deeper level, he may represent the dreamer's father, whose hostility toward him as he was growing up was the original kiss of death. The dream also points to latent homosexual drives.

Knives

Dream: I'm in a strange city. I see a man bleeding on a balcony. I feel terrified. Suddenly a knife whizzes past my head and hits the wall next to me. Another lands at my feet. I run down the street, bullets flying by, and duck into an alley, thinking I'll be safe. Then I see bullet holes in the wall there and fall to the asphalt, covering my head with my hands.

Dreamer: A 23-year-old agoraphobic woman.

Associations: Her father was an avid hunter. As a child she had recurring nightmares of gorillas. She had not been able to go outside her apartment since her father died in a car accident.

Interpretation: The dream indicates the source of the dreamer's agoraphobia. She had murderous wished toward her father (the man bleeding), which she normally defended against through a reaction formation of extreme concern for him. The agoraphobia stems from a projection of these murderous wishes onto the environment, which were seemingly granted when his car crashed. In the end she huddles in an alley (mother's womb).

Knots

Dream: Jim and I were on a sailing boat. He was trying to tie a knot and couldn't. I had to do it for him.

Dreamer: A 28-year-old woman.

Association: For some time she had been wanting Jim to propose.

Interpretation: Jim was not ready to "tie the knot."

L

Labyrinth

Dream: I was in a labyrinth and couldn't find my way out. It was dark and made of narrow hallways. I woke up terrified.

Dreamer: A 20-year-old woman suffering from anorexia nervosa.

Association: The day before the dream she had quarreled with her mother about eating. She felt her mother was too controlling.

Interpretation: The labyrinth represents her mother. The dreamer is terrified that she will be trapped by her attachment to her mother.

Lamb

Dream: I saw a lamb being slaughtered as I passed by a field

Dreamer: A 38-year-old man with masochistic features.

Association: He felt that he was being bypassed while other people at his company were being promoted.

Interpretation: He is his company's sacrificial lamb.

Liberals

Dream: I was at the office and found myself talking like a liberal. Bob and Cindy and the others were there and we were having a nice conversation and we were all liberals.

Dreamer: A 42-year-old political conservative.

Association: He had complained that he was the only conservative in the office.

Interpretation: The dream expresses his wish to be liked by those in his office, even if it means switching his political persuasion and identity.

Life

Dream: I was a scientist and I was engaging in the study of various forms of life. I had a laboratory, and there were jars of insects and frogs and cages with monkeys.

There were some odd-looking animals that had ears where their eyes should have been and eyes where their mouths should have been, and mouths on all sides of their heads.

Dreamer: A 33-year-old man with an eating disorder.

Association: His mother used to tease him that he should have been born with two mouths so he could eat faster.

Interpretation: The "life" he is really studying is his own. The various forms of life, especially the strange animal with mouths all around, are the dreamer.

Lighthouse

Dream: I was swimming in an ocean at night. Suddenly I saw this lighthouse in the distance and swam toward it. I climbed up the rocks and went inside but there was nobody there. Then I walked up the circular stairs to the top and found some old trunks and boxes of books and some old navy hats.

Dreamer: A 29-year-old male narcissist.

Association: His father was a merchant marine who had hats like the ones in the dream.

Interpretation: The lighthouse is a phallic symbol. The ocean symbolizes mother. The dreamer wishes to break his overly strong attachment to his mother and be initiated into the masculine world and be accepted by his father and other men (reading the books, wearing the hats).

Lightning

Dream: As I slept I sensed a flash of light. I opened my eyes and saw three flashes of lightning outside the window.

Dreamer: A 27-year-old woman suffering from infertility.

Association: She and her husband had been trying to have a baby for some time. She prayed to God every night before bed.

Interpretation: The lightning denotes God's intervention and perhaps a divine (immaculate) pregnancy.

Line

Dream: I saw a line that had a squiggle at the end of it.

Dreamer: A 23-year-old schizophrenic man. As reported by Kafka (1980).

Association: The dreamer had the dream after he had taken LSD.

Interpretation: The dreamer interpreted that the line represented the course of history, and the squiggle symbolized the Nazi holocaust. This dream illustrates how the schizophrenic interprets his own abstract dream symbols.

Lion

Dream: I sealed up my wife's body in a container that had the figure of a lion.

Dreamer: Philip of Macedonia, father of Alexander the Great. Reported by Plutarch (110a).

Association: He had this dream soon after marrying Olympias.

Interpretation: Aristander, a Greek dream interpreter, interpreted this dream to mean that Olympias was pregnant and that the child would prove to be as courageous as a lion. The dream may also indicate Philip's fears of his wife's power (the lion symbolizing her power or her animal nature) and his wish to protect himself by sealing her up. His fears were actualized later when Olympias, a violent and jealous woman, conspired with her son, Alexander, against her husband.

Dream: As I drove along a country road, I suddenly saw a mountain lion kill a deer. When I got to a service station I called my mother and told her about it. She was amazed.

Dreamer: A 30-year-old man.

Association: His mother called him every day and spoke to him in a teasing seductive manner.

Interpretation: The lion represents his libido and the scene in the country symbolizes his wish to rape his mother, at whom he is in a rage. His guilt about this rape results in his calling her on the phone to get her reaction (her blessing). She is amazed with his prowess.

Dream (fictional): The dreamer dreamed about Africa when he was a boy "and the long golden beaches and the white beaches, so white they hurt your eyes, and the high capes and the great brown mountains." He could hear the surf roar and see the native boats come riding in. He could smell the tar of his own boat as he slept and he could smell Africa in the dream. "He only dreamed of places now and of the lions on the beach. They played like young cats in the dusk and he loved them. . . ."

Dreamer: Ernest Hemingway, through the character of the Old Man in *The Old Man and the Sea* (1952).

Association: The old man in the novel noted that "he no longer dreamed of storms, nor of women, nor of great occurrences, nor of great fish, nor of fights, nor of contests of strength, nor of his wife."

Interpretation: The lions on the beach symbolize his youth and vitality, which are now in decline. The wish in the dream is to be young again and regain his former vitality. However, on another level, Hemingway, the author of this literary dream, is noted for writing about heroes who exemplify masculine strength (masculine narcissism), and the old man represents his portrait of such a hero in old age. Hemingway admitted that he wrote this book, as he had many others, on the heels of being rejected by a woman, who had made a parting remark disparaging his writing. The book, and the dream, may be a literary reply to the effect that, "I'm still strong and vital, even if I'm getting old."

Love

Dream: I dreamed the music of love.

Dreamer: Franz Liszt, Hungarian composer, who wrote a composition entitled "Love Dreams."

Association: He wrote that the theme of "Love Dreams" came to him in a dream.

Interpretation: Sometimes creative ideas can germinate in dreams, when the pressures of waking hours have subsided.

Dream: Bill and I are strolling in a meadow. We see another couple lying in the clover, naked. They are embracing one another madly, and they look very much in love. For a moment I feel very sad that Bill and I don't have that kind of love and passion in our lives anymore; then I think, who cares?

Dreamer: A 37-year-old woman.

Association: The night before the dream her husband had once again dozed off almost as soon as he got into bed and she had once again fallen asleep feeling sad and frustrated.

Interpretation: This is a common dream by married women who regret that passion has waned in their relationship. The ending of the dream—where she at first feels sad and then thinks, "Who cares?"—parallels her waking relationship: she has been denying how much she actually does care. The dream is like a wake-up call.

Luggage

Dream: Somebody gave me a white cat to care for at my parents' house, but I forgot to feed it. I was walking to my grandmother's house and I had a lot of luggage.

I was approaching Grandmother's house, but I didn't go in. I stood on the street. It was nighttime. I felt confused and paralyzed. I hadn't fed the cat in two days.

Dreamer: A 31-year-old woman with a borderline personality.

Associations: She had recently visited her parents and had left after a few days because of the unpleasantness. She had been sexually and physically abused by her mother and stepfather as a small child. Her grandmother had been her only solace.

Interpretation: The white cat represents her innocence and spirit, which were crushed by the traumas that she experienced in her parents' house, and which she cannot now, as an adult, repair (take care of). The luggage symbolizes this trauma, which she must carry with her, the weight of which paralyzes her. This is a "state-of-her-life" dream.

Dream: I went down to the cellar and found an old trunk and some other suitcases there. I was afraid to open them.

Dreamer: A 27-year-old man.

Association: He had just begun therapy.

Interpretation: The luggage in the basement symbolizes the repressed memories of his unconscious.

Mandala

Dream: I had a strange dream last night. It was as if I were looking through a kaleidoscope. I kept seeing these beautiful, colorful patterns. Each one was circular and perfectly symmetrical.

Dreamer: A 32-year-old woman with multiple personalities.

Association: She often complained about the confusion and disorder of her life.

Interpretation: The kaleidoscope is probably a mandala with perfect symmetry, representing the dreamer's wish for order and clarity in her life. Jung (1971) viewed mandalas as universal symbols of harmony that could be found in nearly all cultures, ancient and modern, and considered dreams such as this significant turning points in the dreamer's progress.

Mane

Dream: As we sat in a restaurant my girlfriend's neck grew longer and hair sprouted from it, falling down around her face, neck, and back like a mane. I told her, "You ought to see this." She looked in a mirror and said she had to admit it was quite beautiful.

Dreamer: A 40-year-old man.

Association: His girlfriend had recently gotten a new hairdo, which was parted down the middle. He had remarked, "It looks like a mane," and she was offended.

Interpretation: The dream represents a wish by the dreamer that his girlfriend had been able to appreciate his remark about her hair looking like a mane.

Mania

Dream 1: I, my husband, and my previous therapist were on a boat, touring the world. I gave advice to this previous therapist that he should acquire some light-weight clothes like my husband's. I woke up feeling manic.

Dream 2: I opened the door and saw my husband and another patient in bed under the covers. I closed the door and fled.

Dream 3: Both brothers of mine were in a new car, which had a nose like an airplane. I was sitting on the hood.

Dream 4: I was looking for a hatpin in my husband's factory. Men there, very brawny, tried to attack me. I ran.

Dream 5: I was estranged in a motel with my dog. I was afraid.

Dreamer: Miss A., a 30-year-old manic-depressive, as reported by Pao (1980).

Associations: After reporting the first two dreams she spoke of her husband's affairs; after the third and fourth dreams she devalued her femininity and talked of her envy of her brothers and of her attempts to make her husband more manly; after the fifth dream she talked of her fear of aggressive, biting dogs, and of her own aggression. These dreams all occurred during the patient's depressive phases (she did not dream during her manic episodes).

Interpretation: According to Pao, Dream 1 alluded to her fear of involvement with her new therapist; Dream 2 indicated her rageful thoughts about her husband's infidelity, corresponding to a similar triangle in the therapy situation (with the therapist's other patients); Dreams 3 and 4 underscored her grandiose fantasies attached to identification with her oldest brother, compensating for feelings of inadequacy; and Dream 5 expressed her conflict over aggressive impulses. These five dreams covered most of her basic conflicts, which would continue to be articulated during her therapy.

Marriage

Dream: I was marrying Carmen, but I was confused. I was driving to the wedding in the wrong car. The car let me off at the wrong place. I tried to call Carmen just to let her know where I was, but my mother answered the phone. I asked to speak to Carmen, but she wouldn't let me talk to her. She said it wasn't appropriate to talk to the bride on the wedding day.

Dreamer: A 32-year-old obsessive-compulsive man.

Association: He and Carmen had spoken about marriage the night before.

Interpretation: The confusion in the dream is an indication of his indecisiveness about the prospect of marriage. His indecisiveness has to do with his mother's disapproval of his fiancée, shown at the end when she refuses to let the dreamer speak to Carmen.

Dream: I dreamed I married my mother.

Dreamer: A 40-year-old man with an oedipus complex.

Association: He felt disgusted whenever his mother called him, which was almost daily.

Interpretation: The dream is an obvious wish, related to the emotional incest he has experienced from his mother since early childhood and which still continues. This incest is disgusting to him on the surface, but this disgust masks a deeper desire that makes him feel guilty.

Masculinity

Dream: I was at a party. There was a tall, muscular man in the corner watching me. We went into a side room. It had some kind of loft bed, which we had to climb up to. He forced me to take off my clothes and said, "Now I'm going to make you into a man." He proceeded to have anal sex with me. I was very upset, but afterwards I noticed that my cock had become larger.

Dreamer: A 29-year-old man suffering from ego-dystonic homosexuality and a masculinity complex.

Association: His father had been a tall, muscular man who had been hostile toward him.

Interpretation: The dream embodies the dreamer's wish to achieve masculinity by being "initiated" into manhood through anal rape by a muscular man (his father). This act assuages oedipal guilt and means acceptance by the father (who in the dreamer's childhood was hostile).

Dream: My father and some other men were trying to pick up a refrigerator, but couldn't. I lifted it for them and put it on the other side of the kitchen. They were surprised.

Dreamer: A 37-year-old narcissistic woman.

Association: Her father had always favored her two brothers.

Interpretation: Lifting the refrigerator expresses her wish to outdo her father and brothers in the masculine realm.

Masochism

Dream 1: A woman asked me to go with her to her apartment. Then she said she was going to shit in my mouth. I said, "I don't think so. I'm not a masochist." But I lay down and she sat on me and I got very excited. She laughed at me when I ejaculated.

Dream 2: Three women were kicking me. When they were finished I looked at them and they said they were sorry.

Dream 3: I went into a store and I was very angry at the female clerk about something. She didn't take my anger seriously. Then she made me stoop over and she gave me an enema. I told her she'd be sorry.

Dream 4: A mother and daughter invited me for tea and then began having sex in front of me. They giggled as I watched.

Dream 5: I went home to visit my mother. She pulled out my penis and made it hard and pointed at it. She called my sister and they both pointed at it. I walked out in a huff.

Dreamer: A 40-year-old man with masochistic features.

Association: His mother invited him to Thanksgiving dinner but he refused. Someday he would prove to everybody who had mistreated him what kind of person he was.

Interpretation: This series of dreams indicates the progress of the dreamer's therapy. In the beginning there is more distortion: he dreams about strange women sexually degrading and dominating him. By the end it is his mother and sister. His father's disappearance soon after he was born left him in the clutches of his mother and sister, who dominated and degraded him, leading to his development of a masochistic character.

Massage

Dream: Mr. A., one of my patients, begins to massage my back. I'm sitting on a folding chair and he is standing behind me. At first I have clothes on, then I'm naked. He slides his hands down and rubs my thighs. As he massages my inner thighs, his fingers graze my testicles a couple of times. Suddenly he stops and walks away, smirking at me.

Dreamer: A 53-year-old male psychotherapist.

Associations: The patient had brought in slides of his new paintings during the previous session and the therapist had praised them. The dreamer recalled an incident from his childhood when he was 11 and his younger brother had massaged his penis while they played "doctor." The game was interrupted when his mother called from the other room to ask why they were so quiet.

Interpretation: The dream is a wish for male bonding with the patient. The massage represents the maternal soothing the dreamer did not get from his mother, but which his younger brother had sometimes supplied. As in the childhood memory, the massage in the dream is interrupted. The patient walks away smirking as his mother did when she played her sons and husband against one another, stirring up competition among them and preventing them from bonding. Hence the patient was both mother and brother in the dream.

Masturbation

Dream (painting): His own profile, shriveled up over a barren landscape. A woman's head and shoulders grow out of one of his cheeks. She is leaning toward a man's torso, her mouth near his genitals. A lily and two little demons sprout out of other parts of his face, and a grasshopper hangs from beneath his nose. Where his mouth should be, there is nothing. A fishhook hangs from the top of his head, with some kind of fleshy substance hanging from it. A tiny couple stands underneath his face, embracing, and an egg lies on the ground in the forefront.

Dreamer: Salvador Dali, Spanish surrealist painter.

Associations: He described his painting, *The Great Masturbator,* painted when he was 24, as "the expression of my heterosexual anxiety." At that time he was still a virgin, inhibited by deep fears of female sexuality and anal obsessions.

Interpretation: The embracing couple symbolizes Dali's parents and the egg is the one they laid when he was born. The woman leaning toward genitals expresses Dali's sexual urges, and the demons growing out of his face and the grasshopper under his nose probably symbolize the conflicting feelings of guilt and self-hatred that gnaw away at him and prevent him from achieving a union with a woman. The hook at the top of his head may show that he is hooked—that is, fixated to his unresolved past. In many of his paintings he depicted his head as shrunken and gnarled, perhaps an indication of self-hatred and inferiority, as well as of genital inferiority (small, disgusting penis).

Matricide

Dream (Greek myth): Clytemnestra killed her husband, King Agamemnon, in order not to give up her lover Aegisthus. Orestes, her son by Agamemnon, avenged his father's death by killing his mother and her lover. The gods of Mount Olympus convened and tried Orestes for murder, and he was acquitted.

Interpretation: Matricide by a son, in psychoanalysis, is the result of a negative Oedipus complex. In the "positive" Oedipus complex, the son wishes to kill his father and marry his mother. In the negative complex, he wants to kill his mother and unite sexually with his father. There is a homosexual element in this myth.

Dream: My mother was flying in an airplane and it crashed. I woke up alarmed and concerned.

Dreamer: A 28-year-old woman.

Association: Her mother was scheduled to take a flight the next day. The dreamer assumed that her dream was a prophecy and called her mother to ask her not to go.

Interpretation: The dreamer's concern about her mother was a reaction formation, masking a death wish. The mother had been overcontrolling of the daughter all her life, and the daughter unconsciously wished to get rid of her.

Men

Dream: The dreamer is lying at Adler's feet and reaching out with her hands to touch the material of his silk dress. Adler makes a sexual advance. Then the dreamer says, smilingly, "You aren't better than other men." He nods affirmatively.

Dreamer: A woman patient, as reported by Adler (1917).

Association: The patient experienced a similar situation with her father when she was a child. At the time of the dream she was having an affair with a married man.

Interpretation: The dreamer, according to Adler, suffers from a masculinity complex, and the dream is an enactment of her masculine protest—her wish to have male power. She sits below the man and reaches at his silk dress (makes him into a woman). By seducing him and proving that he is no better than other men, she reverses the scale of power.

Dream: I was taking a shower when suddenly a group of men came into the bathroom. I asked them to leave but they wouldn't. I was really annoyed.

Dreamer: A young hysterical woman.

Association: She had five brothers who used to tease her as she was growing up.

Interpretation: The men in the dream symbolize her brothers and all men in general, who she feared would be intrusive like her brothers.

Dream 1: I was in a factory. There were other men. A woman was working alone, very pretty. I talked to her and she liked me. I started kissing her. The other men were glaring at me.

Dream 2: A beautiful woman and I were on a pile of wood. She was naked and I was about to fuck her. Then some men came and grabbed her and took her away.

Dream 3: I was in a house. I was trying to have sex with a woman, but there were some other men in another room and I kept getting distracted.

Dream 4: Swimming with a naked woman. Some men on the shore.

Dream 5: Walking with a woman. A crowd of men surrounds us.

Dream 6: I'm in a shop of some kind. There's a beautiful girl behind the counter. We talk for a while and she invites me behind the counter. We begin making love on the floor. I look up and my brothers are standing there, glaring at me.

Dreamer: A 34-year-old man with oedipal features and multiple symptoms of sexual dysfunction.

Association: He had had dreams with this recurring theme for as long as he could remember. He had been his mother's favorite and his brothers were jealous.

Interpretation: The variations of this dream occurred over several years of therapy. The dreamer, the youngest of four brothers, suffered from intense castration fears due to a sometimes violent rivalry with his brothers and father that was fueled by his mother's babying of him and his brothers' envy of that favoritism. The castration fear associated with his brothers (strange men) underlay his problems with impotence.

Migraine

Dream 1: I'm sitting in bed reading. Bob comes in and says he has a migraine. He starts kissing me and I say, "How can you make love if you have a headache?" Suddenly it isn't Bob anymore but an older man, a black man with a goatee. Then I notice a woman is staring at us from the window disapprovingly. I wake up with a migraine.

Dream 2: I'm on the street. A lot of young men are leering at me and I'm afraid. I wake up with a migraine.

Dream 3: I see a man with an erection. He's holding his hands on his temples as if he has a headache. I wake up with a migraine.

Dream 4: I'm kissing my father. I wake up with a migraine.

Dreamer: A 32-year-old woman with a history of migraines.

Association: She recalled that when she was 5, her father, an alcoholic, fell into bed with her after an argument with her mother.

Interpretation: These four dreams reveal the dreamer's father fixation (the older man, the black man), which is the source of her migraines. The unconscious erotic feelings that were aroused when her father slept at her side, and which still linger, are in conflict with her conscience. This psychic conflict causes her to avoid sex with her husband and fear sex in general, and it produces the tension that leads to the migraines.

Mirror

Dream (Greek myth): A beautiful young man named Narcissus was punished for rejecting the love of the nymph Echo by being made to gaze at his own reflection in a pond. He fell in love with his reflection, dove in, and drowned.

Interpretation: Narcissism has come to mean an excessive self-love or concern for the self and lack of concern for others. According to Freud, narcissism is an aspect of homosexuality, causing individuals to choose as sexual objects those most similar to (reflections of) themselves. In the myth, Narcissus develops a preoccupation with himself after rejecting the love of Echo (rejecting heterosexual love). The end result of his self-preoccupation is that he drowns (gets overinvolved) in his own reflection. This happens with narcissistic people in general.

Dream (fairy tale): A queen regularly looks in her mirror and says, "Mirror, Mirror, on the wall, who's the fairest of them all?" Generally the mirror answers, "You, my queen." However, one day the mirror replies that Snow White is the fairest, whereupon the queen casts Snow White out of the castle and leaves her in the woods to die.

Interpretation: The story of the queen is a symbolic description of a narcissistic personality. Such personalities tend to harbor grandiose ideas about themselves, and if those ideas are challenged, they feel affronted and react with fits of rage. Psychoanalytically, this tale can be seen as a parable about a certain kind of mother who, due to her narcissistic pride and vanity, competes with her daughter and degrades her. Philosophically, it can be viewed as a morality tale of good and evil, the queen representing spiritual corruption while Snow White stands for honesty and purity. In such tales, good prevails against evil; in life it often does not. Yet such tales show children the way toward healthy relating.

Dream: I was gazing at the mirror when suddenly it cracked, splitting my face into fragments.

Dreamer: A young woman with multiple personalities.

Association: She had seven personalities, which took possession of her body at different times.

Interpretation: The mirror here, as in many dreams, symbolizes honesty (as in, "the mirror doesn't lie.") In this case it reflects, by cracking, the fragmentation of the individual's personality.

Money

Dream: My father showed me his financial statement. He had a large sum of money in the bank, more than I thought. My brother and I would get a good share when he died.

Dreamer: A 30-year-old man.

Association: For some time he had been struggling with a marginal level of sustenance. He had recently visited his father, who had shown rare kindness.

Interpretation: This is a simple dream of a wish to inherit money from his father to relieve his current dire monetary predicament.

Dream: I was walking on the beach and saw some coins in the sand. I picked them up and found more. I dug a hole and found a whole treasure trove of coins. I was rich.

Dreamer: A boy, who had this dream from the ages of 4 to 8.

Association: He recalled the abusive family environment in which he had been raised.

Interpretation: Recurring dreams of finding a treasure or of winning the lottery represent the wish for liberation from some unpleasant situation. The boy's wish to find a treasure trove was such a wish. It signified a way he could escape from his oppressive familial environment.

Dream: I was paying a priest some money I owed him.

Dreamer: A 23-year-old obsessive-compulsive man.

Association: He had recently "sinned" by having an affair.

Interpretation: He had to atone (pay) for his sin.

Dream: I was dropping coins all over the ground.

Dreamer: A 27-year-old man with an impulsive character disorder.

Association: His wife accused him of philandering.

Interpretation: Dropping coins means dropping seeds (his sperm) everywhere.

Dream: I was spending money all over town.

Dreamer: A 30-year-old woman.

Association: She was afraid to buy a new dress because her husband would complain.

Interpretation: She wanted to liberate herself from her husband's control.

Dream: I had a lot of money in a bowl. There were silver dollars, half dollars, and quarters. A woman wanted me to contribute something to charity but I refused.

Dreamer: A 32-year-old man with an anal-retentive personality.

Association: The woman looked like his mother.

Interpretation: He would hold on to his feces (money) and not go to the potty for his mother.

Monsters

Dream 1: I was at my drawing class. The nude male model suddenly got off his chair and turned into an angry monster. He suddenly had to kill me. I kept running from him and was afraid he would catch me.

Dream 2: I was at my drawing class. Suddenly some kind of monster that I couldn't see was trying to kill me. I ran out of the room but he seemed to be in the air around me.

Dreamer: A 37-year-old schizoid woman.

Association: She had this recurring dream whenever she had her menstrual period. She felt attracted to the nude model in the dream.

Interpretation: The monster represents her father, who had been physically abusive during the oedipal phase and had denigrated her femininity during her adolescence. The monster also stands for her mother, who was competitive with her. Finally, it represents the conflict between her own internalized objects and her own internalized hatred of her femininity. Attraction to a man (to her father) is taboo, arousing fears of annihilation. This internal conflict is heightened by her menstrual period, which to her is an omen of bad luck, and a reminder of her femininity.

Dream: While he is sleeping at his desk, reason disappears and monsters that hunt and fly by night—owls, bats, and lions—surround him.

Dreamer: Francisco Goya, Spanish painter. As depicted in his painting, *The Sleep of Reason Produces Monsters*.

Association: The painting is reportedly a reproduction of one of the painter's nightmares.

Interpretation: The beasts of prey that surround the painter as he sleeps perhaps symbolize the pangs of his own conscience—that is, his guilt and the fear of reprisal due to the projection of self-hatred onto external forces (the monsters).

Monument

Dream: "A great image, whose brightness was excellent, stood before thee; and the form thereof was terrible. The image's head was of fine gold, his breast and his arms of silver, his belly and his thighs of brass. His legs of iron, his feet part of iron and part of clay. Thou sawest till that a stone was cut out without hands, which smote the image upon his feet that were of iron and clay and broken. Then was the iron, the clay, the brass, the silver, and the gold broken to pieces together, and became like the chaff of the summer threshingfloors; and the wind carried them away, that no place was found for them; and the stone that smote the image became a great mountain and filled the whole earth."

Dreamer: King Nebuchadnezzar, the ruler of ancient Babylon who built the hanging gardens. Reported in the *Bible* (Daniel).

Association: The dream was a recurring one that interfered with his sleep. It troubled him so much that he forgot the dream and threatened to kill all the wise men of Babylon unless they could remember it. Daniel, a Jew, had a vision one night and told him his dream and its meaning.

Interpretation: Daniel's interpretation spoke of the successive kingdoms that would follow Nebuchadnezzar's, symbolized by brass, silver, iron, and clay, being of weaker and weaker dispositions. Psychoanalytically, the dream could be seen as an anxiety dream. The monument with feet of iron and clay perhaps symbolizes the king's fears about his own vulnerability and mortality (something many ancient kings of Babylonia and Egypt seemed obsessed with). The stone that "smote" him and becomes a mountain that fills the earth expresses the fear that somebody else (one of his sons?) will succeed in doing what the dreamer wanted but failed to do: rule the whole world.

Dream 1: I returned to my brother's condo. The condo was gone, and instead there was a monument. The grounds were full of his belongings. I picked them up. His girlfriend was there but she wasn't picking anything up. The monument looked like a pile of flowers shaped like a casket. His girlfriend's two boys were riding around in a golf cart. I didn't ask them to leave.

Dream 2: I went to the cemetery where my brother was buried and found a large monument shaped like a golf cart.

Dreamer: A 33-year-old man in mourning.

Association: His brother had died of cancer. The two of them used to play golf together. His brother's girlfriend lost the condo after he died.

Interpretation: These two dreams, which the dreamer had successively on the same night, represent the dreamer's attempt to mourn the loss of his older brother. The monument perhaps stands for masculinity (the phallus), and denotes the masculine bond he had formed with his brother, and the hopes attached to it, which were left unfulfilled at the brother's death. The golf cart in both dreams is a symbol of their bond and also represents masculinity. The image of the two boys riding in golf carts may be a wish that he could relive his own childhood with his brother, under the watchful eye of a kind mother (the girlfriend). The condensation of monument, coffin, and flowers is an indication of the tender reference and idealization of the dreamer for his brother.

Mother

Dream: The dreamer saw his mother, with a peculiarly peaceful, sleeping expression on her features, being carried into the room by two (or three) people with birds' beaks and set down upon the bed.

Dreamer: Sigmund Freud, at age 7 or 8. Reported in Freud (1900).

Associations: He recalled seeing pictures of tall figures with birds' beaks in an illustrated *Bible*. He remembered an illustration of an Egyptian funeral, and a bier that looked like a bed. He also recalled an older boy named Philipp, who had taught him the vulgar word for copulation. He had read about a case of another boy who had dreamed about a man with a hatchet chasing him after having seen his parents having sex when he was 9 years old.

Interpretation: The dream is an oedipal dream. Freud's association to the other boy's dream about being chased by a man with a hatchet alludes to what Freud probably thought would happen to him if his father found out about his forbidden, incestuous thoughts about his mother. The reference to Philipp confirms the sexual nature of Freud's unconscious thoughts, and hints that like Philipp, Freud might also have witnessed the primal scene. Hence, the dream is a warning that if he pokes his nose in his parents' sexual relations and sexual desires for his mother, both he and his mother might die.

Dream: I was in a big country house. Mark came in and said something about bad guys in a car. Then he left and I was outside of the house by myself. There was a pond covered with ice. I saw some female bodies lying on top of the ice, their eyes bulging like fish eyes. Then I said, "Go to sleep, Mom, you're dead!" The ice melted and the bodies slipped under the water. I ran to the house scared and yelled, "Let me in."

Dreamer: A 43-year-old alcoholic man

Association: His mother had died when he was 9. The house reminded him of New Jersey Victorian houses where he used to play in a band with Mark.

Interpretation: This is a mourning dream. The bad guys in the car may represent a displacement of his guilty feelings about his mother's death. Seeing her dead, lying on an icy pond, perhaps denotes how the memory of her death has been frozen in time. Telling her she is dead and seeing the ice melt and her body sink represent the fact that he is emotionally letting go of her at last. She and the females with fish eyes suggest symbols of death, of which the dreamer is terrified.

Dream: I was at a big white house. There was some kind of party. The hostess was planning to murder all the guests. My brother and I began to arm ourselves. The hostess, who looked like my mother, aimed a gun at me and pulled the trigger but fired blanks. I tried to shoot her but my gun also fired blanks.

Dreamer: A 39-year-old depressed male.

Association: My gun was smaller than my mother's.

Interpretation: The dream indicates the murderous wishes the dreamer has toward his mother, and which he projects onto her. That her gun is bigger than his suggests primitive ideas about the phallic mother, derived from castration fear. The fact that both guns fire blanks indicates the ambivalent nature of their relationship. Having his brother as an ally in the dream reverses what happened in real life, when his brother was his mother's favorite.

Dream: I was in a massage studio, in a private room. A young girl was lying on a table and I was supposed to massage her. But I saw a shadow in the corner. It looked like my mother.

Dreamer: A 30-year-old anal-narcissistic man.

Association: He had had a sexual encounter with a woman that weekend, and afterwards felt disgusted with her.

Interpretation: The dream denotes how the memory of his incestuous relationship with his mother lingers in his present, interfering with his love life. The disgust he felt for the woman he had sex with in his real life alludes to the disgust he felt for his mother, which was connected to the guilt about his incestuous wishes, as well as to the way his mother felt about him when he was born (she had wanted a girl).

Dream: Mike and I were riding on bicycles through a musty tunnel. We got to an open place. Two women were there with G-string bathing suits. Their behinds were showing and we thought they were hookers. Suddenly my mother appeared. Then I was getting bogged down in some kind of swamp. I went to a sink to wash my clothes and they had shit all over them. Some of the shit got in my mouth, and there were worms in the shit.

Dreamer: A 37-year-old man suffering from depression and perverse sexual tendencies.

Association: He had recently read an article in a magazine about tapeworms. He had the sense that his mother saw his penis as a worm.

Interpretation: The dreamer and his friend are riding their bicycles (phallic symbols) through a musty tunnel (his mother's vagina). They see two sexy women. Then his mother appears and he finds himself in a swamp of excrement and worms, some of which gets into his mouth. The swamp of excrement and worms symbolizes his inferior feelings about his own genitals, feelings which he introjected from his mother's negative attitude toward him and his masculinity from an early age. These images suggest a regression to primitive pregenital ideation. This image also may indicate his use of anality as a defense against his incestuous impulses, harking back to the stage of anal eroticism.

Dream: I wish to be hanged. . . . I have torn them to pieces, drunk out their blood. . . . I have opened all hearts and eaten them up. . . . I am a funnel, I have devoured all men, but you can tear me to pieces, prick me with needles—I shall not defend myself. . . . I see myself breaking strange people to pieces and taking the bones into my body. . . . I did not know my mother; perhaps, if I knew my mother, I would have obeyed her. . . .

Dreamer: A 26-year-old psychotic woman, as reported by Schilder (1942).

Association: She used to live with her mother. Her psychotic breakdown began with a hypochondriacal idea of being incapacitated and unable to cook. This idea was related to a problem with overeating and with sadistic wishes about her mother.

Interpretation: The dream shows the extreme guilt of the dreamer about death wishes toward her mother. She feels that she has killed all people and is responsible for all the world's misfortune. The introjection of persons the dreamer hates (all representing aspects of the mother) is portrayed as an oral incorporation (cannibalism). This is a feature common to dreams of psychotics, traceable to a regression to the earliest of infancy, when a baby physically chews on everything in order to possess it. The patient's extreme guilt reveals a sadistic superego that exacts punishment on the patient (she must be hanged, torn to pieces).

Dream: The dreamer had sexual intercourse with his mother.

Dreamer: Julius Caesar, dictator of the Roman Empire, reported by Freud (1900).

Association: An ancient Roman oracle prophesied that the man who first kissed his mother would conquer Rome.

Interpretation: The dream interpreters of Caesar's day saw this dream as a favorable omen that he would take possession of the earth (Mother Earth). Psychoanalytically, it perhaps also indicates an oedipal wish to take possession of his mother.

Dream: The dreamer lay with his mother and they made love.

Dreamer: Hippias, Ancient Greek General. Reported by Freud (1900).

Association: The night after he had this dream, he led the Persians back to Marathon.

Interpretation: Hippias interpreted this dream as a sign that he should return to Athens, recover his power, and die an old man in his motherland. Psychoanalytically, this is an oedipal dream of possessing his mother. Freud wrote, "I have found that people who know that they are preferred or favored by their mother give evidence in their lives of a peculiar self-reliance and an unshakable optimism which often seem like heroic attributes and bring actual success to their possessors" (1900, p. 434).

Mourning

Dream 1: I wake up and go to the kitchen. My husband is there making breakfast.

Dream 2: I visit my husband's grave. As I sit there I hear a faint voice inside. "Get me out of here," it says.

Dream 3: My husband is buying some fruit at the corner store.

Dream 4: I'm walking along on the street where my husband had his heart attack. He's still lying there on the street. He looks meek. I shout at him, "Get up. How dare you abandon me in this way."

Dream 5: My husband knocks on the door. I know it's him, but I don't want to see him. "Go away," I tell him, angrily.

Dream 6: I'm dozing and I wake up to see my husband lying on my bed. He looks pale, barely alive. "It's all right," I tell him tenderly. "You can go now."

Dreamer: A 49-year-old narcissistic woman who is in mourning.

Association: Her husband died of a heart attack about a year and a half earlier.

Interpretation: This series of dreams indicates the evolution of the dreamer's mourning, which lasted several years. In the first few dreams she has not accepted his death. In dreams 4 and 5 she expresses her anger about his "abandonment" of her. In the final dream, she finally accepts his death and lets him go. Dream series such as this one represent a gauge of therapeutic progress.

Mouth

Dream 1: I was in a small room. I couldn't tell if I was standing or lying down, or looking up or down. I saw a step covered with sand. I could feel the texture of the sand in my mouth.

Dream 2: I was in the woods. A child was with me. I had a glass in my hand, a crystal glass. I put it in my mouth. The whole top part was in my mouth and I couldn't get it out. The glass broke and cut my mouth.

Dream 3: I was on a path in the woods. I saw a goat and stood there looking at it. Then a man came by. He was wearing a marshmallow shirt. I thought it was a great idea. It was so soft against his skin. "How'd you do that?" I asked. "I melted them down and molded them," he said. I wondered how it would be on my own skin, and eating it.

Dreamer: A 29-year-old schizoid woman.

Associations: She had recently found out that she had a tumor in her brain that her doctor ascribed to too much lactose in her body. She had recently had an abortion against her wishes.

Interpretation: This series of dreams, all dreamed during the same night, expresses her oral wishes and alludes to the circumstance of finding a tumor in her brain due to her body's production of too much lactose (milk). The excess lactose, in turn, stems from frustrations of her wishes to nurse a baby (the recent abortion). The dream also harks back to her infancy, when her own nursing was traumatically interrupted. The marshmallow shirt in the last dream seems to condense oral (eating) and anal eroticism (marshmallow = feces).

Murder

Dream: "I dreamed that the pinnacle that the Senate had erected on our house as a monument to Caesar had tumbled down, and then I was holding my husband in my arms, butchered, and was weeping about his murder."

Dreamer: Calpurnia, wife of Julius Caesar. Reported by Plutarch (110b).

Association: She had the dream on the night before he was murdered, and begged him not to go to the Senate that day.

Interpretation: Soothsayers of the time considered this dream to be a forewarning, which it was. Various rumors had been flying about Caesar's assassination; Calpurnia must have heard them, and they probably influenced this dream.

Dream: I fought a duel with my father. We shot at each other with guns. When my ammunition gave out, I ran away. Father kept shooting at me. I shouted, "This is not dueling any more, this is murder."

Dreamer: A male patient suffering from an eye tic, reported by Stekel (1911).

Association: He had spoken of animosity toward his father.

Interpretation: The eye tic was related to the patient's unconscious wish to shoot his father, the tic having to do with aiming a gun. The dream indicates his fear of his father's wrath, and of his father having more ammunition (potency) than he.

Dream 1: There's an ambulance in front of my house. Somebody's been murdered. I think it's my parents.

Dream 2: Father has shot someone in the bedroom.

Dream 3: My parents are in prison. They murdered somebody. I feel afraid.

Dream 4: Father is lying dead, face up, in the bathtub. He had been murdered.

Dream 5: I was going swimming. My mother's body was lying on the bottom of the pool. I went to tell my father and he said, "Don't worry, she'll keep."

Dream 6: I see both parents lying in a pool of blood in the cellar. I feel a shadow behind me.

Dreamer: A 24-year-old woman suffering from multiple phobic symptoms.

Association: She was angry at both parents for abusing her as a child. Her mother used to wake her up at night and fly at her in an alcoholic rage. Her father was weak and appeasing of the mother. She was left with a continual state of anxiety.

Interpretation: The wish in these dreams is that somebody (not herself) will murder her parents so that she can be free. In one dream her father murders her mother; in another she is the murderer; in others an unknown assailant has murdered both of them; in another they are both in prison for murder. The last dream helps explain her phobic symptoms; the shadow (mother? father? her bad internal object?) is angry at her for having murderous thoughts.

Dream 1: I was with two people I didn't know. We came out of the subway and then somehow we were in a house. A mother had left her two children and I held my hand over their mouths and smothered them. It was sort of an accident. I felt no remorse. We went back down to the subway; we had to hide from the mother. Then we found a small pickup truck and drove to another house. We hid there for a while and then somehow I was alone. I saw the police outside and I realized what I'd done. I felt despair.

Dream 2: I killed somebody—a female—and I think I'd done it to see if I could do it and get away with it. Left a telltale clue. Afterwards I felt real despair.

Dreamer: A 43-year-old passive-aggressive man whose father had abandoned him, his sister, and his mother soon after marriage.

Association: He had recently written a letter to his mother complaining about her emotionally abandoning him as a child. She replied that he was always complaining and showed no remorse.

Interpretation: Partly due to his never having had a father, the dreamer had never learned to assert himself. His mother had displaced her anger at the father onto the son, treating him with subtle disdain. In his dreams, he treats others with disdain, but just as he does in his waking life, he disowns his murderous rage. In the first dream, the murder is an accident; in the second, it is an experiment. In the first he kills two children (perhaps himself and his sister), identifying with his aggressor mother. The subway may be seen as a womb symbol (he had had other more direct dreams of his mother's womb), showing his wish to go back to the womb for more nurturing. In the second dream, however, he is able to acknowledge that the murder was intentional—a more healthy attitude. In both dreams, he feels despair—the despair, perhaps, he once felt as a boy upon feeling abandoned by his father (physically) and mother (emotionally).

Dream: I was on the phone with my mother. Suddenly I heard a shot. Somebody had shot her. It was her sister's boyfriend. She died while I was talking to her on the phone. I realized she must have died.

Dreamer: A 25-year-old passive woman whose mother had hysterically stifled and abused her.

Association: She had talked to her mother the day before the dream and felt annoyed, as usual. She was friendly with the boyfriend of her aunt.

Interpretation: The dream is a wish for her mother's death. The reference to her mother's sister's boyfriend harks back to a situation that prevailed when she was growing up, during which there was animosity between her mother and this boyfriend. In actuality the dreamer has murderous wishes toward her mother, which she cannot acknowledge to herself. Hence she displaces them onto the boyfriend.

Muscles

Dream: I'm in some home, and this man is there with a very long penis. He's very muscular. There's something uncouth about him. He's dark, manly, and rough. And we're in bed and I want him to fuck me and he won't. However, he had me by the penis and there's a rush of excitement. Then I think other people are coming into the room, interrupting us. Then later he's still lying in bed eating a salad. The salad is on his chest but I dump it all over his head because he wouldn't fuck me. I'm so angry. The salad turns into a jellylike substance, like sperm, I guess. Then we start kissing each other.

Dreamer: A 23-year-old ego-dystonic homosexual male. Reported by Socarides (1980).

Associations: Y. had come over the night of the dream and he had been very attracted to Y. but unable to get him into bed. He became severely anxious and depressed and went cruising in order to fill the emptiness and relieve the tension linked with his dread that he might go out of control.

Interpretation: Socarides notes that this dream portrays explicit sexual activities with little distortion, activities similar to those the dreamer pursued in his fantasy life every day. It expresses the dreamer's desire to play the female role with a muscular (powerful) man and thereby acquire the partner's long penis and masculinity through incorporation. It also shows his aggressive impulses (dumping the salad). This and similar dreams served to restore the dreamer's self-representation.

Music

Dream: The dreamer sold his soul to the devil, who then picked up a violin and played a sonata of exquisite beauty with consummate skill.

Dreamer: Tartini, famous eighteenth-century Italian composer and violinist. Reported by Freud (1900).

Association: When he awoke from this dream, he at once wrote down what he could remember of the music. The result was his famous "Trillo del Diavolo."

Interpretation: Without knowing more about Tartini's life, we can only speculate that he was struggling with a Faustian conflict between spirituality (his soul) and personal gain. In the dream, a compromise is worked out wherein he is able to sell his soul but still obtain the fruits of spirituality (the beautiful sonata).

Dream: Recurring dreams have told me, "Be a musician."

Dreamer: Socrates, ancient Greek philosopher. Reported by Plato (420 B.C.).

Association: He recalled having these dreams a few days before poisoning himself while in prison. He had been charged with undermining the morals of youth.

Interpretation: Socrates interpreted the dreams to mean that he should be a philosopher: music symbolized philosophy. However, in view of the troubles his philosophizing brought him, perhaps the dream could be seen as a warning that he should put his creativity into a different, less controversial, channel.

Mutilation

Dream: People were having amputations, being mutilated, and there was blood everywhere.

Dreamer: Eleanor M., a schizophrenic woman, as reported by Kafka (1980). She had hundreds of recurring dreams dealing with complex images of gore.

Associations: Her first acute episode came after her mother had demanded that she be present in the operating room in which her mother was "opened up" and found to have widespread cancer. One of her delusions was that she had given her mother a sedative that killed her. During her stay at the mental hospital she hallucinated and was preoccupied with violence, was wildly agitated, prone to exposing herself, smeared herself and the walls with menstrual blood, destroyed property, and assaulted people. However, during times of remission she was a rather high caliber wife, mother, and participating member of the community.

Interpretation: Kafka's method of dealing with the dreams of schizophrenics is to emphasize not the dream's latent content, but the dreamer's experience. The themes of mutilation, amputation, and blood that permeate this dreamer's dream could, of course, be interpreted in terms of their indications of paranoid ideation, megalomania, narcissistic rage, and the castration complex. Incidentally, in treating her, Kafka developed a technique of using "gory" language in discussing her dreams and impulses, a technique he compared to the showing of war movies to soldiers who returned from World War II suffering from battle fatigue.

N

Nakedness

Dream: I was at a party and I was naked. Everybody else was dressed except me. I went to get a glass of wine from the kitchen and the butler joked with me about the "cheap wine" and then I was sitting on a couch talking to a couple. They didn't seem to notice that I was naked. Nobody else did either. It all seemed perfectly normal.

Dreamer: A 28-year-old woman with hysterical features.

Association: She didn't like parties because she didn't like the sexual approaches she invariably got from men at parties. Her father once said she looked cheap.

Interpretation: The dreamer's nakedness and its acceptance as normal represent her wish to be accepted by people for who she is (a beautiful, sensual woman), without her attractiveness being overemphasized. The couple in the dream stand for her parents, who in real life pressured her about her appearance and criticized her if her clothes were too revealing. The joke about cheap wine refers to her father's remark, during her adolescence, that she looked cheap.

Dream (painting): An elderly doctor dreams that a winged demon instills licentious wishes into his mind. A naked woman appears at his side and beckons to him. Meanwhile, a little Cupid plays on stilts at his feet.

Dreamer: Albrecht Dürer, sixteenth century German painter, in his painting *Dream of the Doctor.*

Interpretation: The naked woman probably represents the dreamer's forbidden wish for sexual intercourse. The demon symbolizes his guilt feelings about such a wish. The cupid is likely his id (his inner child) wanting to romp.

Dream: The dreamer was walking through the college grounds when suddenly he sensed all eyes were upon him. Looking down, he discovered that he was naked.

Dreamer: A male college professor. Reported by Faraday (1974).

Association: This recurring dream usually appears right after he has published a paper. He notes that he cleverly uses other people's ideas in his papers.

Interpretation: The dream expresses his fear that he will be exposed (naked) as a fraud.

Dream: My wife and her sister were sitting in the kitchen. I entered and heard her sister ask my wife, "When Cal sleeps, does he wear pajamas or does he sleep naked?" My wife informed her that I sleep naked and they both shuddered. Then Jim, the sister's husband, walked in naked.

Dreamer: A 32-year-old male with a castration complex and perverse sexual impulses.

Association: He expressed frustration that his wife did not want to touch his penis during sexual intercourse.

Interpretation: Nakedness in the dream denotes masculinity. The dreamer felt that his masculinity had been offensive to his mother, as it now is to his wife. The dream represents his wish to have his masculinity accepted. Jim's nakedness lends support to this acceptance.

Dream: The dreamer was very incompletely dressed and was going upstairs. He was going up three steps at a time and was delighted at his agility. Suddenly he saw a maid-servant coming down the stairs. He felt ashamed and tried to hurry, and then became inhibited. He was glued to the steps and unable to move.

Dreamer: Sigmund Freud, founder of psychoanalysis. Reported in Grinstein (1980).

Associations: The night of the dream he had climbed the same stairs after taking off his collar, tie, and cuffs, and thought, "What if I meet a neighbor?" He also remembered how he sometimes would spit on the staircase because there was no spittoon, and a female concierge would often reprimand him for doing so. *Spucken* (spitting) in German is similar to *Spuken* (haunting). Then he recalled a nurse who had cared for him until the age of 2½. She was his first instructress in matters of sex, and used to insist on his cleanliness, although she bathed him in her own bathwater first. She also chided him for being "clumsy."

Interpretation: Freud interpreted this dream as exhibitionistic. His associations to the concierge who caught him spitting and the nurse who told him he was clumsy and insisted on his cleanliness point to a wish that he might be caught masturbating (spitting = masturbation). The paralysis represents a conflict between his libidinal desires and his superego injunctions against them. The pun (*Spucken, Spuken*) linking spitting and haunting suggest that Freud might have felt haunted by the memory of his father, who might punish him for his forbidden infantile oedipal wishes. The neighbor might also symbolize his father.

Dream (daydream): The dreamer saw herself in church. As the organ thundered out hymns, she would throw off her clothes and stand naked for God and everyone else to see. She would feel no shame or sense of sin.

Dreamer: Marilyn Monroe, American movie actress, who committed suicide at age 39 and was famous for her "dumb blonde" roles, as reported in Zolotow (1960). She had these recurring fantasies when she was 6.

Associations: She recalled that when she was 4 she and her brother, Lester, took off all their clothes in the backyard and played doctor. Taking off her "orphan's clothes" made her feel more normal, but then the neighbors saw them and complained. Their adoptive fundamentalist mother, Ida, blamed Marilyn for the incident, saying she was the bad one who had seduced her two-month younger foster brother. Marilyn also recalled that when she was 13 months old her grandmother tried to suffocate her in her crib. The grandmother was later admitted to a mental hospital. Marilyn never knew her father.

Interpretation: The daydream above may offer clues not only to Marilyn's drives but also to her character formation. The desire to go naked in the church and be absolved of sin by God shows an exhibitionistic trend that would dominate her adulthood and lead to her specializing in sexy, exhibitionistic movie roles. These roles might be seen as a compulsion to repeat the earlier exhibitionism (in her backyard) for which she was punished and made to feel bad. Going naked before God was also perhaps her way of shedding her orphan identity and of searching for a father (God), who would protect her from suffocating women.

Names

Dream: The telephone rang and I said hello. The person asked for someone named Mary.

Dreamer: Elizabeth, a 33-year-old obsessive-compulsive woman defending against a schizoid core, as reported by Seinfeld (1993).

Associations: This is a recurring dream. Each time the phone caller asks for a different person. Sometimes it is Mary, sometimes Bill, Alice, or John. The dream reminded her that she was called upon to take care of various things—a new job, her boyfriend going away for a few weeks, and so on. She wished it were someone else called upon to do these things. She always appeared able and willing, but underneath felt overwhelmed and wanted to be left alone.

Interpretation: The dreamer interpreted that having the caller ask for another person was a way of protecting herself from intrusion; if the call was for somebody else, she did not have to respond. Seinfeld, who comes from the object relations school of psychoanalysis, interprets that the dreamer's false self—that part of her willing to face whatever demands arise—may well have developed in reaction to intrusions. The ring of the phone might also symbolize the demands of early childhood, when she first developed the false self that performed as expected while screening the true self that wished to be left alone.

Navel

Dream: I went to the mirror and saw that my navel was gone. For some reason that made me feel free.

Dreamer: A 43-year-old passive male.

Association: On the day before, he had spoken to his mother and she had reminded him, as she often did, of what a difficult time she had had in giving birth to him.

Interpretation: The navel symbolizes the dreamer's connection to his mother (the umbilical cord). Its disappearance perhaps represents his wish to separate from her emotionally and, at the same time, to have never been connected to her (born from her) so that she could no longer complain about his birth.

Niceness

Dream: I was with my friend and her brother. Her brother seemed disappointed in me. He knew I was not a nice person—that I was capricious, opinionated, and mean.

Dreamer: A young woman with a hysterical personality.

Association: She had recently been fired from her job because of a conflict with her male boss, whom she had accused of sexism. She felt this boss thought she was capricious.

Interpretation: This is a dream of self-revelation. In it, she displaces judgments about herself—judgments which her former boss made (and which her father once made), and which she has warded off during her waking hours—onto her friend's brother. Since it is her friend's brother who is saying them, she takes the judgment more seriously.

Dream: A man tried to kiss me and I slapped him. I told him I was a nice girl.

Dreamer: A young woman with erotophobia.

Association: When she had walked on the street the day before she saw many men leering at her and resented it.

Interpretation: The dream reveals her fear of sexuality and its characterological basis. Her obsessive-compulsive behavior defends against a fear of her inner badness (sexuality and aggression).

Night Terror

Dream (night terror): The dreamer began screaming in terror in the middle of the night. She imagined that Larry was somewhere in the room. She thrashed on the bed, screaming, "Clyde, Clyde! Larry's going to kill you!" She then sat bolt upright and opened her eyes. "Larry's gonna kill you!" Her psychiatrist ran in, but she wasn't talking to him. She looked right past him into space. He decided, on a hunch, to talk to her. "Miss T.," he said, "It's Dr. F. Can you hear me? . . . You're having a dream. Tell me about it." "They're all here. Larry's gonna kill Clyde. He told me not to tell. Now he's gonna kill my brother, and you, and everyone." "Where is Larry?" "Right here in the room. Can't you see him?"

Dreamer: Miss T., a woman suffering from night terrors. Paraphrased from Friedmann (1980).

Associations: She had been raped when she was 11 by "Larry," the father of a child for whom she was babysitting. He then threatened to kill her younger brother (Clyde) if she ever told about the rape. For twenty years the trauma was locked up inside her. From then on she had night terrors, in which she would thrash around on her bed, scream out loud, and wake up sweating.

Interpretation: The night terrors were repetitions of the original trauma. Their aim was to master a situation in which her ego had been flooded and she had not been able to respond as she would have liked. Friedmann points out additional earlier factors (she was raised by her father to be a man, despising her own femininity) that contributed to the intensity of her feelings about the rape. Freud once noted, "Every wishful impulse which creates a dream today will reappear in other dreams as long as it has not been understood and withdrawn from the domination of the unconscious" (1911, p. 94). The wish in this night terror is to be rescued.

Noose

Dream: I was at work and I opened the drawer of my desk and found a noose in it. I asked Jane if she knew how it had gotten there and she said she didn't. I threw it into the garbage and when I looked again it turned into a snake and slithered away.

Dreamer: A 49-year-old man with phallic-narcissistic features.

Association: Jane, his co-worker, had been angrily refusing his sexual advances. He had a reputation of being a womanizer.

Interpretation: This is a warning dream. The noose symbolizes the dilemma in which the dreamer may find himself if he does not mend his philandering ways. The rope/snake is a phallic symbol.

Nose

Dream: I dreamed that I was sitting in a restaurant with Phil when my nose began to bleed. He was trying to be nice about it, but I was very irritated with him.

Dreamer: A young woman with hysterical features.

Association: The night she had the dream she had begun to menstruate.

Interpretation: The bleeding nose symbolizes menstruation and her irritation about having to be a woman and not having a male appendage instead (the nose symbolizing a penis).

Nothing

Dream: I walked around all day and thought of nothing.

Dreamer: A young woman, as reported by Lewin (1948).

Association: She said she had never faced reality since the day she was born.

Interpretation: Nothing, according to Lewin, symbolizes the female genital. The reality that the patient never faced is the reality of her disappointment at not possessing a penis; it seems to her she had nothing.

Dream: I went into the classroom and sat down to take the exam, but I could think of nothing. My brain was completely empty.

Dreamer: A 30-year-old businessman.

Association: He had been under pressure by his boss to finish a project.

Interpretation: Nothing symbolizes the dreamer's sense of inadequacy to live up to his boss's expectations. He has the same feelings about his parents, who always had unreal expectations for him and were consequently always disappointed by him.

Nuts

Dream: I saw a drop running out of a nut.

Dreamer: A schizophrenic woman, described by Schilder (1942).

Association: The patient supposed that the nut was the uterus.

Interpretation: The dream apparently was one of rebirth.

Dream: I was with my boss and some co-workers. We were at a restaurant somewhere near the company headquarters. I wanted something from him, but I didn't know what it was. I noticed that in another part of the room people were playing poker and I could see huge piles of chips. I looked back up at my boss and his head had changed into a large nut. I knew it was him because I could still see his blue eyes.

Dreamer: A 37-year-old man.

Associations: He had been trying to work up the courage to ask his boss for a raise. One of his co-workers had remarked about the boss: "He's a tough nut to crack."

Interpretation: The nut symbolizes the boss's rigidity. The poker game with huge stacks of chips represents the risk the dreamer must take in order to get a raise (stack of chips) that he so badly wants.

Oasis

Dream: I was in a desert with three other men. We were walking for many days. One by one the other three men died. Then I saw this valley and walked through it and there was this beautiful oasis, with a large green meadow and a little pond down on the other side.

Dreamer: A 40-year-old man with depressive symptoms.

Association: He had not had sex with a woman in two years. In previous dreams he had killed off his brothers and father.

Interpretation: The oasis, which lies in a valley, symbolizes the female genitals of the universal female/mother; the meadow denotes the pubic hair and the pond the vagina. The three other men in the dream who die are the dreamer's father and two brothers, with whom he had a great deal of rivalry as he was growing up. The unconscious remnants of that rivalry still interfere with his sexual performance.

Obstacles

Dream 1: I took a cab to LaGuardia Airport. On the way we ran into a traffic jam. The driver, a fat woman, and I began arguing over which was the best route to take.

Dream 2: My sister Dolly and I took the subway to the bus station, but when we got there we couldn't find it. Instead there was a thing called "Disney Space Mountain" that resembled a lot of indoor roller coasters. It seemed we would have to go through this obstacle course to get to the airport.

Dream 3: I took the bus to the airport, but the bus kept circling around and coming back to where I started.

Dreamer: A 40-year-old woman with strong narcissistic, oral-dependent features in her personality.

Associations: She had recurring dreams about wanting to go somewhere and running into obstacles. She recalled her mother's disapproval of all the boys she had wanted to date.

Interpretation: These recurring dreams are an example of Freud's *compulsion to repeat* in dream form. The dreams of going somewhere represent her wish to separate from her mother, on whom she is still orally dependent. The obstacles are probably symbols of her mother's intrusiveness. In the first dream, the woman cab driver is her mother; in the second the "Disney Space Mountain" may be a breast symbol (denoting her oral dependency); in the third, the bus may be seen as her mother's womb in which she is trapped or as her self, beset with conflicting internal objects that have her going in a vicious circle.

Older Man

Dream 1: I'm in a bar with some buddies. I see Mary and go up to speak to her about my career plans. She walks away and sits down with an older man. I wait for her to come back. They talk for a long time and I'm getting angry. I leave and come back and the older man is standing alone. I want to talk with him but don't have the nerve.

Dream 2: I'm in bed with a woman. I'm naked but she has her clothes on. I try to take them off but she stops me. I go to the bathroom and when I return an older man is in bed with her and they're both naked. I say "What's up?" They don't seem to notice me.

Dreamer: A 32-year-old passive male.

Associations: He had been in bed with a new woman that weekend and had experienced partial impotency. He remembered wishing he had been able to discuss such things with his father.

Interpretation: The older man symbolizes the dreamer's father. In real life his father has always been competitive with him, never a pal as he had wanted. In these dreams, his father takes away the woman (his mother, sisters). This scenario repeats what happened in his childhood and denotes a repeating pattern in his present life, linked to his past rivalry with his father. This recurring dream is his attempt to master this past situation and discharge feelings about it.

Oranges

Dream: I saw two oranges in the sand. I picked one up and bit into it. It tasted sour.

Dreamer: A young man with an oral fixation.

Association: His mother always nagged him about drinking plenty of orange juice when he was sick. He recalled that she had confided recently that he had been an unwanted child.

Interpretation: The two oranges signify breasts—specifically, his mother's breasts. The image harks to a traumatic time in his infancy when his mother's milk turned bad and he felt rejected.

Paddle

Dream: Bill and I were in a canoe on a beautiful river. There were mountains all around and we could see trout jumping everywhere. Suddenly there were rapids and the boat shot down them. We tried to keep the boat from turning over, but Bill lost his paddle. The boat went sideways and rolled over and we were swept away by the current. I woke up trembling.

Dreamer: A 27-year-old woman with hysterical features.

Association: She had been arguing with her husband about money and had fears about their economic future. She found herself looking at other men.

Interpretation: The metaphor of being "up a creek without a paddle" imparts the economic situation of the dreamer's marriage as she sees it. She does not feel that she can depend on her husband, nor does she think he is manly enough (paddle = phallus) to satisfy her (keep the boat in the water).

Pain

Dream: The dreamer was trying to paste a newspaper clipping into an album. But "he wouldn't go to the place," which caused him much pain.

Dreamer: Hanns Sachs, Viennese psychoanalyst. Reported by Freud (1900).

Associations: He had been pasting newspaper clippings the day before, and went to bed with a bad cold. He went to sleep thinking that he did not want to get out of bed during the night. He awoke with a pain in his bowels.

Interpretation: Sachs noted that the dream, in its capacity of guardian of sleep, had given him the illusion of a fulfillment of his wish to stay in bed by means of a symbolic representation. Instead of the pronoun "it" (for the news clipping) he substituted "*he* wouldn't go to the place."

Dream: Tom and I went away for the weekend with Herb and Ellen. Ellen and I were resting in bed and she touched my vagina. At first it felt good, then I had a terrible pain. I awoke and had to urinate.

Dreamer: A 32-year-old woman with homosexual impulses.

Association: The day before the dream she had a momentary thought that Ellen was attractive.

Interpretation: The dream expresses her conflict about her homosexual impulses. At first she feels pleasure (id gratification), then pain (superego guilt).

Paradise

Dream: I was in some kind of paradise. It was a terribly peaceful, beautiful place, with strange tall flowers and huge trees with exotic and colorful fruits, and birds so big they could carry me inside their beaks, and velvety grass on which I could roll and somersault. There were coconuts that had chocolate milk in them and I drank them and was laughing. I never wanted to leave.

Dreamer: A 32-year-old woman with an eating disorder.

Association: She had loved chocolate milk as a child.

Interpretation: The paradise refers to the dreamer's wish to return to the responsibility-free simplicity of early childhood, where her oral-narcissistic impulses were immediately gratified without attending guilt.

Dream: I woke up and saw a new trap door under my bed that I hadn't seen before. It led through a tunnel and then out into a meadow. The meadow was like a paradise, with beautiful, naked young women romping playfully like deer. Three of them came toward me and I made love with them.

Dreamer: A 25-year-old passive male.

Association: He regretted feeling inhibited sexually.

Interpretation: The paradise under his bed denotes the hope that he can unleash his sexuality and find happiness. The tunnel may symbolize his need to separate from his mother first.

Party

Dream: I was at a dance party in a big hall. There were a lot of people there but I didn't know them. The scene changed. I was shopping with the mother of a girl. The mother was in a purple velvet dress, plain but dressy, and I was in a similar dress in blue. The scene changed again and I was rushing to take an examination.

Dreamer: Miss B., a 25-year-old manic-depressive, as reported by Pao (1980).

Associations: She remembered a dance party at the hospital. The girl at the dance reminded her of a neighborhood girl in the house where she had been living when her mother died. That was when her father had married her stepmother and she had had an affair with her uncle. She cried, "If my mother had lived, I could be married like the girl in the dream and probably would not have become psychotic."

Interpretation: The dream expresses the wish that her mother was still alive and she could go shopping with her, learn to affirm her femininity, and not have affairs with uncles or be psychotic. The rush to take an examination relates to her fear of therapy, linked to her fear of involvement with another man. The party in the big hall where she didn't know anybody pertains to the time her new stepmother moved in and the wedding was held.

Path

Dream 1: A path in the woods. I didn't follow the path, but went across the bridge to the city instead. It was a leafy path, which got dark.

Dream 2: I passed the spot where the greenhouse was supposed to be. I climbed a rock. . . . I held out my arms and felt the damp leaves and ran over the path.

Dream 3: I was riding on a horse bareback. I was on a sandy path and I walked up to the rear of the horse. It wanted to bite me.

Dream 4: I was riding a bicycle along the path to our old house. There was a long snake in the driveway.

Dream 5: I was with my sister, riding on an old merry-go-round. . . . We were peering over the bench; we had our arms around each other.

Dream 6: You were making sexual advances toward me and I was dismayed and pleased at the same time. . . . It was more like physical closeness, like hugging.

Dream 7: I am walking very snugly with my husband. "I really do love you," he says. "I love you, too," I say back. It was a cross between our local market today and the house where I grew up, that same leafy area....A darker section of the path made me feel hesitant.

Dreamer: Anne B., a 40-year-old married woman with multiple personalities, as reported by Marmer (1980).

Associations: The patient had three personalities: Jane, Child, and Witchy. Dreams 1 and 2 were Child's. Dream 3 was Jane's dream about which she related to intercourse (riding a horse). Dream 4 was a Child dream about an enema (snake). Dream 5 was Child and Jane as two children. Dream 6 was a Jane dream. Dream 7 was Witchy's, and alluded to the period when her father died.

Interpretation: The path in these dreams generally denotes a regression back to a period of childhood, often to the childhood home and the leafy surroundings. In fact, all of the dreams led back to associations of the primal scene trauma, when the patient was about a year and a half old (riding a horse, snakes, enemas, sexual advances, a dark section of the path). It was around Christmastime and she awoke and walked into her parents' room to find them engaged in intercourse. Her father jumped from the bed wearing a nightshirt, his penis erect and exposed, and grabbed her by the right arm and put her roughly back to bed, shouting at her loudly. She turned to her stuffed dog, masturbated, chewed on the dog's ear, and gagged herself until she vomited. Her parents were so annoyed by this additional disturbance that they threw away the dog. She had been dreaming about this incident in symbolic language ever since.

Pearl

Dream: I caught a large fish. When I pulled the hook out of its mouth, I found a small oyster. I opened up the oyster and there was a beautiful pearl. I felt very happy.

Dreamer: A young, pregnant woman.

Association: She had visited her doctor the day before, and he had said, "You're going to have a very healthy child."

Interpretation: The pearl signifies the dreamer's wish to give birth not only to a healthy child, but to a valuable and cherished "jewel."

Pedophilia

Dream: I was in a playground like the playground near the home where I grew up. Some boys were playing nearby. As I watched them I suddenly developed X-ray vision; I could see their little penises through their pants. Then I found if I looked really intensely at one of their penises, I could make it get hard.

Dreamer: A 38-year-old pedophile.

Association: He recalled that when he was a boy, an uncle had touched him and masturbated him on several occasions.

Interpretation: This is a fairly straightforward dream of wish-fulfillment. The dreamer regresses back to the stage in which he himself was molested. The familiar playground suggests a desire to regain the childhood and playfulness that he lost. The boys in the playground are symbolic of himself, and making them erect through eye contact (not physical contact) is a way of restoring his lost masculinity and undoing what his uncle had done.

Dream: My mother is washing under my foreskin.

Dreamer: A 37-year-old man suffering from impotence.

Association: His mother was preoccupied with washing under the foreskin of his penis when he was a child. His penis would become erect and she would say, "You naughty boy."

Interpretation: The dreamer had been aroused by his mother's washing of his penis and had this recurring dream about it. The incestuous washing ritual interfered with his sexual functioning as an adult.

Peeping

Dream: Nancy and I were in her house. We went to bed and there were people peeping down at us from the skylight. Nancy complained that I was scratching her.

Dreamer: A 38-year-old schizoid man with paranoid features.

Association: He reported brooding about his ex-wife, Nancy, when he had gone home to visit his parents for a weekend.

Interpretation: The people on the roof peeping at the dreamer were the dreamer's parents, who had often interfered in his marriage. The skylight probably symbolized his vulnerability. In the dream Nancy complains that the dreamer is scratching her while making love, yet he is not aware of doing so. This perhaps indicates his dissociation from his own aggression.

Pen

Dream: I was with a Chinese girl. I think I'd been seeing her for a while, and she was giving me a blow job. Meanwhile my friend from work starting fucking her from behind. He had a detachable red penis that was long and narrow like a fountain pen. The penis would come off and he would hold it nonchalantly as he fucked her.

Dreamer: A 34-year-old male with narcissistic and latent homosexual features.

Association: A week before, this friend had lent him a pen and was nonchalant about wanting it back. He was a young man in his early 20s, and the dreamer envied his youth.

Interpretation: The pen is a phallic symbol, and the fact that the young friend is nonchalant about his penis coming off and on denotes a security about his masculinity that the dreamer envies. The wish is that he could somehow bond with the young man and absorb some of his youthful potency.

Dream: I was writing a letter to a famous actress, with whom I was in love, but my pen kept running out of ink.

Dreamer: A 32-year-old man.

Association: He had always admired this actress, but did not think she'd like him.

Interpretation: The pen running out of ink stands for his lack of confidence (impotence) with regard to desirable women.

Penis

Dream: I dreamed I was sucking my own penis.

Dreamer: A 34-year-old man with latent homosexual and transvestic tendencies.

Association: When he awoke he had homosexual fantasies about a male friend.

Interpretation: The act of sucking his own penis is like the archetypal symbol of the snake devouring itself: it represents both death and rebirth. At the same time it has a narcissistic meaning of self-absorption and union with another male who is similar to himself—also has a penis.

Dream: My girlfriend called me and said I should come right over, she had something amazing to show me. We went into her bedroom and closed the door. Then she pulled up her skirt, and there was a small penis sticking out of her vagina. "Look what I found. It was inside me all the time."

Dreamer: A 42-year-old woman with an hysterical personality.

Association: She thought of her recent reluctance to have sex with her husband, and her revulsion toward his penis.

Interpretation: This is a simple wish-fulfillment dream. The dreamer wishes to have a penis, and displaces that wish onto her friend. The dream of having a penis inside the vagina harks back to childhood fantasies that psychoanalyst Melanie Klein (1932) discovered were common among little girls.

Dream: My husband and I are at another one of our dinner parties. The bread-basket is passed around to the women only. When it gets to me, I see not bread inside it but my husband's penis.

Dreamer: A young woman, as reported by Delaney (1994).

Association: The woman had long suspected her husband of having an affair.

Interpretation: The penis in the breadbasket is a telltale clue that her husband's penis is not her own possession, but is being served to all the other women at the table. (After the dream, the dreamer's investigations proved that her husband had indeed had affairs with nearly all the women at the table.) The dream may also be an indication of her anger and desire to castrate her husband.

Dream: I found a lump on my inner thigh and discovered I had a penis hidden there.

Dreamer: A 29-year-old borderline woman with multiple personalities.

Association: The "male" personality, Tom, had this dream.

Interpretation: Tom, one of seven personalities, is the one who carries the feelings of penis envy and wishes that he had a penis like "his" father. In the dream his wish is granted.

Perfume

Dream: I was in a car with Father, driving to Philadelphia for a conference. We were going to stay in the same room, but when we got there things changed. I found out I had to stay in a room with another woman. Dad stayed someplace else and I never saw him again. I went to the room where the other woman was. She said I could have any room I wanted. I went into the bathroom and tried on the complimentary perfumes. Then I heard a man knocking and asking for the other woman. It seems he wanted to rape her. I yelled for security guards and they took the man away. Then I went back to play with the perfumes.

Dreamer: A 38-year-old borderline woman.

Association: She had visited her father that weekend. She used to play with her mother's perfume bottles.

Interpretation: The dream represents a symbolic re-creation of traumatic events in her childhood. She was abandoned by her mother at 4, and her father remarried a younger woman. In the dream, going to the hotel with her father and then finding she had to leave her father's room and sleep with the other woman probably denotes having to give up the oedipal intimacy with her father upon her stepmother's arrival. The man who wanted to rape the woman perhaps symbolizes her father and demonstrates an anger at her father, projected onto him in the dream. This may also allude to the violent way small children think of sexual intercourse. The fact that she was "playing" with perfume is another clue to the childhood sources of the dream, and shows her longing for her mother. Perfume bottles may also represent her father's penis, which her mother possesses.

Pigs

Dream (fairy tale): There were three pigs. The first built a house of straw, the second a house of wood, and the third a house of brick. Soon a wolf came by and stopped at the house of straw. "Let me in," he said, "Or I'll blow your house down." The first pig refused and the wolf did as he warned and ate the pig. He went to the house of wood and did the same thing. When he got to the house of brick, he could not blow it down, and the third pig was saved.

Interpretation: The three pigs symbolize vulnerable children, who, like pigs, are easy to catch and eat. The wolf in this case symbolizes all the evil of humankind. The houses stand for not only external boundaries, but strong selves.

Dream: I got a very young pig to eat. I cut its head off and pushed it away, lest I see that it was pork meat I was going to eat. . . . It tasted very good. Suddenly I felt disgusted and awoke.

Dreamer: A middle-aged Orthodox Jew. Reported by Gutheil (1951).

Association: He recalled that in a jealous tirade he had forced his youngest daughter to break up with her boyfriend.

Interpretation: The very young pig represents two forbidden objects—pork, which is forbidden to observant Jews, and the daughter, for whom the man had incestuous feelings. The dream allows this prohibited pleasure, but not without feelings of disgust (guilt).

Playground

Dream: I went outside in my robe. A woman was with two children. They ran up to me, a boy and a girl. The girl approached me and said, "You know, it would be good of you to get rid of that garage and make a playground."

Dreamer: A 29-year-old woman suffering from anxiety.

Association: She recognized the woman as a friend of her mother's.

Interpretation: The dreamer had always felt she had been deprived of a normal childhood. Her parents were both quite strict and physically abusive. The children perhaps symbolize the child inside of her, and the playground stands for the children she never had. The garage may contain all the repressed memories of that dark childhood.

Dream: Jim and I were driving along when suddenly we saw this amusement park called "Playland." He stopped the car and we went inside. He kissed me as we went through the gate.

Dreamer: A 27-year-old woman.

Association: She had just met a new man toward whom she had romantic hopes.

Interpretation: The amusement park represents sexual intercourse, which psychodynamically is *a regression at the service of the ego.* "Playland" indicates this regression.

Plumber

Dream 1: I was in the bath, and then the plumber came and let the water out. Then he took a big drill and stuck it into my stomach.

Dream 2: The plumber came, and first he took away my behind with a pair of pincers, and then gave me another, and then the same with my weewee-maker.

Dreamer: Little Hans, a 5-year-old boy. Reported by Freud (1909a).

Associations: Little Hans had a phobia about horses; he was afraid to go out on the street for fear one would bite him. He also was obsessed with his penis and with his mother's vagina, and was always wanting to sleep with his mother at night.

Interpretation: It was the case of Little Hans that helped Freud confirm his theory about the Oedipus complex. Little Hans's dreams reflect this complex. He wants to sleep (bathe) with his mother, but his father (the plumber) interferes. In one dream the plumber bores a hole in his stomach with a drill (i.e., rapes him with his big penis); in another he takes away the boy's behind and penis and gives him another one. Upon being questioned about the dream by the father, Little Hans reveals that the plumber has given him a bigger behind and penis, like his father's.

Police

Dream: A prostitute accosted me and I ran to the police to report it, but they arrested me instead.

Dreamer: A 43-year-old fetishistic man who frequented prostitutes.

Association: He complained that he had been spending too much money on prostitutes and wanted to stop.

Interpretation: The police symbolize the dreamer's superego – his wish that he will have the resolve to stop his addiction.

Dream: I was at my mother's house, sleeping. My friend Seth came over, then somebody else came over who looked like my brother, only he had a Russian accent. He had killed a police officer and needed a place to hide out. Then he and Seth eloped and left me there to take the blame from the police.

Dreamer: A 33-year-old paranoid man.

Association: His brother's name was also Seth. "Eloped" was a word used by doctors at the hospital where he worked to describe patients who ran away from the hospital.

Interpretation: The police officer who was killed probably represents the patient's mother, toward whom he is enraged. His older brother left home after high school and went to live in Russia, leaving him to cope with his murderous rage and guilt. In the dream he projects this rage onto his brother, then feels unfairly blamed for the murder. The word "eloped" signifies the brother's escape from a crazy house (mental ward), and perhaps also denotes the dreamer's projection onto the brother of his latent homosexual urges.

Pool

Dream: Bill and I were playing pool. The felt on the pool table was as thick as grass. I couldn't get the ball in the hole because of the thick felt.

Dreamer: A middle-aged, depressed male.

Association: He thought of his father and how his father had refused to play pool with him as a child.

Interpretation: His inability to get the ball in the hole because of the thick grass symbolizes his fear of competition with other males, which relates to his father's discouragement of competition. At the same time, the dream may be seen as symbolizing a conflict about sexual prowess—the stick representing a phallus and the hole a vagina.

Dream: I was in the basement with a fat woman. She took one of my father's pool sticks and threw it at me. It stuck in my back.

Dreamer: A young male with a fetish for high heels.

Association: He recalled that his girlfriend had bought a new pair of high-heeled shoes that weekend.

Interpretation: Fetishes such as those involving high-heeled shoes are often linked with castration fear and the associated primitive fantasy that mothers (and women) have penises. This dream represents such as wish; the woman with a pool stick symbolizes the phallic woman who penetrates the dreamer with her phallus.

Pregnancy

Dream: I'm pregnant. I want to have the baby, even though I'm single. Mother goes with me to a doctor's office. We have to fill out forms to receive benefits. Mother insists on filling out the forms, and I notice she doesn't fill them out completely. When we leave I tell her, "You didn't fill the forms out correctly. Now I won't receive any benefits." She denies it and we have an argument.

Dreamer: A 27-year-old borderline woman with a mother complex.

Association: She recalled other dreams about objects in her belly and remembered that her mother had had a history of miscarriages. She spoke of how her mother never liked any of her boyfriends.

Interpretation: The pregnancy symbolizes both a passage to womanhood and to feminine power. The dreamer's memory of the mother's history of miscarriages and dislike of all her daughter's boyfriends points to a recurring theme of the dreamer's waking life. Her mother had always sought to keep the daughter dependent on her and prevent her from separating. She was proud of her own beauty and constantly denigrated her daughter's looks and discouraged any relationship with a man, including her own father. (It may be that the mother, through projective identification, anticipated that her daughter would have the same problems with childbirth that she did.) The dream is a cautionary tale about the mother's manipulativeness and intrusiveness.

Dream: My friend Barbara was pregnant and she had a very difficult labor and was in a great deal of pain. I felt sorry for her and brought a dozen roses when I visited her.

Dreamer: A 25-year-old woman.

Association: She was due to give birth at any moment.

Interpretation: This dream is a striking example of dream displacement. The dreamer displaces her own imminent delivery onto her friend, so that her friend must endure the difficult labor that she herself anticipates.

Dream: My sister came to me and said, "Feel my belly." I felt it and realized she was pregnant.

Dreamer: A 32-year-old man.

Association: When he was 6 years old his mother has been pregnant with his sister, and she had pulled down her dress to allow him to feel her belly.

Interpretation: The dream imparts the dreamer's oedipal attachment to his mother via this displacement of the memory onto his sister.

Dream: I was pregnant and gave birth to a demon-child.

Dreamer: A 22-year-old woman with paranoid features.

Association: She did not think she should have children.

Interpretation: The child is an externalization of her inner demon (repressed rage), and an outgrowth of paranoid grandiosity.

President

Dream: I was in a cave. It was snowy and icy outside. There was somebody else there with me and he was sleeping on a sleeping bag and I was on a mat. We were both teenagers, but I saw that the other person had a teenaged body but [President] Bill Clinton's face. I was supposed to guard the President. I walked to the edge of the cave and saw that it led to the ocean. I dived into the water in order to find out something. The water was freezing, below zero. I started to become afraid of what would happen and went back to the cave. Other people were there and wondered why I'd left my post. President Clinton made excuses for me.

Dreamer: A 33-year-old man with an eating disorder.

Association: His father looked like Bill Clinton. The body of the other teenager looked like that of his brother.

Interpretation: The dream is about the rite of passage to manhood. President Clinton with a teenaged body is a condensation of the dreamer's father and older brother, who in real life were pals and excluded the dreamer from their "club." In the dream he is not only included, he is their protector. The warm cave may symbolize the womb; the cold outside and ocean might stand for adulthood, responsibility, manhood. In real life he is an oral-dependent person whose grandmother had cultivated a fear of adulthood in him. President Clinton's (his father's) making excuses for him represents the fulfillment of a wish that he had gotten more support from his father.

Priest

Dream: There is some kind of archaeological excavation. I'm digging in a corner when I discover some old bones. I'm about to pick them up when a priest warns me not to touch them. I pick one up anyway, and as I do my nose starts to bleed.

Dreamer: A 47-year-old obsessive-compulsive man.

Association: His father was an archaeologist.

Interpretation: The dream is about competition with his father. The priest represents both his father and his own superego (an introjection of his father's moral injunctions). If he tries to compete with his father (become an archaeologist) or delve too deeply into his unconscious (the excavation), he will be punished by castration (the nosebleed).

Prince

Dream (fairy tale): The pretty girl was feeling bad that her mother and stepsisters could go to the Royal Ball and she couldn't. Then her fairy godmother appeared and created a beautiful gown for her to wear and a carriage to take her to the Royal Ball, but she warned her that at the stroke of midnight the gown would turn back into rags and the carriage would shrink back into a pumpkin. While at the ball, she danced with the prince and he fell in love with her. At midnight she had to rush off. While she was running down the stairs, one of her glass slippers fell off. The prince found the slipper and had his men search the kingdom to find the foot that fit the slipper. When his men came to her house, they found that her foot was the perfect size. She became the prince's wife and they lived happily ever after.

Interpretation: "Cinderella" is popular and universal because it is a common dream of many women. The fairy godmother represents the dreamer's wish to find a loving mother, and the prince not only symbolizes Cinderella's elevation to a status higher than her mother and sisters (fulfilling narcissistic needs) but also Cinderella's father returning and coming to her rescue. Her father had treated her like a princess, thus engendering in her the need to continue to be treated that way, while he and she provoked the hostility of her siblings. This is perhaps the prototypical rescue fantasy. It also dramatizes what can and does happen in some stepfamilies.

Princess

Dream: A news report blares out from the television set that Princess Anne has been eaten by a lion that has escaped from the zoo. I sit up and watch the news, and there are two different endings to the story. In the first, Princess Anne is saved by a taxi driver. In the second, the taxi driver stands idly by and allows her to be eaten. The workers pick up bits and pieces of her body and put them on a stretcher.

Dreamer: A 34-year-old schizophrenic man severely abused by his mother.

Associations: His mother had trained horses and was once visited by Princess Anne, who had been naughty to her and demanding about which horse she would ride. He recalled once getting his finger caught in a door, and his mother hysterically screaming about it.

Interpretation: Princess Anne symbolizes the dreamer's mother. The dual endings of the dream indicate his ambivalence toward her. The lion represents his rage; the two taxi drivers denote the idealizing and devaluing parts of himself. He idealizes his mother in the dream by associating her with a princess, which also reflects his own grandiose ego-ideal (the prince). The final ending, however, is the one that wins out, showing the depth of his rage at her. The memory of getting his finger caught in the door is a screen memory linked with earlier physical abuse by his mother.

Prison

Dream: I am in a prison. I am naked. The guards try to force us to have sexual intercourse with them. I watch them rape a girl in the cell next to mine, but for some reason they don't bother me. I hear somebody being killed down the hall. I try to remain cheerful.

Dreamer: A 24-year-old woman who was sexually abused as a child.

Association: She recalled that whenever she was abused she would think to herself, "This isn't really happening to me; it's happening to somebody else."

Interpretation: The dream represents a compulsion to repeat a past trauma, master it, and discharge some of the shock still connected with the memory. In the dream, as she fantasized in real life, she has the sexual abuse happen to somebody else, not her. The prison symbolizes her family environment, and the guards her father and brothers, who terrorized her.

Prune

Dream: I looked under my pillow and found a prune. For some reason I put it on the shelf, as if it were a trophy.

Dreamer: A middle-aged woman.

Association: She was going through menopause and felt relieved.

Interpretation: The prune denotes the drying up of her ovaries, which she views as a triumph (trophy).

Pun

Dream 1: The dreamer was at a restaurant where only one meal was offered – "Wild Boar"—at $12. She thought it was too expensive and decided not to order it.

Dream 2: A stubborn dog was "gnawing at the sole" of one of the dreamer's sandals.

Dream 3: The dreamer was dressed in fencing clothes and was fencing with a small, delicate tree.

Dream 4: Bob Hope, the comedian, came bouncing down a street on a pogo stick.

Dream 5: The dreamer took a huge mouthful of Chinese food. It burned her tongue and she had to spit it out.

Dreamers: Various students and acquaintances of Faraday (1974).

Association: The associations for each of these dreams showed that they revolved around verbal or visual puns.

Interpretations: (1) On the night of the dream, the dreamer had stayed up to review a book that cost $12 and was a "bore"; (2) Something was gnawing at the dreamer's "soul"; (3) The dreamer had had a fight with his girlfriend, Teresa—pronounced *Treesa*—the night before the dream; (4) The dream expressed the dreamer's feeling that "Hope springs eternal!"; (5) The dreamer had "bitten off more than she could chew" when she signed up for a recent course in Asian studies.

Punishment

Dream: I'm in a dungeon. My sister's friend Jane is whipping me. She wears black high-heeled shoes and nothing else. I get a huge erection and she whips me even harder. I ejaculate.

Dreamer: A 29-year-old masochist and fetishist.

Association: He spoke to his sister on the phone and had a brief erotic thought about her.

Interpretation: The punishment in this dream, as it is in most dreams, is a wish fulfillment. It serves to gratify an incestuous wish for his sister (symbolized by his sister's friend), while at the same time assuaging his guilt for having such wishes (by being punished).

Dream: There is a war and I'm captured behind enemy lines. Since I'm a high officer, they imprison me and torture me. I'm tied to a table and three men take turns interrogating me. When I refuse to talk, they punish me by pressing lighted cigarettes against my skin. Somehow, it doesn't hurt.

Dreamer: A 49-year-old obsessive-compulsive man.

Association: When he informed his father of a promotion at his job, his father did not seem pleased.

Interpretation: The punishment is the fulfillment of a wish by his superego. He feels guilty about the promotion, as it arouses castration fears related to having been his mother's favorite and thereby provoking the enmity of his father and brothers (the enemy torturers in the dream). The cigarette burning perhaps denotes anal penetration.

Pyromania

Dream: Someone has set fire to my parents' house. The fire trucks come and I rush up to help them. I take one of the fire hoses and arch the water high over the roof of the house where their bedroom is. I feel very afraid but very excited. Then all of a sudden one of the firemen turns to me and says, "Hey, you're in your underwear."

Dreamer: A man with pyromaniacal impulses.

Association: He had been having fantasies of burning up shops and buildings. His father had owned a shop most of his life but was now retired.

Interpretation: Freud linked fire with bed-wetting, noting that the urge to wet the bed was aroused by the urge to put out the fire – the sexual fire. In the case of this pyromaniac, there was a link between an experience in early childhood when he had witnessed his parents having sex and a later desire to start and put out fires. The "someone" who starts this fire is the dreamer, and he then helps put it out with a hose (penis) in which the water arches high (urinal exhibitionism) over the roof to the parents' bedroom (location of the primal scene). He is in his underwear and he is "very afraid but very excited," as he was back in his childhood when he witnessed the primal scene.

Queen

Dream: The dreamer had a recurrent dream that the British Queen Mother kept dropping in unannounced at all hours of the day. In one dream the Queen Mother arrived as usual and proceeded to teach her how to make chicken soup, despite protestations that they were both on a reducing diet. She woke up crying with anger and frustration.

Dreamer: Ann Faraday, British psychologist. Reported in Faraday (1974).

Association: She had this dream whenever her mother-in-law visited.

Interpretation: The Queen Mother symbolizes the mother-in-law who so often visited and tried to dominate the dreamer. Such recurrent dreams are attempts to discharge frustration and master a repeatedly frustrating situation.

Dream: I am in a dark room trying to make love to Mary. I notice a figure sitting in the corner. It is Queen Elizabeth. I lose my erection.

Dreamer: A 31-year-old man.

Association: He recalled that his mother continually scoffed at all the women he dated.

Interpretation: Queen Elizabeth represents his mother, whom he idealizes. His attachment to her gets in the way of his being able to enjoy sexual success (potency) with other women.

Queer

Dream: My father and I were watching some birds. We were standing on a lookout tower somewhere in the country. Then he saw something through his binoculars and said, "That's queer." I asked him what he meant, but he didn't answer.

Dreamer: A 22-year-old homosexual man.

Association: He had been wondering whether he should tell his father that he was homosexual. He was afraid of his father's reaction.

Interpretation: The dream expresses the wish that his father will somehow discover (the binoculars) that the dreamer is homosexual without his having to tell him. The term *queer,* with its negative connotation, denotes the dreamer's anticipation of the father's disapproval. The act of standing on the lookout tower (a phallic symbol) watching birds (women) may also denote a wish to bond with his father, and the fact that his father sees something queer perhaps designates the homosexual nature of the bond.

Quiche

Dream: I dreamed my mother served quiche.

Dreamer: A 27-year-old man with latent homosexual features.

Association: He thought of the title of the book, *Real Men Don't Eat Quiche.*

Interpretation: The dreamer is afraid that his mother has turned him into a homosexual.

Rabbit

Dream: I was in a basement somewhere and I saw something white in the corner. I walked over and discovered a bunch of white rabbits. It was a mother and six little ones. Then, as I was watching, a seventh little one popped out. I felt really happy and excited for her.

Dreamer: A 27-year-old woman.

Association: Her menstruation was overdue and she thought she might be pregnant. She planned to have a lab test to find out.

Interpretation: The pregnant rabbit in the basement symbolizes her hope that there is something growing in her own uterus. Rabbit also refers to the rabbit test, by which pregnancies used to be ascertained. The number seven perhaps denotes the wish that her future offspring will be fortunate.

Radio

Dream: I was listening to the radio, and I heard on the news that you'd been arrested for practicing without a license. I was being interviewed as one of the fake therapist's patients.

Dreamer: A 30-year-old-man.

Association: The dream was about his therapist, whom the dreamer's insurance company had recently turned down because he lacked the necessary credentials.

Interpretation: This dream is a fairly straightforward dramatization of the patient's fears about his therapist's legitimacy.

Dream: I was sitting in the living room when the radio went on by itself and I heard my neighbor's voice. He was talking to his wife about me, about how he was going to kill me. I had the sense that he knew I could hear him, and that he was deliberately transmitting it to my room through the radio.

Dreamer: A 42-year-old man with paranoid features.

Association: He had been terrified of this neighbor for some time.

Interpretation: The radio represents a transmitter of telepathic communication. The dreamer, in his paranoia, disowns his own aggression and projects it onto people in his environment, in this case the upstairs neighbor. He fears that this neighbor knows about his latent homosexuality and will kill him because of it. This replicates the quality of his relationship with his father.

Rape

Dream: It was like I was watching a movie. I was watching it and I was in it. I was on a street in New York, a dark, industrial, film noir kind of street. I was scared. "Get a grip on yourself!" I told myself. Then I saw a woman. She was also scared. I could see how agitated and upset she was. Seeing her made me even more afraid and worried about her. I stepped louder to show her I was there and she wasn't alone, but she didn't see me. She was walking hurriedly and I followed her. Suddenly we were in a children's playground. We passed a mother with a baby in a stroller. Then we went past the playground to a building on the other side. She went down some stairs into the building. I knew there was going to be trouble so I followed her. Then I heard her scream. I rushed through the building and out the back and saw that she was on a hill behind the building and was being raped. I saw a long birch log and picked it up, then tried to scream at the rapist but no words came out. "Get . . . out . . . of . . . there . . . !" I screamed. He turned to me and I yelled again, "Get . . . off . . . of . . . her . . . !" I could scarcely get the words out. My throat was paralyzed. But he heard me and he stood up and I thought, this is good. I can vanquish this oppressor. "Get lost . . . you . . . fucking jerk . . . !" He moved slowly away and I woke up feeling great. The dream was so intense.

Dreamer: A 37-year-old homosexual man with a castration complex.

Associations: The woman in the dream was himself, and the man was his brother. He had the dream the night after group therapy, when he talked about how his older brother would pin him down to the ground and call him a fag and make him say "I love you Tommy." His therapist used the word "rape" to label the scene.

Interpretation: This is a breakthrough dream—a dream that signals a breakthrough in therapy as well as in terms of the dreamer's repression and understanding of a significant childhood trauma. The intensity of the emotions in the dream underscores its significance and also points to the intensity of the traumatic event itself. The fact that the dreamer is both an observer (watching it like a movie) and a participant parallels how in real life he had defended himself then through splitting, and still does in his everyday life through an intellectual detachment. Another parallel is how he is protective of women both in his real life and in the dream. He has a strong identification with his feminine side (via a strong identification with his mother); therefore it is not he but a woman (his anima) who is being raped. The dark industrial street at the beginning symbolizes the threatening world of masculinity; the children's playground denotes a regression to his childhood. The birch log that he picks up is a phallic symbol. He has finally vanquished his older brother, something he could never do as a child.

Dream: I was in the kitchen with a large fat woman, and she was smiling at me in a teasing way. Suddenly I pulled out a knife and jumped on her. My cock was so hard that it pierced her panties and entered her vagina. I held the knife at her throat and fucked her so hard blood starting pouring out. When I came, my sperm was so hot it scorched the inside of her vagina so that she couldn't have any more babies. When I got up she was still smiling, so I cut her head off. Then I felt repulsed and ran out into the street. When I turned around, I saw her head rolling on the ground toward me, like some tumbleweed. I kept running but the head kept chasing me.

Dreamer: A 29-year-old sociopath who had committed several rapes.

Association: The kitchen in the dream was his mother's kitchen. The woman in the dream had a body (fat) like his mother, but her face was that of a pretty girl.

Interpretation: The rape victim is the dreamer's mother, who gave him up for adoption when he was 3, then came to reclaim him when he was 12. She lived with him for a year and was drunkenly seductive with him, then sent him off to a boarding school, where he was treated cruelly and raped by older boys. The rape in the dream is a reversal of the emotional and actual rapes that he had to endure throughout his childhood. The acts of rape and murder show not only incest and hate, but also the dreamer's need to bolster his insecurity about his manhood (the phallus-knife, his erection so hard it pierced her panties, etc.). His sperm scorches her so she can have no more babies—this demonstrates his rage about his mother having him and not taking care of him. The disgust following the act and the rolling head denote his guilt feelings.

Dream: I was watching a football game with Ted and our two friends, Louise and Bill. Suddenly I felt a hand running up my thigh. I look around and see a blond-haired man sitting behind me. Then I feel my skirt being lifted from behind and I feel his penis going between my legs from behind. I feel him lifting my ass up and inserting his penis. I pretend to keep watching the game so that Ted and the others won't see what's happening. The man is raping me right there in broad daylight. I wake up excited.

Dreamer: A 42-year-old woman.

Association: She had spoken of how boring her sex life was. She complained that her husband was too passive.

Interpretation: The blond-haired man in the dream represents her older brother, with whom she played "doctor" as a small child, and who also has blond hair. Football symbolizes male aggression. The dream is a simple wish-fulfillment, harking to the sexual excitement she felt about her brother and the fantasies she had about him.

Rapture

Dream 1: I dreamed I enjoyed indescribable beauties of music.

Dream 2: I dreamed that I was floating and flying with the rapture of an eagle up toward distant mountain peaks.

Dreamer: Friedrich Nietzsche, German philosopher. Reported in Kaufmann (1953).

Associations: One of the main themes of Nietzsche's writing is his concept of the *will to power* by which he meant the desire to master oneself and others. He posited that this will to power was not only the basic urge of humans, but also the fundamental drive of all living beings: "Whenever I found the living, there I found the will to power."

Interpretation: The two dreams above are both symbolic of aiming for superior achievements. In the first, the dreamer hears music that is indescribable in its beauty; in the second, he flies to the mountain peaks. The eagle represents power and potency. In primitive societies, eagles have been associated with the sun. To fly to the top of the mountain is to achieve the ultimate power, to be godlike, that is, a sun god. Both dreams coincide with the main theme of Nietzsche's philosophy—the will to power. And they substantiate observations by Nietzsche's peers that he was a grandiose individual who had been both pampered and belittled by a family household in which he was the only male among four women.

Rats

Dream: I was lying in bed reading and I saw something moving under the covers. I became terrified and clamped my legs together. Suddenly a rat jumped from the edge of the bed and ran out of the room.

Dreamer: A 32-year-old married woman who was frigid and suffered from migraine headaches.

Association: She recalled that her grandfather used to touch her genitals and she remembered the odor that always came from his body. She thought of the saying, "I smell a rat."

Interpretation: The rat symbolizes the incestuous touching by her grandfather. Her disgust about this has now taken the form of a generalized aversion to sexual intercourse with her husband and with all men. To have sex is to smell a rat.

Dream (hallucination): The dreamer saw animals like rats and pigs coming toward him.

Dreamer: Edgar Allan Poe, American poet and writer who suffered from depression and alcoholism.

Association: Poe had hallucinations about rats and pigs in between bouts of drinking.

Interpretation: Insects, rats, mice, and other little animals that are seen in the dreams and hallucinations of alcoholics represent aggression turned against themselves in the form of guilty self-reproaches.

Dream: I was running along the seashore with a small rat in my hand. I tossed the rat into the sea and it turned into a shaggy dog. I walked the dog in the park and showed it to my friends.

Dreamer: A 30-year-old schizoid man who had an emotionally incestuous relationship with his mother.

Association: He thought the rat was his heart.

Interpretation: The rat symbolizes his guilty heart, which is exposed and vulnerable (held in his hand). The sea perhaps represents purification, baptism, or it could symbolize his mother. The shaggy dog denotes a spiritual transformation. It is a dream of redemption.

Dream: A rat was biting my ass.

Dreamer: A 23-year-old obsessive-compulsive man.

Association: He thought of his strict and stingy father.

Interpretation: The dream has two layers of meaning. The rat denotes oedipal guilt and could represent the father's phallus (anal penetration by the father), which the dreamer, as a boy, fantasized as a way of assuaging his guilt at being too close (incestuous) with his mother. It could also represent feces, harking back to the anal stage, when the father oversaw the dreamer's toilet training and was overly strict.

Republicans

Dream: I was practicing serving, only instead of a tennis court I was on a field, like a football field, and the net went all the way across the field. I threw up a tennis ball and it turned into a little human. I looked up and it was Richard Nixon, with a scowl on his face. I slammed him across the net. I threw up another ball and it was Ronald Reagan, and another turned into Newt Gingrich. Then I looked on the other side of the net and there were all these little Republicans with mean little faces and they were rushing toward me as if they wanted to bite my toes. I ran off the court and woke up anxious.

Dreamer: A 44-year-old man suffering from political narcissism (his narcissistic grandiosity was bound up with his "liberal" identity).

Associations: He felt upset when the Republicans won a recent election and took over both houses of the United States Congress. He had recently had an argument over politics with his tennis partner.

Interpretation: The dreamer's obsessive and narcissistic preoccupation with Republicans is dramatized in this dream. All that the dreamer denies in himself—his own prejudice, aggression, and envy, is projectively identified as belonging to Republicans. He makes himself a giant compared to them (indicating his narcissistic grandiosity), then has them attack him in mean little clusters (demonizing them). There is also an oral-homosexual motif (biting his toes, which are phallic symbols).

Ring

Dream: Mother shows me her sapphire ring. We compare rings. Her ring is of lesser quality than mine. My ring is a deeper blue.

Dreamer: A 30-year-old schizoid man who was abused by his mother.

Association: He recalled that his mother devalued him as a child, often telling him he would never amount to anything.

Interpretation: The ring symbolizes self-worth. As an adult, the dreamer now shows his mother that he has more self-worth than she has (reversing what occurred in his childhood). The deep blue signifies eternity (the sky, ocean) or spiritual completeness.

River

Dream: I was at a river and needed to get to the other side. Finally I found a small rowboat and was able to paddle across the river.

Dreamer: A middle-aged woman.

Association: She was in a crisis and could not make a decision that would solve the crisis.

Interpretation: The river symbolizes a crisis that the dreamer wishes to resolve. The rowboat represents the solution. This is a simple wish-fulfillment dream.

Rock

Dream (Greek myth): Because of his many offenses when he was King of Corinth, Sisyphus was condemned in the underworld eternally to roll a huge rock up a hill, from which it rolled down again.

Interpretation: The metaphor of the myth of Sisyphus, that of eternally rolling a huge rock up a hill, from which it continually rolls back down, may stand for various kinds of neurosis, which involve self-sabotage. For example, an obsessive-compulsive continually washes his hands, yet they keep getting dirty again; the hysteric continually has fits, yet they never serve to assuage her deepest anxiety and must be followed by more fits; the alcoholic continually gets drunk, then feels guilty and remorseful, then gets drunk again. These conditions result from childhood situations that engendered guilt and for which the neurotic feels he or she must atone through ongoing rituals. Hence, the rock symbolizes the burden of guilt.

Dream: I went home but instead of my house I found a huge boulder. It was magnificent.

Dreamer: A 56-year-old man.

Association: He continually derided himself as weak.

Interpretation: The rock symbolizes strength. The dreamer's house is himself. The dream is a wish for strength.

Rome

Dream 1: The dreamer was looking out of a train window at the Tiber and the Ponte Sant' Angelo. The train began to move off, and it occurred to him that he had not even set foot in the city.

Dream 2: Someone led him to the top of a hill and showed him Rome half-hidden in mist; it was so far away that he was surprised that his view was so clear.

Dream 3: There was a narrow stream of dark water; on one side of it were black cliffs and on the other meadows with big white flowers. The dreamer noticed a Herr Zucker (whom he knew slightly) and decided to ask him the way to the city.

Dream 4: The dreamer was in Rome and saw a street corner and was surprised to find so many posters in German stuck up there.

Dreamer: Sigmund Freud, as a young man. Reported by Grinstein (1980).

Associations: Writing to his friend, Fliess, of this last dream, he noted, "I awoke and immediately realized that the Rome of my dreams was really Prague (where it is well known that there is a demand for street signs in German). Thus the dream had fulfilled my wish to meet you in Rome rather than in Prague. Incidentally, my longing for Rome is deeply neurotic. It is connected with my schoolboy hero-worship of the Semitic Hannibal and in fact this year I have no more reached Rome than he did Lake Trasimene."

Interpretation: Freud's dreams of Rome stemmed both from a longstanding, unfulfilled wish to go there, and from an infantile and narcissistic desire to "conquer" Rome as his hero, Hannibal, had done. There may also have been an unconscious fear of going to Rome that related to an oedipal conflict. Freud alluded to an oedipal dream by Julius Caesar of sexual intercourse with his mother. Hence, he seemed to interpret that Rome to him symbolized his father, whom he wanted to conquer in order to take possession of his mother.

Room

Dream: I'm in a dark room. I see something in the middle, like a trunk. I go over to it and unlock it and begin to examine the things inside of it. I find some old photographs, clothes, toys. They look familiar.

Dreamer: A 29-year-old professional woman who has just begun psychoanalysis.

Associations: She had left the previous session of therapy feeling excited about the therapist's request that she remember her dreams. She recalled that the photographs, clothes, and toys in the dream were those of her childhood, belonging either to her or to her siblings.

Interpretation: The room symbolizes the dreamer's self; the trunk in the middle her repressed memories. The dream is a wish to cooperate with the therapist in exploring her unconscious thoughts and memories.

Dream: I saw my old bedroom in the house where I grew up, but it was distorted. It was much larger and had stained-glass windows instead of the regular windows, and the roof curved downward in the middle, as if it was going to cave in.

Dreamer: A schizophrenic male.

Association: He noted that his dreams had not contained these kinds of distortions before. He said in the past when he dreamed of his bedroom it was just as it had been in real life. He did not understand these new distortions.

Interpretation: K. R. Eissler (1953) was one of the first to notice that during times of greatest delusion in their waking life, psychotics tend to dream realistic dreams. In the above instance, the fact that the schizophrenic dreamer had begun to dream in the distortions that are normal for nonpsychotic individuals was a sign that he was improving.

Dream: I stood up and found that my head hit the ceiling. Then I realized that the room was getting smaller. I squatted down in a fetal position and the room closed in on me. I was scared.

Dreamer: A 23-year-old woman with claustrophobia.

Association: Her father, who was a religious fanatic, had berated her earlier in the day for her heathenism.

Interpretation: The metaphor of the room getting smaller and the dreamer squatting in a fetal position suggests a back-to-the-womb motif. It also perhaps represents her father's oppression.

Rose

Dream: I'm being stalked by a tall man with gray hair and glasses. I run through an old house. The stalker is shooting at me with a gun. I hide behind a sofa. The stalker shoots and I see the bullet coming toward me. It hits my brain. Pink fluid comes out of my brain and turns into a rose.

Dreamer: A 30-year-old man with a borderline personality who had an emotionally incestuous mother and an absent father.

Associations: The stalker reminded him of his father. The house was not a familiar house, but the sofa in it was the sofa of the house where he grew up.

Interpretation: The old house represents the house where the dreamer was born (with the same sofa). The stalker is his father, who is angry at him because of his emotionally incestuous relationship with his mother. The bullet that hits the brain, which releases pink fluid that turns into a rose, represents the father's jealous attack on the son's superior intellect (his brain). The pink fluid that comes out of his brain symbolizes his feminine side (his anima), toward which the father harbors resentment. The rose harks back to folklore and myth, as in the medieval legends of fair maidens being unjustly executed and then having roses grow from the ground above their graves.

Running

Dream: I was going up some stairs to change trains. I felt that the train was already on the upper platform, and it actually was. I had indecision about whether I should run for it or whether I shouldn't bother. I decided at once, of course. . . . There was another girl with me running for the train, but she was running for it only half-heartedly. I decided to make a real run for it, but it was a tremendous effort to run. Every step was a great effort. My legs and feet were leaden. I felt that I was getting old. . . .

Dreamer: A depressed patient, as reported by Bonime (1980).

Associations: She said she was really struggling hard to miss the boat, holding back, then noted, "I don't want to give myself to my husband." She recalled her mother's threats as a child, "Stubborn devil, I'll show you stubbornness," and how it made her all the more stubborn.

Interpretation: The dream represents the dreamer's effort to overcome her depression. She runs to the train (to get on with her life), but is held back by "leaden feet" (a symbol of depressive psychosomatic retardation). The dreams harks back to her war of control with her mother (the woman in the dream perhaps representing her mother), and alludes to her "dragging her feet" with respect to giving herself to her husband.

Rust

Dream: I went to turn on the faucet and found that it had turned brown and rusty, and the water that came out was also full of rust.

Dreamer: A 33-year-old soldier who had just returned from serving seven months in war.

Association: He had not slept with a woman during the time he had served.

Interpretation: The rusty faucet symbolizes the dreamer's fear that he had forgotten how to perform sexually.

S

Sacrifice

Dream: I was tied to a tree, naked. I had to be sacrificed. There was a tribe of men, women, and children standing around and they had these beatific, loving smiles. They were going to do something sexual to me and then kill me by driving a wooden stake through my heart. I tried to be brave.

Dreamer: A 28-year-old woman with borderline personality.

Association: She complained of feeling victimized in every aspect of her life.

Interpretation: The dream indicates the dreamer's sense that she is a martyr who has to sacrifice herself sexually and emotionally (the stake in the heart) in order to be loved (the loving smiles of the tribe). This also alludes to her situation in her family of origin, where she was sexually abused by her father as her mother smiled lovingly on and did nothing.

Sadism

Dream 1 (fictional): "A man flogs a pregnant woman's belly."

Dream 2 (fictional): "A man watches a pregnant woman give birth, discharging semen on her as she does so. He then murders the infant before the mother's eyes, and does so while pretending to caress it."

Dream 3 (fictional): "A man causes an enormous weight to fall on the pregnant woman's belly, thereby crushing her and her fruit at one stroke."

Dreamer: Marquis de Sade, eighteenth-century French writer who was the prototypical "sadist." Reported in his (1814) book *120 Days of Sodom*.

Associations: Although not much is known of de Sade's childhood, statements he made about his mother and about women indicate a deep hatred of her and point to extreme cruelty at her hands. The above fragment, among the milder of his scribblings, was written while he was serving an eleven-year sentence in prison for criminal perversity.

Interpretation: In these dreams, as in numerous others, de Sade tortures pregnant woman. This recurring theme suggests a deep womb envy—a hatred of women and women's nurturing capacity. The wish in such dreams is revenge on the mother who bore him and, it may be safely conjectured, who inflicted unheard-of torture upon him during his earliest infancy and childhood. The infant symbolizes not only his mother's "fruit" and her soul, but also himself as an infant; hence he is killing, in effigy, both his mother and himself along with this entire memory.

Salamanders

Dream: I saw these salamanders, bright green. They were chasing each other and became all entangled, like an Escher drawing. Then they changed into corn cobs and started spinning around. They were spinning and spinning.

Dreamer: A 29-year-old hysterical woman.

Association: Her husband was pressuring her for more sex.

Interpretation: The salamanders represent phalluses. The change into corn cobs is an allusion to her father, who was a farmer who grew corn. In her unconscious mind, her husband and her father are one, and she cannot separate her incestuous feelings about her father from her sexual feelings about her husband. This conflict makes her dizzy, causing the salamanders to spin.

Salt

Dream: My husband was chasing after me with a salt shaker. He kept throwing salt on my neck.

Dreamer: A 24-year-old woman.

Association: She recalled that her husband had complained that their sex life needed some spice.

Interpretation: The salt is the spice that their sex life needs. It may also be an allusion to the folk saying that "To catch a bird put salt on its tail. . . ."

Satyr

Dream: I dreamed I saw a satyr mocking me. Finally, after much effort, I caught him and got him into my power.

Dreamer: Alexander the Great. Reported by Plutarch (110a).

Associations: He had surrounded Tyre with his men, was trying to conquer it, and was disturbed with how long it was taking.

Interpretation: Aristander interpreted the dream by dividing *satyr* into two words (in the Greek): *tyre* and *yours*. He said the dream meant "Tyre is yours." The satyr, in Greek mythology, is a god shaped like a horse or goat with a man's head, and symbolizes potency. Hence, psychoanalytically, the satyr represented Alexander's wish to be potent.

Scar

Dream: I was in the bathtub washing myself. I discovered I had a scar on my belly, as though from an operation.

Dreamer: A 40-year-old schizoid man.

Association: He remembered that when he was a child his mother used to taunt him by showing him the scar on her abdomen, saying, "See what you did to me when you were born."

Interpretation: The scar on his own belly is a way of atoning for his guilt feelings, not only about his mother's labor, but also about having something—a penis—that she does not have. (Little boys often imagine that the vagina is a castration scar.)

Scream

Dream 1: I was watching TV and saw a report about a revival of the musical *The King and I*. They were going to do a production in Japan, which would include the scene of the silent scream. They play was controversial because of its anti-Japanese theme.

Dream 2: I was in a restaurant waiting for Teresa. I explained to the waiter that this red-haired woman was coming. I saw her down the hallway working on something. Then I was outside on the street. There was an accident. A handsome, blue-eyed officer was lying unconscious. I put my arm around him and then was kissing him. His blue eyes opened but he was paralyzed.

Dreamer: A 37-year-old homosexual man.

Associations: His mother's favorite musical was *The King and I*. When he was a child, he used to want to scream, but had to remain silent. The unconscious officer reminded him of his brother.

Interpretation: The dreamer had these two dreams consecutively on the same night. The first, *The King and I*, symbolizes his bond with his mother, and probably refers to his rage (the silent scream) about the fact that his mother was so passionate about a play but paid little attention to his feelings. The play being anti-Japanese is an allusion to his belief that his mother was "anti" her son. In the second dream, the redhead again represents his mother (who is working and not paying attention to him); the officer is both his brother and father, about both of whom he had homosexual fantasies. The officer is paralyzed (castrated, powerless) at the mercy of the dreamer, reversing the actual situation of his childhood.

Dream (painting): The distorted image of a man stands in the middle of a bridge, screaming. His hands are on his temples as if he has a headache. His mouth is wide open. There are two people in the distance but they have their backs turned and don't see him; he is all alone. The sky, water, and bridge form swirling red backdrops, as though nature itself were awry.

Dreamer: Edvard Munch, Norwegian painter, who suffered from depression, as conveyed in his painting "The Scream."

Associations: He had many family tragedies, among which were his mother's and sister's deaths from leukemia when he was 5 and 17 respectively. In his paintings he strove for subjectivity.

Interpretation: Munch's paintings were a major influence on German expressionism, depicting the alienation and misery of modern man. The scream perhaps also reveals the deep inner torment of Munch as well as the loneliness and sense of abandonment he must have felt after the deaths of both of the closest primary objects in his life. It may be that he never had the chance to adequately mourn either death and hence carried the melancholy inside him throughout his life.

Sea

Dream 1: I was in a house near the sea. The house had three stories. The basement was full of water. I went into the basement. The water was light blue, like the sea. I was amazed to find I could breathe down there.

Dream 2: I saw a beautiful, light blue bay. I went into a building with two little girls, and looked out at the bay.

Dream 3: I was standing on a balcony of a high-rise building. The building came out of the sea. I jumped from the balcony and sank into the sea. It was very peaceful.

Dreamer: A 32-year-old female suffering from chronic anxiety.

Associations: She remembered that her mother told her she did not want her. Her mother said she was "a very ugly baby....Did I give birth to that?" She was abused by her father, and left unprotected by her mother. For twenty days after birth she did not want to eat, and she was often sick.

Interpretation: The sea in these dreams signifies the calm, peaceful fluid of her mother's womb. In one dream, the basement dream, she can breathe under water (as a fetus can exist in liquid). Because of the harshness of her early infantile world, in which she was apparently rejected by her mother, her strongest fixation is at this early stage. Thus this dream is both a wish to go back to the womb and a wish for death and rebirth, both of which promise the comfort and safety she lacked once she was born.

Seduction

Dream 1: You were trying to get me to seduce you.

Dream 2: I came in for a session and you were standing near your desk. You said, "Let's start," but you were standing there smiling at me. I felt your smile was a sexual overture.

Dream 3: I had a feeling of being molested by you. You were standing next to the couch.

Dreamer: A 26-year-old obsessive-compulsive man with latent homosexual features. These three dreams were about his therapist.

Association: In the previous session the therapist had confronted the dreamer about the fact that the dreamer did not respect the therapist's boundaries. "There were no boundaries between you and your mother, and so you don't understand or respect boundaries," the therapist interpreted somewhat angrily.

Interpretation: As a result of the confrontation with the therapist, alluding to the lack of boundaries in the dreamer's relationship with his mother (who had been seductive with him), the patient became sexually aroused by the therapist. He felt slapped down by the therapist for pushing the boundaries, as if the therapist had been telling him he was being seductive like his mother. The wish in these dreams is that his therapist would become seductive and break the boundaries, so that he would not be burned by guilt about his mother, and could feel justified in hating the therapist (the father in transference).

Sensations

Dream 1 (Upon having his face tickled with a feather): A frightful form of torture was being performed; a mask made of pitch was placed on the dreamer's face and then pulled off so that it took the skin off with it.

Dream 2 (Upon hearing a pair of scissors sharpened in his ear): He heard bells, followed by alarms.

Dream 3 (Upon smelling cologne): He was in Cairo, in Johann Maria Farina's shop and had some absurd adventure.

Dream 4 (Upon his neck being pinched): He was given a mustard plaster and remembered a doctor who had treated him as a child.

Dream 5 (Upon a hot iron being brought close to his face): The robbers had broken into our house and were sticking our feet into braziers of hot coal.

Dream 6 (Upon a drop of water being dropped on his face): He was in Italy, sweating violently and drinking white Orvieto wine.

Dream 7 (Upon a candle being shone through red paper): He was in a storm he had once experienced in the English Channel.

Dreamer: F A Murray, nineteenth century French psychologist. Reported by Freud (1900).

Associations: This series of experimental dreams was designed to explore the relation between external sensations and dreams.

Interpretation: The experiment suggested that an external source could affect a dream, but not its eventual plot. In each experiment, a sensation was connected to some anxiety situation, alluding to traumatic events in the dreamer's past or present.

Sex

Dream: Bill and I are in Central Park sitting in a meadow. He insists on having sex although we're in public. I agree, even I really don't want to. He lifts up my skirt and slips his penis into me, but he has trouble getting the right angle. He is positioning himself one way and then the other, and people nearby are starting to laugh at us. He looks up at them and pulls away, and his erection is wilting in front of them all. He is embarrassed.

Dreamer: A 32-year-old passive woman who had an alcoholic father.

Association: She was the daughter whose role was to rescue her alcoholic father.

Interpretation: In the dream, her husband demands sex, as in real life, and she obliges him, even though she does not want to, in order to placate him. He ends up being humiliated. The dream expresses her wish to somehow assert herself with him (in this case having the audience do it for her), and discharge her anger by humiliating him.

Dream: Three friends are at my house and they convince me to have sex with all three of them at once. One of them takes me vaginally, one anally, and I give the other a blow job. It's very exciting. Then, when it's over, one of them calls me a slut.

Dreamer: A 27-year-old borderline woman.

Association: Her boyfriend has a double standard of sexuality for men and women, as did her father: It is all right for men to experiment sexually, but not for women.

Interpretation: The dream is a recapitulation of her husband and father's sexual double standards. The three men symbolize her father, older brother, and boyfriend.

Dream: I am in an elevator by myself. Another man comes in and before I know it he is giving me a French kiss. Then he's having sex with me, unzipping my fly and giving me a blow job. I want to stop him, but it's like I'm hypnotized. By the time we reach the top floor he has finished. I tell him, "I don't want you to ever come near me again!"

Dreamer: A 40-year-old man with latent, ego-dystonic homosexual urges.

Association: A co-worker had approached him seductively recently and he had been repulsed by it.

Interpretation: The dream is a dramatization of the dreamer's ambivalence about his homosexual impulses. The fact that it happens in an elevator shows that such feelings are "still in the closet."

Dream: I'm walking in the woods when a handsome man approaches me. He is beautiful and naked, like a Greek statue, and he is very, very excited about me. I can see his erection pulsing. We kiss and have sex by a rippling stream. I can smell the leaves and the roots and see the blue sky. It's wonderful. It's the most wondrous tryst I've ever had. I wake up feeling excited and alive.

Dreamer: A 33-year-old woman.

Association: She is recently divorced.

Interpretation: This dream is a simple wish-fulfillment dream. The idyllic scene compensates for the depression and loneliness she actually feels during her waking life.

Dream: I was having sex with my girlfriend in a field near the house where I grew up. Then she changed into my sister, then back into my girlfriend again. Each time she'd change into my sister, I'd feel repulsed and want to stop.

Dreamer: A 27-year-old man suffering from retarded ejaculation.

Association: As a boy, his older sister had seduced him.

Interpretation: The dream replicates the seduction of his older sister and indicates the source of his sexual problems: his transference onto his girlfriend of his sister, and the unconscious revulsion the transference brings up.

Dream: I'm paralyzed from the waist down and rolling around on a wheel chair. Suddenly two neighborhood thugs break into my house. They are going to kill me, but I convince them to have sex with me instead. They both urinate on me and rape me; I feel nothing. They are both happy and I'm left with urine and cum all over my body.

Dreamer: A 29-year-old masochistic woman suffering from frigidity, as reported by Delany (1994).

Association: She felt inferior to men and sexually numb from her waist down.

Interpretation: The source of the dreamer's masochism and frigidity is revealed in the dream. She fears that men will rob her (steal her dignity, her soul), and feels inferior to them and unable to protect herself (she is paralyzed and in a wheelchair). Since she feels she is not as good as men, she must perform sexual services for them.

Dream: I'm in a pond with a little girl. She is wearing white panties in the pond. Then I ask her if she'd like to learn about sex. She says yes. I pull down her panties and explain about her vagina and show her how good it feels if I touch it. Then I go down on her and lick it very gently to show her how good that feels. "Is this all right?" she asks. "Of course it is, because I love you," I say. "Anything done out of love is fine." "Okay," she says.

Dreamer: A 45-year-old pedophile.

Association: When he was a little boy, he was molested in a similar way by an aunt who was giving him a bath.

Interpretation: The dream expresses the man's pedophilic impulses and rationalizes them by asserting that the molestation is all right if done lovingly.

Dream: I was lying on the couch. I was relaxed. My therapist came over to me and lay down on top of me and touched me in a sexual way. I was very upset.

Dreamer: A 29-year-old woman with hysterical features.

Association: In the previous sessions she had spoken about how, at the age of 7, she had gotten emotionally close to her father, and her mother had stepped in and told her it was inappropriate.

Interpretation: The dreamer has "inappropriate" erotic feelings toward her therapist (her father in the transference), which she projects onto her therapist in order to relieve herself of guilt. The fact that she is "very upset" signals this guilt. The dream is a replica of what happened in her childhood when she relaxed (trusted and loved) with her father, only to be rebuked by her mother; this caused her to feel betrayed by her father, and in the dream she feels betrayed by her therapist.

Dream: I was having sex with my wife. For some reason I was having rough sex with her. I was throwing her around the bed and saying dirty things to her. She looked hurt and I apologized.

Dreamer: A young, passive male.

Association: He expressed boredom with his wife.

Interpretation: The dream reveals a wish that he could have uninhibited sex with his wife, but also reveals his fear that such uninhibited sex will be too aggressive and hence offensive to her.

Ships

Dream: I'm the captain of a ship. The ship looks like a luxury yacht, but it's really a warship. It's the middle of the night. I'm in the ocean. I have a battle with three other ships—pirate ships. They think my ship is easy pickings, but they are wrong. My ship wins the battle.

Dreamer: A 32-year-old schizoid woman who has three older brothers.

Association: She notes that the pirate ships are her three older brothers, by whom she has constantly felt maligned.

Interpretation: The luxury ship that is really a battle ship represents her mode of defense. On the surface she is calm and caring, but underneath she is ready for battle. She would like to kill off her brothers and have the ocean (mother) to herself.

Dream: I'm on a ship somewhere. I'm feeling anxious because there's nobody around. I run up to the captain and ask where we're going. He shrugs his shoulders. I feel very hopeless.

Dreamer: A 59-year-old man who has long been depressed over the death of his wife.

Association: He said he felt as though he had been drifting since his wife's death.

Interpretation: The ship symbolizes the dreamer's drifting state. The captain (his ego) does not care (shrugs his shoulders) where he is going.

Dream: Somehow I had fallen into the ocean. I held on to a piece of wood as long as I could. Then a beautiful white ship came into view. It looked very peaceful and safe.

Dreamer: A young, single man.

Association: He had recently divorced and spoke of the anxiety of the dating scene.

Interpretation: The ship symbolizes the woman who will rescue him from the ocean of anxiety. White perhaps denotes an angel of mercy.

Shoes

Dream: I was with Jenny. We were taking a tour of a tall building. A dark-skinned guide showed us around. Then he bowed and left us. Jenny said, "Let's go." But I couldn't walk. My shoes were on the wrong feet.

Dreamer: A 38-year-old man suffering from depression.

Associations: He thought of his ex-girlfriend, Jenny, the previous day, when he had read about an earthquake in Mexico, where he and Jenny had once traveled. He used to know a guy who had his shoes on the wrong feet; he was a heroin addict.

Interpretation: According to Freud, shoes may be symbolic of female genitals; hence wearing them on the wrong feet may signify a bad sexual fit. Jenny had broken up with the dreamer because she did not think he had a future and because, as she put it, "You smoke too much marijuana." The dreamer interpreted this to mean he was sexually inadequate.

Shooting

Dream: J and a friend of his were shooting at birds. Mary was there. I had to go retrieve the dead birds and couldn't find anything because it was so dark and I was inadequately equipped. When I returned, J and his friend were dumping Mary over the fence into a pit. "What happened?" I asked. "Well, she got out of hand so I knocked her on the head and threw her over the fence into the pit." I asked if she was dead and he replied, "No, but she will be if we leave her there." I wondered if we should do that, but I was afraid to say anything because I was afraid he'd kill me.

Dreamer: A 32-year-old man suffering from depression and feelings of inadequacy.

Associations: Mary was a girl he had known in high school who had a bad reputation. J was a man he knew who had outspoken views about women, and whose assertiveness he admired.

Interpretation: Shooting symbolizes masculine potency, and the gun is a phallic symbol. The fact that the dreamer does not shoot and is relegated to retrieving the birds (women), like some servile dog, shows his feelings of masculine inferiority. Because he is "inadequately equipped" he cannot even perform this secondary task successfully. Mary symbolizes women's demonic qualities, which the dreamer felt unable to deal with in his family or in his office. He himself would like to do what J does to Mary, but his conscience would not let him.

Sibling Rivalry

Dream 1: A cat ate the baby.

Dream 2: The baby ate the cat and the cat ate the baby's stomach and the baby died.

Dream 3: The baby fell on the floor and the baby's head came off and rolled around the house and the baby's head was still crying.

Dream 4: A wolf jumped into the window and bit the baby and carried him into the woods.

Dream 5: I went to the baby's crib and the baby wasn't there. Some mice were playing with his diaper.

Dream 6: The baby went into the bathroom and fell down the toilet.

Dreamer: A 4-year-old boy whose mother had just brought home a new baby sister.

Association: He kept asking his mother if he could hold the baby, and she refused, saying he might drop her. This made him sad and angry.

Interpretation: This series of dreams is typical of small children who are dealing with the arrival of a new sibling. The sibling rivalry is manifested in wishes to get rid of the child in various ways. Dreams of children are quite transparent and are almost always wish fulfillments.

Singing

Dream: I'm singing in a chorus. It's a fine ensemble that just suits my voice. I awake to the final phrase of the piece, "Glory to the Father . . ."

Dreamer: A young, homosexual man with narcissistic features.

Associations: He had recently visited his father from whom he had been estranged for some time. The dreamer was the soloist in a choir.

Interpretation: Singing symbolizes the joy of his reunion with his father, and also the narcissistic and libidinal investment in both God the Father and his real father.

Dream: My boss came into my office and he was humming a tune. I happened to know the tune and so I began humming it too. We were humming in harmony and then he picked up my telephone and ordered a pizza delivered with extra cheese.

Dreamer: A 43-year-old secretary with musical aspirations.

Association: She expressed frustration with her menial job and her inability to launch her music career. Pizza with extra cheese is one of her favorite snacks.

Interpretation: Harmonizing with her boss represents both a wish for better relations with him and a related wish to be doing something with music rather than secretarial work. The pizza suggests oral (libidinal) satisfaction.

Sirens

Dream (Greek myth): There was an island somewhere in the sea, and on this island were female creatures called sirens, who sang so beautifully they lured sailors to their shores, where the sailors were shipwrecked.

Interpretation: Myths such as this one about sirens are externalizations of primitive fears harking back to early childhood. They probably involve the defense mechanism of splitting, in which the archaic mother is seen alternately as the good mother (angel) and bad mother (witch). Such splitting occurs in response to caretakers who are prone to mood swings in which they are alternately sweet and then harshly punitive to their infants. In the myth of the sirens, the island in the middle of the sea perhaps stands for mother, mother's lap, mother's womb; the beautiful singing symbolizes the angelic mother who sings lullabyes, and the creature of destruction represents the witch–mother posing as an angel.

Dream: I was making love with Jean and suddenly I heard sirens. I looked out the window but couldn't see any cars on the street.

Dreamer: A 42-year-old man.

Association: His girlfriend's father disapproved of the relationship with his daughter.

Interpretation: The sirens represent the girlfriend's father, as well as his own superego's "alarm" at his forbidden pleasure.

Skateboard

Dream: Jim and I were on a suburban street in the middle of the night. We had a self-propelled skateboard and were feeling good. We came to the top of a hill. A crazy, disapproving older man made some comments. My friend insulted him and he insulted us back. We laughed and I said, "Let's go for it." We shared the skateboard and went down the hill. At the bottom we crashed and fell to the pavement, but it was fun.

Dreamer: A 31-year-old man with an Oedipus complex.

Association: He had spoken to his father the day before he had the dream, and his father had, as usual, been disapproving of a new career idea.

Interpretation: The skateboard that is self-propelled stands for a powerful phallus or perhaps for powerful, uncontrollable, latent homosexual urges. The disapproving crazy older man represents the dreamer's father, toward whom he harbors homosexual thoughts. His friend insults the man (father), which is a kind of aggression he was never allowed to show his father. Going down the hill with his friend represents a kind of rebellion toward the father and an enactment of the latent homo-sexuality. The crash at the bottom of the hill indicates his fears about the conse-quences of homosexuality, while his comment that "it was fun" shows his wish to overcome that fear.

Skin

Dream: I walked onto the street and suddenly my skin shriveled up and fell off. I suddenly felt quite vulnerable.

Dreamer: A 39-year-old woman with a borderline personality.

Association: She remembered a telephone conversation with her father the day before, and how nearly everything he said upset her. She wondered why she was so "thin-skinned."

Interpretation: The image of her skin falling off and feeling exposed symbolizes her general oversensitivity due to her father's extreme intrusiveness and criticism throughout her childhood and even at the present.

Skirt

Dream: I was in a basement. I looked in a mirror and saw I was wearing a skirt. Then I saw three women staring at me. They wanted to have sex with me. They want-ed to dominate me. One sat on my face and I had to eat her pussy. It made me gag.

Dreamer: A 38-year-old man with transvestic tendencies.

Association: He recalled wearing his mother's skirts as a boy and feeling ashamed of it, wishing his mother would catch him.

Interpretation: The skirt represents a denial of masculinity, which was offensive to his mother. To atone for his offensive masculinity he must wear a skirt and sub-mit to female domination. The fact that the women's femininity makes him gag reflects his unconscious ambivalence, repressed rage, and incestuous feelings.

Skull

Dream: I saw two human skulls decaying on the floor of a cave.

Dreamer: Carl Jung, psychoanalyst. Reported by Donn (1988).

Associations: Freud and Jung were sharing their dreams during a cruise to the United States in 1909. Early in the trip, Jung had talked at length about using peat bog to keep corpses from decaying in certain primitive cultures. He had been obsessed with aging and death since his boyhood, when he had harbored the psychotic delusion that he was two people, a boy in the present and an old man from a past era.

Interpretation: Jung thought the skulls referred to the collective unconscious—that is, to "the world of the primitive man within myself." Freud, who had thought that Jung's talk of peat bog corpses signaled his death wish for Freud, again interpreted this dream as an oedipal wish by Jung to get rid of Freud (the father of psychoanalysis). Looking at the dream in terms of its symbolism, a cave often represents a womb, and skulls symbolize death, in which case the dream might suggest a wish by Jung that both he and Freud could go back to the womb together (a kind of death). Dreams of going back to the womb are typical of depressed persons.

Sleep

Dream (fairy tale): A witch who is angry that she was not invited to a king's daughter's birth celebration puts a curse on his daughter. The daughter is not to ever use a spinning wheel; if she does, she and the entire castle will be put to sleep for a hundred years. It comes to pass that the king's daughter turns into a beautiful young maiden. Even though the king has banished all spinning wheels from the castle, she finds one in a secret room and begins to spin it. She pricks herself, everyone in the castle immediately falls asleep, and thick trees surround the castle so that nobody can come near it. Finally a prince manages to penetrate the woods and climb the castle walls. He kisses the sleeping beauty, wakes her, and marries her.

Interpretation: "The Sleeping Beauty" symbolizes innocence and sexual repression. The witch stands for the envious mother who wishes to suppress her daughter's sexuality. The spinning wheel denotes passage to adult female sexuality. Upon learning of these sexual secrets, Sleeping Beauty is punished by being put to sleep (repression). The thick trees guarding her castle may represent social mores that enforce sexual repression. The prince stands for the hero/father who rescues her from the clutches of the smothering witch/mother.

Snake

Dream: I bought a snake, and then I realized I didn't really want it; it was the last thing I wanted. I lured it into a plastic container, but realized it couldn't breathe. I punched holes in the lid and the snake escaped through the holes and attacked me. I ran away from it but was trapped in my room. Who would rescue me? My brother? Sharon?

Dreamer: A 34-year-old man with narcissistic features.

Associations: He felt that his brother and his friend Sharon (who was like a sister) both made him feel safe. Snakes were evil.

Interpretation: The snake symbolizes the dreamer's unconscious guilt, including sexual guilt, which he fears will "bite him." As in the biblical story, the snake here brings punishment onto the subject of this dream. He tries to keep the snake contained (repress the guilt) but it gets out anyway, so he longs to be rescued from his internal torment.

Dream: I was watching TV and saw a snake shedding its skin. For some reason I felt relieved.

Dreamer: A 30-year-old woman.

Association: She felt worried that she had contracted a sexually transmitted disease.

Interpretation: The snake shedding its skin represents a rebirth and shedding of guilt (and the disease) by the dreamer.

Dream: The dreamer was sitting at her father's sickbed. She had been dozing. When she awoke, she saw a large, black snake slithering across the wall behind her father's bed, ready to attack him. She tried to keep the snake away, but found that her right arm was paralyzed (it had been hanging over the chair as she slept). She looked in horror at her arm and then saw the fingers of her hand turn into little snakes with death's heads.

Dreamer: Anna O, the first psychoanalytic patient, a pretty and intelligent young woman of 1880s Vienna suffering from hysteria. Reported by Breuer (Freud and Breuer 1893).

Associations: She had to take care of her sick father day and night for many months. During this time she became mentally sick herself and suffered from numerous hysterical symptoms, among them hallucinations such as the one above. At one point, when she dozed off and woke up, she had the thought: What if my father dies when I'm sleeping?

Interpretation: In psychoanalysis, when an individual is overly fearful that somebody near to him or her will die, it masks a death wish. The snake in the hallucination is an externalization of the dreamer's murderous wishes toward her father. The snakes on her fingers and the death's heads at the ends represent her unconscious acknowledgment that she is herself the agent of death. She had become burdened with caring for a father for whom she harbored deep, unexpressed feelings of resentment.

Dream: I saw many snakes. One of the snakes seized its own tail and the image whirled scornfully before my eyes. As though from a flash of lightning, I awoke.

Dreamer: F. A. Kekule, nineteenth century German scientist. Reported by Gutheil (1951).

Association: He had striven for months to express the formula of benzene. When he awoke from this dream, the image of the snake biting its own tail gave him the idea.

Interpretation: This is an example of how dreams can sometimes offer solutions to problems. One may derive an additional interpretation of the dream from the phrase, "the image whirled scornfully before my eyes." Since it is the dreamer who dreamed this scornful snake, it may be a symbol of his superego (conscience) scorning himself for not coming up with this idea sooner. In Jungian terms the image can be seen as an archetypal symbol from the collective unconscious imparting rebirth.

Dream: A friend had put a snake into my bed. I threw off the blanket and tried to kick the snake away, but the snake slithered under my bed and hid there.

Dreamer: A 34-year-old man with latent homosexual tendencies.

Association: In recent days a homosexual friend had kept telling the dreamer he was homosexual and should admit it to himself.

Interpretation: The snake represents another man's penis, forbidden desire (Adam and Eve), and repressed homosexuality, the knowledge of which he struggles against, and at the same time wishes for.

Dream 1: Bob and I were walking along a path. There were snakes all around and we had to tiptoe across them. We saw a car and got inside. It was a big car and Bobby starting driving recklessly down a New York City highway. He did something crazy and I yelled, "Hi, Bob, you're driving really crazy." Finally he pulled over and I relaxed.

Dream 2: Bob and I came upon a lake and a factory with smoke stacks. We thought of swimming in the lake but I was afraid the water was poisoned by the factory or full of snakes. I saw a snake and tried to grab it. It slithered away.

Dreamer: A 32-year-old male with passive homosexual obsessions.

Associations: In previous dreams, snakes had turned into women and women into snakes. Bob was an acquaintance from work whose assertiveness the dreamer admired. The night before the above dreams he had gone out with a "southern belle" who liked to play men against one another.

Interpretation: In these dreams snakes symbolize both homosexuality and women who lie menacing in the dark, and who are elusive (like the "southern belle"), slithering away when he wants to catch one. The reckless car drive and the proposed swim in the poisoned lake (poisoned by the factory with its smoke stacks—phallic symbols) represent homosexual intercourse, which is extremely threatening. The dreams are symbolic enactments of his conflicts between heterosexuality and homosexuality.

Snow

Dream: My cousin Julia and I were meeting at various beautiful resorts in the mountains, forests, lakes. Always at night and always snowing. It was like a travelogue. Fate had us meeting at all these places and it was such a wonderful feeling, the beautiful, cool, snowy nights.

Dreamer: A 32-year-old man with depressive features.

Associations: He remembered that when he was 5 years old, his family went on a skiing trip and he got lost. A forest ranger found him and took care of him. He had had a brief relationship with the cousin in the dream.

Interpretation: This is a dream about regaining his youth and innocence. The snow denotes purity and innocence, and perhaps also being found. Night probably means calm and safety. The relationship with his cousin symbolizes an antidote to the incestuous oedipal feelings he harbored for his mother, making him feel guilty and dirty, and indicates a fresh start.

Sociopath

Dream 1: I went into a store with a large rifle. A woman in the store said she was sorry. I felt antisocial so I shot her anyway and took all the money. I heard police sirens and changed into a woman.

Dream 2: I picked up a prostitute and strangled her. I took all her money and cigarettes. Then I cut open her vagina.

Dream 3: I went into a bank. I was wearing a dress so they wouldn't suspect anything. Then I pulled out a big pistol and shot everyone. I took the money and hid the gun under a skirt.

Dream 4: I went into a familiar house. There was a young woman inside with red hair. I asked her for some pie and when she went to get it I took out a long knife and stabbed her in the mouth. Then I stuffed the pie in her pussy and had sex with her.

Dreamer: A 27-year-old sociopathic male whose father had been a sociopath (convicted murderer) and whose mother was a part-time prostitute who had ten children, of which he was the second.

Association: He often had fantasies of murdering red-haired women. His mother had red hair that she dyed blonde.

Interpretation: The dreamer's masculinity complex (the big rifle and gun), gender confusion (changing to a woman and wearing a skirt), and hatred of vaginas (he cuts one open and stuffs pie in the other) is evident in these dreams. The girl with red hair is his mother, and it is her vagina he hates, because she has used it to have many children (whom she neglected and abused) and to pick up other men and display them before him as a child. Meanwhile, his father was a model for this kind of sociopathy.

Sodomy

Dream 1: I was in a cab. The cab driver, a rough Irish man, said, "Why are you in such a hurry to go home?" He took me to a strange neighborhood and we saw some sleazy women standing around. Then all these rough-looking men came out from everywhere, like in the movie *Deliverance.* I felt terrified.

Dream 2: I was in a porno place looking at magazines, waiting in line to go into one of those booths where you look at naked women. A gay man flirted with me. I took his hand affectionately and was about to sodomize him. We were interrupted by something.

Dreamer: A 31-year-old man with passive-aggressive features.

Association: The rough man in the first dream reminded him of a rough version of his own father. The gay man in the second dream reminded him of himself.

Interpretation: Both dreams are enactments of passive-homosexual impulses. The dreamer, who is heterosexual, nevertheless has passive-homosexual subdrives that rise to consciousness during therapy. Both dreams are about sodomy. In the first, the men like those from *Deliverance* (a movie about uneducated, white, rural men in the South who sodomize a group of men on a river trip) want to sodomize the dreamer. In the second, he (in identification with the aggressor, his father) nearly sodomizes himself (the gay man). The dreamer has such dreams whenever he feels rejected by the women in his life, and they represent wishes to somehow be initiated into the world of men and masculinity.

Somnambulism

Dream: Somebody puts a snake into my bed. I try to kick it out of my bed, so I kick the quilt off. Then I get up with the feeling that the snake is still in my bed. I walk around the bed and I put the quilt on the bed again, and realize at last that all that was a dream.

Dreamer: A somnambulistic man, as reported by Gutheil (1951).

Association: The dreamer was struggling against his unconscious ego-dystonic, homosexual impulses. He had a history of walking in his sleep.

Interpretation: In somnambulism, according to Gutheil, dream thought is converted into dream action. This happens because of the heightened pressure of emotions and a weakness of the ego to defend against them. Generally the actions performed during sleepwalking are those toward which the dreamer's superego disapproves, often involving incestuous wishes toward one parent or the other, or to a sibling. In the above dream, the disapproved theme and the sleepwalking revolved around unwanted homosexual impulses (the snake), which he cannot get rid of. The "somebody" who put the snake in his bed (homosexual thoughts in his mind) is presumably his father.

Soul

Dream (delusion): Well, my mother . . . uh—before she was a baby, I mean when she was a woman, she could think herself—as herself, and hold her face . . . and look very well, and then she would give it to me and I'd look very well; but I was a baby, and she didn't teach me how to really do it, so, uh, it would stay that way, 'cause I was always in a soul—I never had a—really had a body, until—no, it's all soul material. But it fleshed, uh, and that's where we live, on my soul.

Dreamer: Joan Douglas, a schizophrenic woman who was extremely fragmented and was a lifelong patient of Harold Searles. Reported in several of his papers, including in Searles (1979).

Associations: This delusional statement occurred during a session in which Searles had asked if she could assume different forms.

Interpretation: Searles interpreted this and other specimens of Douglas's delusional language as a struggle to be born—that is, to leave her existence as a "soul" and become a fleshed-out human being. This struggle to be born was related to her extreme dissociation from her self, resulting from a severely psychopathological and infantile relationship with her mother. The delusion shows her symbiotic merger with her mother, who "would hold her face . . . and then give it to me." With schizophrenics, their delusions are their daytime dreams, while the dreams they have while asleep are generally more realistic.

Sounds

Dream 1: I was in the woods and heard the sound of a waterfall. It was so striking I couldn't move.

Dream 2: I heard the most beautiful music coming from a speaker somewhere.

Dream 3: A summer breeze whistled past my ears. It was the most exquisite sound I ever heard.

Dream 4: Chimes filled the air. They were all around me. I could have listened forever.

Dream 5: The sounds of people laughing.

Dream 6: I heard a magnificent chorus. It seemed as though there must have been thousands of singers, as though they were singing from heaven. Then I looked at the sky and it opened up and I found myself floating upward.

Dreamer: A 28-year-old man who had become deaf due to an accident at age 12.

Association: He continually regretted having lost his hearing and not being able to hear his favorite sounds.

Interpretation: The beautiful sounds of the dreamer's recurring dreams are simple wish-fulfillments. In the last dream, there is also a death wish and a desire to go to heaven (to join his mother, who had died in the accident in which he had lost his hearing).

Space Travel

Dream (delusion): The dreamer had a delusion that he could travel to other planets. At night, when he was in the privacy of his home, he could will himself to outer space. He kept elaborate records of his travels, including a 2,000-page biography, a 100-page glossary, eighty-two color maps, 161 architectural drawings, twelve genealogical tables, and forty-four folders containing writings such as "The Fauna of Srom Olma I" and "The Transportation System of Seraneb."

Dreamer: Kirk Allen, a schizophrenic engineer, as reported by Lindner (1957).

Associations: The delusion of flight to another planet occurred to Allen while he was engaged in the preparation of a map, and followed his rejection by a woman.

Interpretation: The delusions and delusional systems of schizophrenics are their waking dreams and can be interpreted as such. Kirk Allen's delusion of traveling to other planets and making charts, maps, and journals serves the function of compensating for his feelings of insignificance. In his early childhood, he was abandoned by his mother, and then by a series of nannies, which left him with an extremely fragile ego; most of the time he was left alone with his fantasies. Lindner notes that maps, charts, architectural plans, and other such material often have the unconscious symbolic meaning of the human form, and of curiosity about sexual details. Feeling totally inept about sex, Allen erected a delusional system in which he was the expert.

Spanking

Dream 1 (fictional): "He has two women gently spank him with a martinet; each woman bestows ten stripes, alternating them with asshole friggery."

Dream 2 (fictional): "He has himself whipped by four different girls while farts are being launched into his mouth."

Dream 3 (fictional): "He has himself whipped by his wife while he fucks his daughter, then by his daughter while he fucks his wife."

Dreamer: Marquis de Sade, eighteenth-century French writer for whom the term *sadism* was named, as reported in his book, *The 120 Days of Sodom* (1814).

Association: The above fantasies were written when he was serving an eleven-year sentence in prison for criminal perversity.

Interpretation: Anal imagery and S & M activity have their source in fixations during the anal phase of development. Spankings and farts are common during this phase, as well as perverse primitive infantile fantasies of intercourse between parents and children. It would appear that de Sade had a major fixation during this stage and was most likely treated cruelly by his caretakers. Spankings and other anal-erotic activity by adults are attempts to act out forbidden infantile fantasies and thereby master their still repressed infantile fear, guilt, and rage.

Dream: I was with a woman in a red sweater (the color of his buttocks). A little boy was there, and the little boy said, "Mommy, may I have a spanking?" "Yes, if you like. Get the hairbrush." She got the hairbrush, pulled his pants down over him, and spanked him. "Have you had enough?" "Yes." Then he went off to play. I asked her if the little boy had this spanking before as she put her hairbrush away, and the next moment I was on top of her, excited sexually, kissing her. Watching the spanking aroused me.

Dreamer: A 50-year-old male masochist, as reported by Socarides (1980).

Associations: This dream appeared the night before he was to deliver a lecture in a distant city. He felt overwhelmingly sad at being away from his wife. His separation anxiety was so intense that he locked himself in the bathroom and writhed on the floor.

Interpretation: Dreams of spankings are common for masochistic individuals. In his real life, he would dress in young girls' clothes and pretend to be Linda, a snobbish British young lady, while his sexual partner (his wife) pretended to be a snobbish motherly woman. In the dream he identified with all three figures—the little boy, the mother, and the dreamer (Linda). Spanking fantasies, according to Socarides, serve to ward off the wish for, and dread of, merging with the mother in the primitive mother–child unity, as well as the unconscious homosexual wish to incorporate the father's penis.

Spear

Dream: I was walking in the woods. Some men were throwing spears at a lion. Then the lion turned into a woman.

Dreamer: A 31-year-old man.

Association: He said he could never express anger to a woman.

Interpretation: The spears are phallic symbols. The dream expresses the dreamer's sexual-aggressive impulses, which he displaces onto other men.

Splattering

Dream 1: President Nixon is going to have me shot from a cannon because it is the only way he can get rid of me. I am placed in the cannon and I am shot out. I explode into 1,000 pieces like the atomic bomb.

Dream 2: Someone dragged me to the Empire State Building. They took me to the top and threw me down. I splattered into pieces at the bottom. I was dead and I was looking at the pieces.

Dreamers: Two women suffering from epilepsy, as reported by Levitan (1980).

Associations: Both of these dreams were had on the day following a grand mal seizure. Both were followed by periods in which the dreamer felt depersonalized.

Interpretation: Freud was unable to explain the nightmares of those suffering from traumatic neuroses or post-traumatic stress disorders as the products of wish-fulfillment. Instead, he admitted later in his career that traumatic dreams represent a failure of the wish-fulfillment function. However, it may be that such dreams simply represent a death wish, a wish to obliterate the self in order to be rid of the pain of the stress following such a severe trauma. The fact that such dreams are followed by depersonalization seems to indicate a desire to leave the body.

Split Personality

Dream (fictional): Gentle physician Henry Jekyll discovers a drug that changes him, first at will and later involuntarily, into a monster named Mr. Hyde, who goes on drunken and violent debauches. He develops a split personality and ends up getting shot by police.

Dreamer: Robert Louis Stevenson, Scottish novelist, who suffered from respiratory illness and tuberculosis for most of his life.

Association: Stevenson acknowledged that he got the idea for his novel, *The Strange Case of Dr. Jekyll and Mr. Hyde* (1886), from a dream.

Interpretation: In dreams about split personalities, one person represents the "normal" personality (often the ideal image) while the other is the disowned (repressed) aspect of the personality, projected onto another person. Hence, Stevenson's dream probably alludes to a split in his own personality. Mr. Hyde is in reality the darker, repressed sexual and aggressive impulses lurking in his unconscious, which Stevenson fears will get out of hand. In Jungian terms it would be the shadow.

Dream: Dr. Johnson dreamed he had a contest of wit with an opponent and got the worst of it.

Dreamer: Samuel Johnson, British essayist. Reported by Boswell (1791).

Association: Johnson was known as a witty, contentious person.

Interpretation: The opponent was the split-off aggressive component of his own personality.

Spout

Dream: I heard a noise and saw a spout come out of the wall in my bedroom. Then a reddish liquid came out of it.

Dreamer: A young man suffering from impotency.

Association: He had been with his girlfriend that evening and had not been able to get an erection.

Interpretation: The spout is a phallic symbol. The dream is his wish for potency. The reddish liquid denotes blood, or vitality.

Springtime

Dream: You and a woman were sitting at an outdoor patio table. It was springtime and the birds were singing. I was deciding whether to join you or sit at another table.

Dreamer: A 37-year-old woman whose father favored her sister over her.

Association: The woman had this dream about her psychotherapist.

Interpretation: The man in the dream (her therapist) symbolizes her father, and the woman her sister. The dreamer feels unworthy of joining with her therapist and his woman friend, just as she was made to feel less worthy than her sister of her father's love. Springtime and singing birds may denote the dreamer's unconscious infantile-erotic impulses toward the therapist (father). The dream is a transference dream.

Statues

Dream: I was on a boat with my family down a river. Suddenly my family wasn't there. I didn't know where they were. Then I looked at the bank of the river and I saw all these statues of Greek gods, all toppled over. We reached the end of the waterway and I found my family asleep. I woke them up and said, "Did you see that?" None of them had seen anything. I wanted the crew to turn the boat around, but they couldn't find the route.

Dreamer: A 37-year-old schizoid woman.

Association: She spoke of feeling abandoned by her family.

Interpretation: The statues that are toppled over symbolize the members of her family—particularly her father and two brothers. She had grown up idealizing them, which is why they are seen as gods in the dream. The river the boat goes down represents the river of life. The dream is a death wish about her family.

Dream (Greek myth): A sculptor named Pygmalion created a statue of his own ideal woman and then fell in love with it. He prayed to the goddess Aphrodite that his statue would come to life. It did and he married her.

Interpretation: Myths and dreams of statues coming to life are rooted in primitive magical wishes of children for a beautiful fairy godmother (the good mother) to rescue them from the witch (bad mother). The statue coming to life also denotes god-like powers (narcissistic grandiosity) and immortality. In Jungian psychology, this myth may represent the integration of anima/animus.

Steam

Dream: I was at a party and I saw steam coming out of a woman's ear. She was enjoying it, laughing and showing off, as others at the party looked on. Later a stranger began questioning me and I thought I would be angry.

Dreamer: A 40-year-old schizoid woman.

Association: She said the woman seemed familiar and she really admired her.

Interpretation: The woman represents the dreamer's ego-ideal. The steam coming out of her ear is anger. The woman is quite at home with her anger, enjoying it, laughing about it, and is admired by others at the party. The dreamer who has spent her life repressing her anger, wishes she could be like this woman in the dream and enjoy her anger.

Steel Mills

Dream 1: I was lost in the steel mill and couldn't find my way out.

Dream 2: I was in the steel mill and got trapped in one of the mechanisms.

Dream 3: I was in the steel mill and the doors were all locked and then I found that I couldn't breathe.

Dream 4: The steel mill turned into a maze.

Dream 5: The steel mill became a dark, musty cave.

Dream 6: I tried to escape the steel mill and fell down and broke my leg. Nobody was there to hear me scream.

Dream 7: Part of a machine fell and almost hit me.

Dreamer: A young boy who had these dreams from the ages of 7 to 10.

Association: This was a recurring dream. Both his father and grandfather worked in the steel mills. He had spent most of his time with his mother and two sisters.

Interpretation: The steel mill represented the expectations of his father and grandfather that he be a man and assume masculine responsibilities. These dreams show his anxieties about taking on the masculine role. Having been spoiled by his mother and two sisters, he felt reluctant and inadequate to deal with the masculine world.

Stick

Dream: I'm making love to my wife. A man is watching us through the window. He throws a stick at me and it hits me on my ass.

Dreamer: A young man with a bisexual conflict.

Association: The man in the window reminds him of his father.

Interpretation: The stick is a phallic symbol, his father's penis. Before he can have sex with his wife (or any female who represents a surrogate mother), he must assuage his oedipal guilt by succumbing to his father (a strong male).

Stocking

Dream: I was at a dog-racing track. There was one cute dog, a cocker spaniel. Sand colored. There were hundreds of other dogs and they looked like wolves. They were all chasing the cocker spaniel. I was watching but nobody could help the cocker spaniel. He turned near the fence and a lady picked him up and took him home and put him in a cabinet under her sink. When the other dogs came, they couldn't find him. I felt relieved, and when I went to the sink I could hear him breathing heavily. I opened the door and he was gagged with one of my pink stockings. I didn't like that, but I closed the cabinet door, leaving it open just a crack so he could breathe.

Dreamer: A 29-year-old schizoid woman.

Association: She was the cocker spaniel.

Interpretation: As a child she used to hide in the cabinet under the sink to get away from her abusive stepfather. The wolves chasing the cocker spaniel symbolize the dreamer's fear of men and sexuality. The lady who hides the dog under the sink is herself. The pink stocking that gags the cocker spaniel's mouth stands for her fear of sexuality (pink stocking representing sexuality). It also denotes her general feeling that she cannot complain about anything. That the dreamer observes all of this, standing outside the dream, is an indication of her depersonalization, a defense mechanism she developed in early childhood.

Stone

Dream: I was looking at my face in the mirror when suddenly it turned into a pink, marble-like stone. It looked like a statue from antiquity, like you'd find in a museum, with cracks around the cheeks and forehead.

Dreamer: A 47-year-old narcissistic man.

Association: He remembered looking in the mirror and noticing his gray hairs.

Interpretation: The stone face in the mirror stands for his fear of aging and is at the same time a wish for immortality (becoming a statue).

Storm

Dream (Greek myth): Orion was a giant hunter, noted for his beauty. He was blinded by Oenopion, but Vulcan sent Cedalion to be his guide and his sight was eventually restored by exposing his eyeballs to the sun. He was slain by Diana, and then became one of the constellations in the sky, surrounded by stormy weather.

Interpretation: This myth contains several primitive symbols. Blindness signifies castration. The sun, which sometimes causes blindness in Greek myths, in this one reverses blindness. The stormy weather means anger and unrest. The end of this story, in which Orion is put into the sky where he hovers surrounded by stormy weather, parallels legends and folklore about ghosts of descendants whose spirits hover restlessly in a house.

Dream: I saw a ship being tossed back and forth in a storm, and then it sank calmly into the sea.

Dreamer: A 27-year-old depressed woman.

Association: She had been struggling with suicidal thoughts.

Interpretation: The ship is the dreamer, and the storm imparts the vicissitudes of life that are tossing her about. Sinking calmly into the sea represents both suicide and a flight back to the womb.

Stove

Dream 1: I light my stove, but then I see that it's too close to the bed, which is covered by a pink blanket with white polka dots on it. I don't want the blanket to catch fire, so I extinguish the fire.

Dream 2: It's very cold and I want to light the stove, but I don't have any wood. I call my mother to ask if she has any.

Dream 3: I start the fire in the stove but it won't stay lit. I walk over to my mother's to get warm.

Dreamer: A 39-year-old man suffering from impotence.

Associations: His mother was always calling him to ask about his girlfriends. The previous weekend he had invited a woman to go away for a ski weekend and had been impotent with her. His mother had interrogated him when they got back, wanting to know all the details. It made him sick. The blanket with white polka dots was similar to one he had as a child.

Interpretation: The source of the dreamer's impotence is his attachment with his mother. The stove in all three dreams represents potency. In the first he cannot keep the stove lit (be potent) because it might burn up the blanket with white polka dots (symbolic of his infantile attachment to his mother). The second and third dreams have similar interpretations.

Strawberries

Dream: Anna Fweud, stwawbewwies, wild stwawbewwies, omblet, pudden.

Dreamer: Anna Freud, the child psychoanalyst, at the age of 19 months, as reported by her father (Freud 1900). Freud originally wrote the dream in baby talk.

Association: None.

Interpretation: Freud used this dream to illustrate how undisguised the wishes are in children's dreams.

Dream: I simply saw myself serving you strawberries for breakfast.

Dreamer: A young woman who was skeptical about a dream interpretation, as reported by Fromm (1951).

Association: When the woman told her husband this dream, she prefaced it by saying, "Tonight I had a dream which shows that there are dreams which have no meaning." After hearing the dream, her husband replied, "You only seem to forget that strawberries are the one fruit which I do not eat" (p.149).

Interpretation: The most obvious meaning of the dream is that the wife passive–aggressively gives the husband something he does not like. However, strawberries and other fruits are often symbolic of genitals (male or female), in which case she may be offering him a form of sex that he does not like.

Stuffed Animals

Dream: I was walking past a store window with a man. I saw that the stuffed animals were moving inside, as though they were alive. There was a black panther, a tiger, a dog. They were moving toward the window. Then I saw that there was a hole in the window and they were trying to get through it. I stuck my hand against the hole to keep them from escaping. They tried to bite my hand, but it only tickled. Some crawled out and bit my feet. I woke up laughing.

Dreamer: A 43-year-old schizoid woman whose husband had recently had a heart attack and died.

Associations: She recalled how much fun she used to have as a child, rolling on the grass having play-fights with her pet dogs. As a toddler she had a stuffed black panther and later a stuffed panda.

Interpretation: The dream is a symbolic dramatization of the internal conflict between her childlike impulses—the stuffed animals—which want to break out and have fun, and the adult who must suppress such impulses for the sake of decorum. In Freudian terms, it is a conflict between the id and the superego. The man in the dream is her dead husband (and her father), whom she must continue to mourn.

Stump

Dream: I watched a man molest a girl through the window. Then I went out into the backyard and there was a stump where there used to be a tree. It was quite odd.

Dreamer: A young man suffering from castration anxiety.

Association: He expressed anxiety about his sexual fantasies.

Interpretation: The stump symbolizes castration. He feared he would be castrated because of his aggressive sexual impulses.

Stuttering

Dream 1: I visit a castle. I do not stutter.

Dream 2: I meet a strange man on the street and attack him.

Dream 3: A notary public opens a will and calls for me.

Dreamer: A man who suffered from stuttering, as reported by W. Bircher (in Gutheil [1951]).

Association: The man's stutter was worse whenever he was around his family. He suspected (and confirmed from subsequent information) he was an illegitimate child whose mother kept this fact from him. Whenever he was around her, he wanted to ask, "Who is my father?" but had to stifle it.

Interpretation: This series of dreams reveals the stutterer's unconscious wishes about his father (he owns a castle, he deserves to be killed for abandoning the dreamer, perhaps he left him an inheritance).

Dream: I wanted to say something to Mary and I found myself stuttering.

Dreamer: A 27-year-old man suffering from impotence.

Association: He and his girlfriend had seen a documentary on stuttering. She had been complaining about their sex life.

Interpretation: Stuttering represents the dreamer's sexual problems with his girl-friend, which he displaces upward as a verbal dysfunction. This upward displace-ment may denote an oral-sadistic rage underlying the impotence.

Suicide

Dream: I was on the subway with a bunch of people from my job. We were talk-ing about Senator Dole's chances [of being elected President]. Suddenly we heard a shot. Turns out a man had killed himself in the next car.

Dreamer: A 33-year-old man suffering from depression.

Association: He thought Senator Dole was a complete fake, and had no charac-ter whatsoever. Senator Dole reminds him of his father.

Interpretation: When the dreamer was 4 years old, his father committed suicide by breathing carbon monoxide. However, on the death certificate the death was called an accident, and this is what his mother insisted on believing. The dreamer associates Senator Dole with his father; his father's death was a fake accident, and Dole was a fake Senator. His father had no character (he gave up and took his own life), and neither did Senator Dole. The man who shot himself on another train was perhaps a symbolic re-creation of his father's suicide, which happened sudden-ly in the next building while he and his brother and sister were playing. Due to his mother's insistence that the suicide was an accident, he never had a chance to properly mourn his father's loss or work through his feelings; hence they kept returning in dreams similar to this one.

Dream: I was sitting in the bathroom and took a razor blade and cut both my wrists. Within a few minutes I was dead.

Dreamer: A 17-year-old suicidal girl.

Association: She had this dream on the night before actually attempting suicide by slashing her wrists. She could no longer stand being alive because of problems with her mother.

Interpretation: Sometimes, during periods of high stress, the manifest content of a dream expresses a wish with very little distortion.

Dream: I was in a strange bedroom. A woman came in, dressed in white like a nurse. She was smiling lovingly. "Take all of these and you'll feel better." She gave me a vial of pills. I took them and fell into a deep sleep and died.

Dreamer: A 30-year-old suicidal woman.

Association: She had felt lonely and isolated from an early age, when she had lost her mother to cancer.

Interpretation: The dream is a wish for somebody to help her commit suicide. That someone is her mother (the loving nurse in white), with whom she identified, and whom she must join in death in order to relieve herself of the sense of loneliness, guilt, and isolation that has plagued her.

Dream: I was climbing up stairs. Then I was on a balcony overlooking a garden. It was a beautiful garden with a patio like you find in Italy. There was a canal below, like the canals in Venice, and I thought of the story, "Death in Venice." I thought about committing suicide. I stood on the railing and started to jump, but changed my mind and landed back on the railing. I was too afraid.

Dreamer: A 40-year-old woman suffering from anxiety and suicidal impulses.

Association: She thought of her ex-husband, whom she had recently divorced, and at whom she was still enraged.

Interpretation: Dreams of suicide are common for people who are depressed, as are fantasies of suicide. Here the dreamer romanticizes her suicidal impulses, alluding to the Thomas Mann story, "Death in Venice," about a man who commits suicide. This fact signifies perhaps her narcissistic wish to compensate for an empty life by going out "in style," by jumping into a canal in romantic Venice. The reference to a story in which a homosexual man commits suicide is probably an allusion to her feelings about her ex-husband, whom she suspected of being gay. In reality, it is he, not herself, she wishes to murder.

Sulk

Dream (poem): "My mother groaned! My father wept./Into the dangerous world I leapt:/Helpless, naked, piping loud:/Like a fiend hid in a cloud./Struggling in my father's hands,/Striving against my swaddling bands,/Bound and weary I thought best/To sulk upon my mother's breast."

Dreamer: William Blake, eighteenth-century British poet.

Associations: Blake saw himself as a visionary, noting that he wrote when commanded by the spirits. As a boy he often had visions of God, angels, and various biblical characters.

Interpretation: Otto Rank (1924) was the first psychoanalyst to write about the trauma of birth. Blake preceded him by a century and a half. The dark imagery of "dangerous world," "fiend hid in a cloud," and "bound and weary," are indications of Blake's sense that from birth onward humans are oppressed by the human condition, leading to a repression of their vitality and sexuality. The pun "sulk" (instead of suck), indicative of oral rage and depression, perhaps predates Klein's (1932) concept of the depressive position.

Sun

Dream: I was in a big, sunny apartment building. Bright green trees outside. It was a party. David embraced me and began to kiss me passionately, very sweetly, in an adolescent way. He whispered, "Can you let all your friends know we're lovers?" He was like a cruder version of himself.

Dreamer: A 29-year-old homosexual man.

Association: He recalled a time when he stayed on his father's ship (his father was a merchant marine) when he was a boy. It was the first time he had seen his father's penis.

Interpretation: The sun symbolizes happiness, rebirth, vitality. The kiss by David represents not only this rebirth but also an acceptance by his symbolic father. David's crudeness (a cruder version of himself) is a sign of the condensation of David and the dreamer's crude merchant marine father.

Dream: I was sitting on my balcony watching the sun go down. For a few minutes the sky was dark. Then the sun came right up again. I was amazed and ran inside to tell Bill.

Dreamer: A young woman mourning the loss of her father.

Association: She had thought that her father, who had died of a heart attack, would want her to go on.

Interpretation: The sun symbolizes the father. The setting and then rising sun signifies his death and transformation. The dreamer has transferred the father imago to her husband Bill. This transfer will enable her to do as her father asked: go on.

Dream (Greek myth): Daedalus and his son Icarus made wings out of feathers and wax and were able to fly. However, despite his father's warnings, Icarus flew too close to the sun and the wax in his wings melted. He fell into the sea and perished.

Interpretation: This myth is a parable. The sun is symbolic of life's dangers. Flying represents sexuality, power, and self-indulgence. The fight can also be seen as a rite of passage into manhood. The lesson is that one must practice moderation or else perish (fall back to the womb/sea).

Dream: The sun and the moon merged. There was an eclipse, but it wasn't dark like an eclipse. It was bright green.

Dreamer: A 45-year-old man.

Association: For some time he had been concerned about the circumstances of his own birth, and whether or not his parents had wanted him.

Interpretation: The sun is father, the moon mother, the eclipse is sexual intercourse, and the bright green represents pregnancy, growth, and vitality. The dreamer is conceived under more happy and majestic circumstances.

Surfing

Dream 1: I was at the beach ready to go surfing but I couldn't find my surfboard.

Dream 2: I took my surfboard out to the water, but as soon as the first wave came it cracked.

Dream 3: Dick and I were at the beach. I wanted to go surfing but he kept talking to someone and we never got into the water.

Dream 4: I was at the beach wanting to go surfing, but the police were there and they said the beach was closed because of a shark scare.

Dream 5: I was driving to the beach but every time I thought I was there it turned out to be the wrong beach.

Dream 6: I was going to go surfing, but somebody yelled out that my mother was on the phone.

Dreamer: A 32-year-old phallic-narcissistic man.

Association: He and his father used to go skin diving in the ocean. His mother did not understand his "fetish" about surfing.

Interpretation: This recurring dream in which the wish to go surfing is interrupted alludes to the dreamer's arrested sexual development. He associates surfing with his father and with their skin diving expeditions. It represents masculine sexual assertiveness; the surfboard is a symbol for the phallus. However, the father, who was competitive with him, unconsciously discouraged the dreamer's masculine confidence, and his mother disparaged male sexuality. Hence, the dreamer cannot ever get on the surfboard in these dreams.

Sweater

Dream: I'm wearing my Norwegian sweater in the presence of an older woman. She is standing above me. "Oh, what a beautiful sweater," she says. "That's just like the sweaters that little children wear in Norway. How sweet." I think, "It's an adult sweater," and I feel very defensive.

Dreamer: A 31-year-old man with narcissistic features and ego-dystonic homosexual impulses.

Association: Peter, a friend, was marveling at my photo album the other day, saying, "My God, you look so young." It reminded me that I used to be told how precocious I was as a child. I feel stunted now, like I'm still a precocious child. The woman reminds me of a friend of my mother's.

Interpretation: The dream is a reference to both the recent incident with Peter and to his precocious childhood and all it represents—particularly his mother's infantilizing of him (symbolized by the scene with the older woman). The sweater stands for this infantilization.

Dream: My girlfriend gave me a new sweater.

Dreamer: A 40-year-old man.

Associations: When he was 5, he fell off his tricycle and cut his head. The next day his mother bought him a new sweater. His girlfriend and he had an argument the night before the dream.

Interpretation: The new sweater means he and his girlfriend will patch things up.

Swimming

Dream: I was swimming in the ocean near Fire Island. I was with an older man, in his forties. Suddenly the waves stopped moving. They were suspended in air, and the water had turned to Jello. I said to the older man, "Look at the water, look what it did." He said, "Look where we are." The water had taken us to the steel mill (like the one my father used to work at). I walked out of the water and took a globule of it to show people. I ran home on the railroad tracks feeling anxious about something.

Dreamer: A 33-year-old man suffering from suicidal urges and ego-dystonic homosexual impulses.

Association: His father worked in a steel mill and the dreamer used to have nightmares about it. He had talked to his father the day before the dream and had felt angry at him.

Interpretation: Swimming denotes sexual intercourse—in this case, a homosexual encounter. Swimming in the ocean and drifting may indicate a deviation from the mainstream—into homosexuality, or a regression to his childhood. The older man is symbolic of the dreamer's father (they ended up at the father's steel mill), for whom the dreamer had unconscious incestuous desires. The water that turns to Jello and is suspended perhaps alludes to the dreamer's father fixation, which keeps him suspended and unable to move on in his life, making him weak (like Jello). The "something" he feels anxious about is his guilt.

T

Tail

Dream: Molly and I were in bed, but it was the bedroom in the house my parents bought when I was an adolescent. Suddenly she said, "Look," and lifted up the blankets. There was a little green lizard in the bed. She caught it by the tail and the tail came off. "Why did you do that?" I asked. "It's all right," she answered, and as we watched, the lizard grew another tail.

Dreamer: A 31-year-old man who suffered from premature ejaculation.

Association: His wife had been complaining about his sexual problems. When he was a boy he had a pet iguana.

Interpretation: The dream indicates the source of the dreamer's problem of premature ejaculation: a castration fear toward his wife. It is also a wish that should he be castrated he will be able to grow his penis back. The fact that the dream takes place in the bedroom of his adolescence alludes to castration, the time he first began to masturbate and have castration fantasies.

Taming

Dream: I was in a lion's cage and I was taming two lions that were very ferocious.

Dreamer: A 27-year-old alcoholic man.

Association: He had gone on an alcoholic binge during which he had been physically abusive to his wife.

Interpretation: The taming of the lions represents his wish to tame his own wildness.

Taxi Driver

Dream: I and a strange man go into a room somewhere, like a massage studio. We fuck with abandon but no feelings. I'm in another city, and I'm making love to a bitchy woman. Again, fucking with abandon but no feelings. Then I'm at somebody's house and I'm afraid of her husband. A male taxi driver with a young prostitute girlfriend tries to kill us.

Dreamer: A bisexual male with impulsive features.

Association: The taxi driver in the dream looked like Robert DeNiro in the movie *Taxi Driver*.

Interpretation: The taxi driver perhaps represents the angry, split-off self of the dreamer while the prostitute is his disowned anima. The dream is an indication of the frantic but loveless sexual encounters that, in fact, he has in real life, for which he feels guilt.

Teeth

Dream: A recurring dream of losing teeth.

Dreamer: Stephen Dedalus, hero of James Joyce's (1918) novel, *Ulysses*.

Association: He has this dream throughout the dream sequences of the novel. Dedalus, according to Joyce, was his autobiographical representative. During these sequences Dedalus was pondering some action or another and unable to decide.

Interpretation: Dreams about losing teeth are among the most common, and generally symbolize a loss of power (harking back to the stage when the human infant gets its first teeth and feels the power and pleasure of chewing). In Joyce's dreams, teeth (incisors?) symbolize decisiveness, and their loss, therefore, represents the loss of the power of decisive action.

Dream: I dream that I am at my office, sitting at my desk, when suddenly a tooth falls out of my mouth. I quickly hide it in the drawer, but then another falls, and another. I'm afraid somebody will see them.

Dreamer: A 32-year-old professional woman.

Association: The day before the dream she lost her temper with her boss and began to cry. She felt quite weak and defeated.

Interpretation: To the dreamer, crying means weakness and defeat. Hence, loss of her teeth in the dream means loss of face. It also points to traumatic episodes in her early childhood in which she was often teased to the point of crying by an older brother, and was made to feel powerless. Finally, it may be an allusion to the oral-sadistic stage when she bit her mother's breast and her mother reacted angrily, leaving her hungry (weak) and defeated.

Dream: I was in a modern house somewhere. Suddenly my teeth broke. They crumbled and fell out of my mouth. I was holding these crumbled teeth in my hands wondering what to do. I went to my father and asked him, "What do I do now?" He replied, "How have you been feeling otherwise?" "Kind of tired."

Dreamer: A 39-year-old man suffering from depression.

Association: He had made love with a new woman and found that he could not ejaculate. After a while he lost his erection.

Interpretation: The crumbling teeth symbolize his loss of sexual potency. His sexual insecurity is related to his father, who was not there for him as a child, and in the dream he is again not there for him. The modern house may stand for the new relationship.

Dream: I'm sitting in a restaurant with my girlfriend when my teeth suddenly start to grow. She says, "You look strange. You look like a monster." I look in the mirror and am appalled.

Dreamer: A 32-year-old passive male.

Association: He feels annoyed at his girlfriend because he always has to pay for everything. But he does not think he has the right to be annoyed about that.

Interpretation: The growing teeth represent his anger at his girlfriend. Since he is in conflict about his anger, he is appalled when he sees his big teeth (anger) in the dream.

Dream: My mother brought home a baby. I went to look at him and he was very big and fat and he had teeth. His teeth looked like snake teeth and I was afraid of him.

Dreamer: A 6-year-old boy.

Association: His mother was pregnant and the boy had been expressing anxiety about the imminent loss of his mother's sole attention.

Interpretation: The baby with fangs is an example of projection. The dreamer wants to kill the new baby, but instead he projects that the baby is a monster who wants to kill him. This is also wish fulfillment; if the baby is a monster, Mother will continue to like the dreamer best.

Dream: I was in bed with Sally and she wanted to have sex with me but I had a toothache and couldn't. She teased me, saying I was just using that as an excuse. Then she looked at my tooth and saw that it was bleeding. She took out a tweezer and started trying to pull it out. I woke up with a toothache.

Dreamer: A young man.

Association: He had gone to sleep wanting to have sex with his wife, but because of the toothache had decided against it.

Interpretation: The dreamer's actual toothache and his day residue thoughts were the manifest content of this dream. However, the teasing of the wife alludes to a childhood relationship with a teasing older sister and his resulting castration fears (pulling the tooth).

Terror

Dream: I was walking in the woods with Tom. We were both naked. We came to a cabin and made love. Then I suddenly became terrified. "Does your wife know about this?" I asked. He kissed me passionately. I was excited, but then I was terrified again. I saw my long hair in the mirror and was afraid I'd lose it.

Dreamer: A 33-year-old woman suffering from agoraphobia.

Association: Tom was a friend of hers to whom she was sexually attracted. She'd had an anxiety attack upon talking to him on the phone a week before, and had since feared leaving her apartment.

Interpretation: The dream is an indication of the source of her agoraphobia. Tom symbolizes her father (toward whom she had an intense oedipal attraction); his wife symbolizes her mother (of whom she was terrified). The fear of losing her hair denotes castration fear. Her agoraphobia is a fear of castration by her mother.

Dream: I opened the window and looked up at the sky. It was a very bright blue and for some reason I was terrified. Maybe it was too calm.

Dreamer: A 27-year-old woman suffering from acrophobia.

Association: The window reminded her of the window of her father's office, 10 stories high, of which she was afraid.

Interpretation: The bright blue calm in the dream indicates the calm before a storm. The storm is the dreamer's negative introject (father), which she fears will lure her into falling out of the window.

Testicles

Dream: I was leading a therapy group of men. Suddenly my testicles became disengaged. I tried to put them back on but they wouldn't stay. There was no blood. I tried to keep running the session but was worried about my testicles the whole time. I wondered whether to cancel the session. The men didn't seem to notice.

Dreamer: A 50-year-old psychotherapist who had formed a new men's group.

Associations: He had recurring dreams about feelings of insecurity around other men, or about other men interfering in his relations with women. He traced these feelings back to his relationships with three brothers and a father.

Interpretation: This is a castration-fear dream. The dreamer, the third son, had been his mother's favorite, and his two older brothers and father had been jealous of this favoritism and acted it out by teasing and devaluing him. The men's group referred not only to the actual men's group he was leading, but also to his relationship with his brothers and father, and indicated the castration fear he still harbored toward them, and which he now transferred onto his men's group. The fact that there was no blood may allude to the wish that he could be castrated and yet still be all right (unbloodied) and that it could be fixed.

Therapist

Dream: I was lying on my therapist's couch. I was relaxed. Then my therapist came over and kissed me. I was very upset.

Dreamer: A 25-year-old woman.

Associations: She said she felt quite ambivalent about men. Her mother, a beauty queen, always made her feel that all men, including her father, were off limits to her.

Interpretation: The therapist is a symbol of her father. She wants to be close to him but is afraid he will make a sexual move. Such a move would horrify her, for it might arouse taboo sexual feelings of her own and jeopardize her mother's approval.

Dream: I dreamed I saw a strange figure. It was my therapist's head and a horse's body, wearing a nightshirt.

Dreamer: A young woman. Reported by Ferenczi (1916).

Associations: The nightshirt was one worn by her father when she slept in her parents' room before the age of 4 and witnessed coitus. The horse was one her nurse at the time took her to see, which was mating with a mare.

Interpretation: Her feelings of sexual curiosity, first aroused by her parents and the horse, were now transferred to the therapist. Freud (1900) saw this dream as an example of how a composite image can be condensed from disparate parts with a common link.

Dream 1: I went to your office and you were with a whole group of people—maybe other patients. You didn't seem to notice me.

Dream 2: I woke up and you were in my room, lying in the other bed. I didn't know why you were there. You looked over and smiled, as if to say, "Don't be nervous."

Dream 3: I was on the street and I saw you walking with a man who I supposed was a colleague. I felt jealous.

Dream 4: I went to your office, but instead of an office there was a field and you were playing football with a group of young men. You gestured for me to join.

Dream 5: You were standing over the couch smiling at me.

Dream 6: I came for my session and instead of a couch you had a twin bed. I lay down and you pointed to a fish tank across the room where there were some eels.

Dream 7: You said it was time for my rectal examination.

Dreamer: A 30-year-old passive male.

Association: He complained that he did not know how to assert himself at work. His father had always been distant.

Interpretation: This series of dreams shows the evolution of the father transference. The dreamer's passive-homosexual thoughts about the therapist have their source in similar unconscious thoughts about his father. The wish in the dream is to bond with the therapist (father) in order to appease oedipal guilt and be initiated into the world of men—thereby enabling him to assert himself.

Dream: I was in my therapy session. I had brought in my journal and you were going to read it. I turned and you were talking with Sally, my old therapist. I was about to apologize for my journal. She said, "There are a few pages of really good writing in this journal."

Dreamer: A 33-year-old man with narcissistic features and ego-dystonic homosexuality.

Association: He had originally gone to his old therapist when he was suicidal. Recently he had begun having both suicidal and homicidal urges, and thought of his old therapist with tender feelings.

Interpretation: The therapists in his dreams represent internalized good objects whom he can use to soothe his suicidal and homicidal urges. The journal represents a recording of these urges, about which he is apologetic. His wish is that his new therapist can be as empathic as his old one.

Dream: I went to my therapist's house and her house was gone. There was only an empty lot with dead weeds in it.

Dreamer: A 40-year-old depressed woman.

Association: When the dreamer was 3, her mother died.

Interpretation: The dreamer fears that her therapist will abandon her as her mother had.

Therapy

Dream: It was like something out of *1984*. I was in a strange world where life was very regimented and everybody had to be in therapy. The government and the courts were run by therapists. If you were caught breaking the law, the punishment was having to face your worst nightmare. One day I was watching this court case. A girl was on trial for abusing herself. I don't remember what she'd done—something like taking drugs. She was pronounced incorrigible, and the jury decided she must be raped as a punishment. Citizens drew lots to see who would have to do the raping. A young man was chosen and reluctantly began stalking the girl. I followed her out of the courtroom and said, "Maybe you can hide." "Nobody can help me," she said. "I've been in therapy all my life and nobody can help me." I felt worried about her, so I took her to my house. Then I went back out and I had her purse for some reason. The guy who had been chosen to do the punishment was stalking me. I turned and said, "I'm not going to let you do it!" He sighed with relief. "I didn't want to do it anyway. But what will we tell the authorities?" "I'll go to my therapy session and cry and say that I was raped," I said. We walked down the street together and I said, "Don't you think it's cruel to make people face their worst nightmares?" He replied, "But maybe it's therapeutic." I began to realize that I regarded therapy as a punishment but one that was indeed what I needed.

Dreamer: A 42-year-old woman suffering from paranoid features.

Associations: She had this dream the night after a group therapy session in which she had spoken about her fears of authority figures and another woman had spoken about rape. She said she thought her worst fear would be finding out what her worst nightmare was.

Interpretation: This is a science fiction parable. She is both the observer and the girl who is punished by having to face her worst nightmare. The dream has many levels of meaning. On one hand, it is a portrait of the repressive, regimented atmosphere of her family environment and of her Catholic school upbringing. On the other hand, it represents the nightmarish, paranoid world as she experienced it in her daily life, in which there was the ever-present fear of being overcontrolled by authority. Finally, it signaled her similar fears about being controlled by her therapist. At the same time, the dreamer comes to her own solution: facing her fears of therapy *is* her worst nightmare, because it means "finding out what her worst nightmare is." This is a turning-point dream.

Thirteen

Dream: I'm floating along Route 13 on my way to a town called Princess Ann. I have no body, I'm just a pair of eyes floating along. But I can't get to Princess Ann, because there are too many mountains and rivers in the way. I'm always on the outskirts, looking at the skyline.

Dreamer: A 37-year-old schizophrenic woman.

Association: She went to college in this town and had a terrible time there. She felt lonely and depressed. She flunked out during her senior year. Her mother's name is Ann.

Interpretation: The number 13 means bad luck and Route 13 represents an ill-fated journey. Princess Ann not only stands for the town where she went to college and flunked out, but on a deeper level it also stands for her mother, whom she idealizes as though she were a fairy princess. In real life she was abandoned by her mother at the age of 5, and the depression she experienced at college was probably related to this earlier abandonment. The dream is perhaps a wish to return to her mother (mountains and rivers signifying not only obstacles but females). The fact that she is floating in the dream is a manifestation of her tendency to depersonalize due to the feeling that she was somehow deprived of a self after her mother departed.

Tie

Dream: I'm at a party and a man comes up to me and begins pulling on my necktie. I pull on his tie as well, and I pull it off. Some of the women are laughing.

Dreamer: A 25-year-old borderline man.

Association: When he was at parties, he always felt very competitive with the other men.

Interpretation: The tie pulling represents castration. He fears other men will castrate him, so he must castrate them first. The women laughing may be his mother and sister, who were bemused at the competition that he engaged in with his older brothers.

Tiger

Dream: A tiger jumped into the bathtub and ate my sister. Then he came into my room and he let me ride him.

Dreamer: A 9-year-old boy.

Association: He and his sister had been fighting over a present they had received for Christmas.

Interpretation: The tiger represents the boy's externalized aggression, expressing his wish to get rid of his sister. Riding the tiger means enlisting the tiger's aggression for himself (asserting his masculinity).

Time

Dream (painting): His own shrunken head was hanging over some rocks in a barren landscape. A clock was draped over his head, as though it were melting in the sun. Three more clocks were draped over a table of some kind and from the branch of a leafless tree. One clock, lying face down, had a cluster of ants on it; another had a solitary fly.

Dreamer: Salvador Dali, Spanish surrealist painter.

Association: In his painting *The Persistence of Memory,* Dali was attempting to convey the oppressiveness of time and memory. He claimed that the idea for the painting came to him while he was daydreaming about the nature of Camembert cheese. In many of his dreams, he reported afterwards, he was struggling with guilt about sex and masturbation.

Interpretation: This dream/painting portrays Dali's obsession with time and death—two themes that pervade nearly all of his paintings. The clocks draped over his head and hanging from the table and tree symbolize the weight of time's passing. The barren landscape and the insects may represent the unwanted memories that eat away like insects inside the psyche. The overall effect is a depressive mood, perhaps indicative of Dali's own melancholy. The shrunken head of Dali found in this and other paintings probably denotes not only time passing but Dali's inferiority complex and, perhaps, a sense of oedipal guilt or inferiority (small, disgusting penis). The fact that he was meditating about the nature of cheese when he had this dream may allude to the fact that cheese turns sour over time. So did Dali's inner world.

Dream: I dreamed I was dozing and wanted to know the time. I looked at the radio and saw it was five o'clock. I thought I heard my mother in the other room, and then woke up for real and realized I was in my own apartment.

Dreamer: A 32-year-old depressed woman.

Association: Her mother had died when the dreamer was 5 years old.

Interpretation: Five o'clock in the dream actually means 5 years old. The dreamer returns to the age at which her mother died and harbors the wish that she were still alive. This is an example of dream distortion in which time and age become interchangeable.

Dream: I was rushing to catch a train because I had waited until the last minute. I was afraid I wouldn't get everything done before I left. Each time I started to leave, I found something else I needed to do. However, when I reached the station I suddenly had roller skates on and sped along at an amazing speed. I made the train.

Dreamer: A 76-year-old former ballerina suffering from anxiety.

Association: She was in the process of writing her memoirs. She worried about her health.

Interpretation: The train represents death. "The last minute" stands for the last years of her life. She is afraid she won't be able to finish her memoirs and other projects before she dies, and hopes she can miraculously (roller skates) find a way.

Tinfoil

Dream: Old Brueck gave the dreamer a problem to solve, made a microscopic slide, and picked out something that looked like tinfoil.

Dreamer: Sigmund Freud. Reported in *The Interpretation of Dreams* (1900).

Associations: He associated tinfoil with *staniol*, a Viennese expression for tinfoil, and *Stannius*, a famous psychologist who wrote a pioneering article on the nervous system of a kind of fish. Professor Brueck was his teacher of physiology during his days in medical school.

Interpretation: Dreams in which the dreamer returns to a school he once attended are common. In such cases, the institute or the teachers represent a fixation point in the dreamer's development, to which he returns in his dream. All his life Freud sought encouragement from mentors (the blessings of father figures) as he diverged from the narrow path of medicine to the pioneering path of psychoanalysis. In this dream, tinfoil, according to Freud's association, represents Stannius, the psychologist, so it seems to be a wish that old Brueck (his father figure) would give him his blessing to leave medicine and go into psychology. *Bruecke* in German means *bridge*; hence Brueck may symbolize Freud's bridge from medicine to psychology.

Toys

Dream (play fantasy): The small child ran a toy carriage toward her therapist and said, "I've come to fetch you." She put a toy woman in the carriage, then a toy man, and had them "love and kiss" one another. Then she had another toy man in another carriage collide with the loving couple, run over them, kill them, and roast and eat them up. At another point she took a toy engine with two gilded lamps into her mouth and sucked on the lamps, then asked her therapist to do the same.

Dreamer: Erna, a 2½-year-old girl, reported by Klein (1932).

Associations: Erna's comments led her therapist, Melanie Klein, to believe that her fantasies were usually about her mother, although she denied being angry at her. Her mother said she had toilet-trained Erna prematurely (before the age of one).

Interpretation: Klein interpreted play fantasies as she would the dreams of adults. Hence, toys in play fantasies were interpreted as dream symbols. In the above play she noted the oral-sadistic impulses directed by the dreamer against her parents. The man and woman who "love and kiss" are her parents, and the other man who kills, roasts, and eats them represents the dreamer. Putting the toy engine in her mouth and sucking on the lamps has an oral-erotic meaning. The two lamps "stood to her for her mother's breast and her father's penis" (p. 37). The dream, according to Klein, indicated Erna's paranoid-schizoid position, with megalomaniacal fantasies that led to excessive fear of the mother and contributed to the formation of a harsh superego.

Trains

Dream: The dreamer was in Spain and wanted to take the train to a place called Daraus, Varaus, or Zaraus.

Dreamer: Havelock Ellis, British psychologist, as reported by Freud (1900).

Associations: A few months after having this dream he found out that Zaraus was in fact the name of a train station on the line between San Sabastian and Bilbao, through which his train had passed about seven months before he had the dream.

Interpretation: The instigating agent of the dream is the experience in Spain when his train passed through Zaraus. Probably this station is a screen memory for something that happened in the past to which he is fixated. Confusion about a station may represent some confusion in his life.

Dream: I'm sitting in the engine of a train. The train goes into a tunnel. At the end of the tunnel is a brick wall and my mother is tied up against the wall. The engine crashes into her and I wake up in a fright.

Dreamer: A 28-year-old woman with multiple personalities.

Association: She recalled that her mother sexually abused her as a very small child, sticking her fingers and the necks of whiskey bottles into her vagina.

Interpretation: This is a dream of revenge. The tunnel represents her mother's vagina and the engine symbolizes phallic aggression by the patient's male personality, who violently rapes and kills the mother.

Dream: I was naked and sitting on the bumper of the engine of a train that was rushing down a track. The train was going through a forest on Long Island where I grew up. It went over a pond and a snake jumped out and bit me.

Dreamer: A 31-year-old man who was a recovering alcoholic and had voyeuristic and exhibitionistic tendencies.

Association: He said the snake was his mother and that the pond reminded him of the pond at an elementary school he attended. He said the train was also driven by his mother.

Interpretation: The train symbolized his phallic-narcissistic sexuality (including his voyeurism, exhibitionism, and other perverse drives). His mother had "driven" him to this form of perverse sexuality by relating to him in an inappropriately sexualized way (she herself being an alcoholic), but she had also castrated him by refusing to let go of him and undermining his confidence (the snake biting him).

Dream: I was trying to get to the train, but my feet were stuck in something like glue.

Dreamer: A 39-year-old woman who is burdened with taking care of her elderly parents.

Association: The night of the dream she had been invited to go to the country with friends for the weekend and had to decline.

Interpretation: She was "stuck" to her parents (dependent), and feared she was "missing the train."

Dream: I was waiting at the train station. A woman next to me said, "I've been waiting for 45 minutes." I went home to ask my father for his car. I found him naked on the bed in his room, reading the newspaper. I asked for the car keys and he gave them to me with a strange look in his eyes.

Dreamer: A 27-year-old hysterical woman.

Association: She recalled that her father made noises when he ate soup or drank coffee, and these noises would excite her and she would go to her room and masturbate aggressively. Her father would look at her embarrassedly when she was an adolescent.

Interpretation: The train she is waiting for perhaps represents her father or her father's phallus, as do the keys to the car. The dream is a wish for her father's acceptance, which she thinks she may get through sexual surrender to him. Oral associations (her father's noises) may relate to repressed memories of witnessing the primal scene.

Dream: I was on a train going somewhere. I kept going from car to car. I couldn't find my sleeping compartment.

Dreamer: A 45-year-old woman.

Association: The dreamer had recently lost her apartment.

Interpretation: The dream reflects the dreamer's current homeless condition.

Dream: I was at the train station and I kept getting on one train and then getting on another. As soon as I got onto one train, I'd think, "No, this isn't it." And then I'd find another and another. Each train didn't seem like the right one.

Dreamer: A 36-year-old computer analyst.

Association: She had been feeling that she was behind in her work as an analyst.

Interpretation: She interpreted that the metaphor in the dream of going from train to train and never feeling it was enough was a visual pun telling her that she needed more "training" in computer analysis so that she could keep up with her job.

Dream: I was in a train that kept stopping and starting. Each time it stopped, new passengers would step aboard. I resented these new passengers, because I felt they were keeping me from getting to my destination.

Dreamer: A 31-year-old obsessive-compulsive man.

Association: Whenever as a child he took a car trip with his mother, she was always making unscheduled stops and it irritated him.

Interpretation: The stopping and starting of the train, taking on new passengers, harks back to his early childhood when his mother gave birth to one new sibling after another, which prevented the dreamer from reaching his destination (arrested his development). The memory of his mother stopping and starting is a screen memory.

Transplant

Dream: I was on an operating table and they were giving me a heart transplant.

Dreamer: A 45-year-old narcissistic male.

Association: His girlfriend had recently accused him of being "hopelessly cynical."

Interpretation: The transplanted heart represents a rebirth of innocence.

Transsexual

Dream: My girlfriend gave me a gift certificate to a transsexual movie house. When I got there I found that I was supposed to have sex with a transsexual. I felt betrayed by my girlfriend.

Dreamer: A 32-year-old male with transsexual impulses and gender-identity confusion.

Associations: He expressed a fear that his girlfriend was a lesbian. As a boy, he had been displaced by two younger sisters. He was made to feel that he was the wrong sex; if he were female, his mother would still love him.

Interpretation: The transsexualism symbolizes the dreamer's wish to change his sex in order to be loved by his girlfriend (his mother and sisters). At the same time, he feels betrayed, just as he had once felt betrayed by his mother when she favored his two younger sisters over him.

Trap Door

Dream: I was walking over the roofs of houses. I went into the window of one of the houses and saw this trap door partly hidden by a rug. I pulled up the trap door and it led down a spiral staircase to a woman's bedroom. She was taking a shower. I asked her where the Appalachian trail was, and she gave me directions. I found some yellow sneakers, just my size. A man came in and said, "You know what those sneakers are called? Boat shoes." He and I walked onto the roof.

Dreamer: A 40-year-old man with voyeuristic tendencies.

Associations: The day before the dream he had thought about asking his father to buy him a pair of sneakers for Christmas. He had always been intrigued by trap doors. The woman reminded him of his mother.

Interpretation: Houses symbolize women, and the trap door often signifies entry into women's erotic secrets (their vaginas). The woman taking a shower is perhaps his mother. She gives him directions to the Appalachian trail, which perhaps signifies the path to manhood—the dreamer and his father had been fond of hiking and camping. The man in the dream is the dreamer's father, and wearing his sneakers means "wearing his father's shoes." He had always felt inferior to his father in real life, so this dream represents his oedipal wish to separate from his mother and bond with his father.

Traumatic Stress

Dream 1: I'm walking on a street. A car races around the corner and is about to hit me. I wake up trembling and sweating and all stressed out.

Dream 2: A motorcycle spins out of control and races toward me.

Dream 3: My car stalls on the train tracks. I hear a train whistle.

Dream 4: I'm in a building and it suddenly collapses.

Dream 5: I'm walking along a beach when the tide suddenly rises and a huge tidal wave knocks me down.

Dream 6: I'm walking on a wooden footbridge. The boards are rotten and I fall through.

Dream 7: A rock falls from a building a few feet in front of me.

Dream 8: A bus flips over but I get away.

Dream 9: A car comes toward me but I jump on top of the hood and ran my feet into the windshield, killing the driver.

Dreamer: A 40-year-old man suffering from post-traumatic stress disorder.

Association: He had been hit by a car as he was crossing the street and had been hospitalized for several months.

Interpretation: This series of dreams shows the dreamer's therapeutic progress as he works through the traumatic stress of the accident. Such dreams are attempts to master a situation that originally overwhelmed the ego and left it in shock. By the last dream, he had managed not only to get away but also to kill the driver (discharging the anger connected with his injury).

Tree

Dream (Chinese parable): Nan Po was walking along when he came upon a large and unusual tree. But when he looked at the branches, he saw that they were so twisted that they could not be made into boards or posts; the trunk was so gnarled it could not be made into a coffin or boat. When he licked the leaves, his tongue was cut and bleeding. When he sniffed the air, the odor of the tree was horrible and his mind became drunk and frantic. "Ah, yes," he said, "this tree is indeed good for nothing, and so it has become one of the largest trees of all."

Dreamer: Chuang Zi, in his ancient Chinese parable of "The Useless Tree."

Association: He was a follower of Lao Zi, who wrote of a stoic life.

Interpretation: The tree here symbolizes a kind of man and a philosophy of life. In Taoist philosophy, uselessness is considered a virtue. Uselessness, psychoanalytically, perhaps means not having neurotic or narcissistic needs to be smart, to be helpful, to be rich, to be loved, to be powerful, to be famous, et cetera—needs that can be exploited by others and result in the loss of the self. It means keeping a low profile, not flaunting oneself, or overextending oneself, and staying centered in oneself.

Tribe

Dream: I'm part of a tribe and we're all wonderfully naked. One of the men leads me down into a fertile valley and whispers, "You're free." He kneels to drink the syrup between my thighs. I hear people yelling up on the hill, but I don't care. Then I'm in a garden and there are flowers bursting into bloom all around me. My own vulva blossoms into a yellow flower. On the hill I hear the tribe chanting, "Yes, yes, yes!" I wake up masturbating, feeling immensely excited. The dream remained vividly in my mind for days.

Dreamer: A 32-year-old woman.

Associations: The man in the dream reminds her of her brother, John. She has always been attracted to her brother and envious of his lack of inhibition. Her parents seemed to give him much more freedom than they gave her.

Interpretation: This is a breakthrough dream, connoting the dreamer's separation from her parents (the people yelling on the hill) and her sexual and spiritual liberation. The intensity and vividness of the dream underscore its significance to the dreamer and perhaps point to the unleashing of formerly repressed feelings. The naked tribe probably signifies both a regression back to the archaic innocence and nakedness of early childhood and family life, and the primitive passion of sexuality. Her brother, whose freedom she envies, serves as the springboard to her own liberation.

Tunnel

Dream: I was crawling through tunnels. They were in an embankment by a river. I crawled in and out of the tunnels. I sensed that my mother was observing me as I did so. At one point a baby rabbit chewed on my finger, but it didn't hurt. Next I was in my house and I had a diagram explaining the tunnels.

Dreamer: A 32-year-old man with severe narcissistic features.

Association: His mother had not wanted him and tried to abort him. When she was angry, she would pull up her skirt and show him the birth scar from her Caesarean operation, yelling, "See? See what you did to me?"

Interpretation: The tunnels perhaps symbolize his mother's vagina. The rabbit whose bite doesn't hurt denotes benign pregnancy. The dream represents his wish to go back to her uterus and be born again. Perhaps if he learns how to exit the correct way (through the vagina), without causing so much pain, his mother will accept him. The diagram connotes his wished-for expertise at the birthing process.

Dream: I was walking down a long tunnel. It kept getting smaller and smaller and I couldn't breathe.

Dreamer: A 27-year-old woman suffering from claustrophobia.

Association: She thought about going to church with her mother. She always felt hemmed in at church, and wished her mother would stop making her feel guilty when she did not want to go.

Interpretation: The tunnel represents church and her mother's suffocation of her through guilt induction.

U

Umbrella

Dream: I was on a park bench. A woman walked up and sat on the other end of the bench. She had a white umbrella and placed it on the bench so that it was pointing toward me. I got an erection and became agitated and had to leave.

Dreamer: A 28-year-old man with an umbrella fetish.

Association: When he was a little boy, his mother had a white umbrella like the one in the dream.

Interpretation: The umbrella is a phallic symbol; hence the woman with a white umbrella represents an innocent woman with a phallus (his idealized view of his childhood mother). The dream is a straightforward dramatization of the dreamer's umbrella fetish. Fetishistic objects often denote the unconscious wish by the fetishist that his mother and all women have penises, which assuages guilt and castration fear.

Underwear

Dream: I was in a strange house looking in a chest of drawers. I found a pair of men's underwear and was disappointed. A woman lived upstairs in the house, but she wasn't there. Then I was walking through a field and came upon a pond. A woman was swimming in the pond, and she had a small child with her. I hid behind a bush so she wouldn't see me. She was wearing a bathing suit that looked like underwear. Suddenly she saw me and said, "You've been following me around." I squirted her with a water gun.

Dreamer: A 37-year-old man with transvestic and voyeuristic tendencies.

Associations: He recalled that when he was a teenager he and his friend would break into houses. The house in the dream was like the house in which he grew up.

Interpretation: The dream expresses his tranvestic and voyeuristic tendencies. He is disappointed to find the men's underwear, but attracted to the women's underwear (which, in real life, he wears and is for him a fetish). The imagery harks back to the situation in his early childhood when he was displaced in his mother's affection by the arrival of a new sibling. He found himself distanced from the mother and her new child (as he was in the dream), and had to be content to gaze at them from a distance. Squirting her with the water gun perhaps denotes his wish to have sex with her (possess his mother).

Dream 1: I was in a house and there was a party. Two older women were flirting with me. They were dangerous, involved in illicit activities. One said to me, seductively and confessionally, "We were both going to bed with you before." Then they both left the room. I went upstairs and looked through their underwear drawer.

Dream 2: I was sitting on a blue sofa. There was a woman sitting on the other end of the sofa in her underwear. I got excited; then I realized it was my mother and I felt guilty.

Dreamer: A 40-year-old obsessive-compulsive man.

Association: His mother had a blue sofa. She was an alcoholic who used to walk around in her underwear in front of him.

Interpretation: The seductive older women in both dreams stand for his mother, who had been inappropriately seductive as he was growing up. He had developed a fetish for underwear, and that fetish is explained in this dream, as a curiosity and obsession with his mother's sexuality, with which she teased him. Freud saw such fetishistic objects as phallic symbols; that is, the underwear represents the phallic woman common in the fantasies and dreams of little boys. Such fantasies compensate for guilt about possessing a member that the mother does not have.

Unicorn

Dream (medieval myth): The unicorn had the legs of a buck, the tail of a lion, and the head and body of a horse, with a single horn in the middle of his forehead. His body was white, his head red, his eyes blue. He was so strong that he was the only animal that could attack the elephant. The only way hunters could catch a unicorn was to place a young virgin nearby. No sooner did the animal see the damsel than he ran toward her and lay down at her feet, allowing himself to be captured.

Interpretation: According to medieval folklore, the unicorn symbolized Christ while the virgin represented the Virgin Mother, who bore him, and from whose womb he sprang in order to take on the sins of the world. Psychoanalytically, the unicorn is a symbol of purity and masculine vitality (the horn denoting an erect penis).

Dream: I was sitting with Anne. We heard something in the back yard and looked around to see a unicorn.

Dreamer: A 32-year-old passive male.

Association: He had problems of impotency with Anne, his girlfriend.

Interpretation: The unicorn represented a wish for potency.

Urine

Dream (fictional): After his shipwreck he was washed ashore on a land called Lilliput, where the people were about the size of mice and he was a giant. One evening he was awakened by cries of hundreds of people at his door. Several of the Emperor's court entreated him to come immediately to the palace, where the queen's apartment was on fire due to the carelessness of a maid of honor. When he got there the fire had grown so fierce that the little buckets that were handed to him—the size of thimbles—did little good. Fortunately, he had the evening before drunk a good deal of a delicious wine called glimigrin, and the heat of the fire began to operate on his urine, which he "voided in such a quantity, and applied so well to the proper places, that in three minutes the fire was wholly extinguished..."

Dreamer: Jonathan Swift, through his character Gulliver, in *Gulliver's Travels* (1726).

Association: Swift had a reputation as a misanthropist. He never married nor did he even, it appeared, have sexual relations with a woman, although he carried on a distant amorous correspondence with a younger woman.

Interpretation: Swift's fantasy of Gulliver, a man who towers over everybody else, is the kind of fantasy that is common in children who in their dreams compensate for resentment about being smaller than adults. In the fragment paraphrased above, the queen's apartment is on fire and the giant dreamer douses it by urinating on it. This may be an oedipal fantasy. The queen symbolizes the mother and the king the father. Fire represents passion—in this case, passion gone wild. It may also symbolize the dreamer's anger at his mother and women. The dreamer's mode of rescue of his mother harks to boyhood fantasies in which phallic prowess is associated with urinating long and far. It may also allude to bed-wetting and shaming in Swift's own childhood. Freud (1905) linked bed-wetting with "playing with fire."

Dream: The dreamer was in bed and urinated. A woman was lying in bed looking on. She was red and stout. He grabbed at her breasts; she did not object. She showed him her vagina; it was ugly. He did not want to have anything to do with her.

Dreamer: Emanuel Swedenborg, the Swedish scientist who suffered from paranoia. Reported in Gutheil (1951).

Association: Swedenborg had a fear of women, which he traced back to a problematic relationship with his mother.

Interpretation: The red and stout woman represents the dreamer's mother. Her vagina is ugly because it arouses the dreamer's phallic guilt (at having a penis) and his disgust of incest. The bed-wetting perhaps stems from scenes in childhood during which he wet the bed as a means of getting attention and sympathy from his mother. It was then that he probably first had feelings of shame about his incestuous urges.

Vacuum

Dream: I was floating around in a vacuum somewhere in outer space. There was nothing but blackness and not even a sound. I felt very lonely.

Dreamer: A 37-year-old woman suffering from depression.

Association: Her mother had died while giving birth to her. She had been raised by her father and stepmother. She kept a picture of her real mother in her purse and looked at it often. She wondered what it would have been like had she not died.

Interpretation: The vacuum stands for several things. First, it represents the physical sensation of depression, which feels like a dark, empty, isolated existence. Second, it represents a wish to reunite with her mother, to go back to her womb. Third, it perhaps imparts the state of suspended growth (like a vacuum) in which she was put following her mother's death, never having had a chance to mourn and work through the feelings of loss, guilt, and anger.

Vagina

Dream: The dreamer dreams of Aunt Annie Heller, Deaconness of the old Presbyterian Church. She is lying on top of a rumpled bed in a restaurant, right alongside the cash register, which is being constantly rung up. Her nightgown is pulled up over her thighs, exposing her completely. She calls to him to join her in the bed, insisting that he strip right in front of the guests who are at the tables surrounding the bed. He is shocked by this indecency and protests, but to no avail. Finally he crawls in and forgets entirely about the environment. Then he notices her vagina. By some magic she has but to touch it and it is transformed—like little Japanese papers in a glass of water, which open up before your eyes into magnificent and astounding shapes.

Dreamer: Henry Miller, American author. The dream was recorded in his *Nightmare Notebook* (1975) when he was in his late thirties.

Association: Miller notes that this aunt in reality had absolutely no sexual appeal, and was physically ugly, ignorant, narrow, and tight-fisted. She was completely opposite to his mother.

Interpretation: This dream represents a displacement onto his aunt of the emotionally incestuous relationship Miller actually had with his mother. In the dream, he defends against his guilt by attributing the sexual impulses to an aunt who is in fact antisexual. (In Miller's early childhood, during the phallic narcissistic stage, his mother had sexually teased him and then accused him of being "naughty." This led to his fixation with phallic sexual themes in his novels. This fixation and how it was transformed into a creative release can be detected in the image of Aunt Annie's phallic vagina, with its "magnificent and astounding shapes.")

Dream: I was lying somewhere and my balls and penis had fallen off. I tried to put them back on, but they wouldn't stay. I was very sad about it. I felt really dejected. Then I looked down and there was a big opening like a vagina between my legs.

Dreamer: A 42-year-old man suffering from alcoholism and paranoia.

Association: The day before the dream, he had had an argument with his boss, whom he saw as a father figure.

Interpretation: The dreamer's mother had been an alcoholic who had, when drunk, attacked her son's masculinity. His father had been overbearing and competitive. The dream indicates the man's unconscious retreat from the masculinity that had been so scorned by his mother and had provoked his father's competition. He transfers both mother and father onto his boss, toward whom he attributes murderous wishes. He can escape the murderous wishes of this boss—and his parents—by becoming a woman.

Dream 1: I'm in a room. It's an unusual room, because it's sort of L-shaped and there's half a wall in the middle of it.

Dream 2: A long rectangular room with a window at each end.

Dream 3: A room with a high ceiling that spirals around and around like a beehive.

Dream 4: I walk down a hallway into a room and I see somebody sitting on a rocking chair.

Dream 5: I'm in a dark, closed in place. I can't breathe.

Dream 6: I'm in a large, narrow loft. I can see a woman in a window across the alley.

Dream 7: I'm in bed with Sally. I go down on her, and suddenly I shrink and become very small and I'm able to stick my head inside her vagina. Then I find that by squeezing my shoulders together I can actually climb inside. Then I get even smaller and I'm able to crawl up her vagina into her uterus.

Dreamer: A 38-year-old narcissistic man with a birth trauma.

Association: His mother had a rocking chair like the one in the fourth dream. The woman in the window looked like his mother.

Interpretation: This series of seven dreams, which were had over a period of several years, show the progress of the analysis. In the beginning, the dreamer's symbols were abstract—just bare rooms symbolizing the womb. Then there were clues such as his mother's rocking chair and the woman in the window (both symbolizing his mother). Finally came the last dream, which emerged during an intense relationship with a woman toward whom he had a mother transference. Recent research (Piontelli 1992) using ultrasound has shown that the fetus is very much alive inside the mother's womb, playing, kicking, sucking its thumb, masturbating, and responding to the mother's moods and movements. Infants and toddlers apparently retain a memory of the womb, and adults likewise retain it in their body ego. Research has also indicated that traumas can occur during gestation or the birth process (i.e., lengthy deliveries are more likely to cause a mother to be initially rejecting, thereby causing a birth trauma to the infant). The dreamer's mother was perhaps of this variety.

Dream: I dreamed that I was curled up on the floor in the corner of my room, and then I slipped off my panties and began to slither up my own vagina. It was strange.

Dreamer: A 25-year-old woman with homosexual impulses.

Association: She complained that she did not enjoy sexual intercourse with her husband and found herself looking at other women.

Interpretation: The image of a woman "slithering" up her own vagina is akin to the archetypal symbol of the snake devouring its tail, which stands for rebirth. At the same time, it can be seen as an indication of narcissism (falling in love with herself), which at the same time represents homosexuality (falling in love with somebody similar to oneself).

Vampire

Dream: I was in an ambulance and I was dead. Lying beside me was a black girl and she was still alive. I took a syringe and stuck it into her neck and sucked out her blood. She died and I came alive, like a vampire. Then I was at my mother's house. She was there with some women friends. I did the same thing to them, sucked out all their blood, and they died and I lived.

Dreamer: A 30-year-old schizoid and homosexual male.

Associations: The day of the dream, he had encountered an aggressive, black bank teller who had been rude to him. He recalled how his mother had ignored him after she had divorced his father, and had formed a close relationship with his younger sister. He had always felt left out.

Interpretation: Dreams of vampires are common among a certain type of passive male. The dreamer's deadness represents his feeling that his life or blood had been sucked from him in his early childhood, particularly after his parents' divorce, which he was never allowed to mourn. His mother displaced her anger at the dreamer's father onto the dreamer himself, attacking his masculinity and aligning herself with her daughter against her son. A reversal occurs in the dream wherein he first sucks the blood out of the black woman (symbolizing both the rude bank teller and a shadow image of his mother), and then his mother and her friends (his mother and sister).

Dream: A vampire broke into my bedroom while I was sleeping. He lay on top of me and bit into my breast. Suddenly blood was all over the place. I knew I was going to die if I couldn't get help. I called out for my uncle, who was sleeping in the same room, but he didn't hear me.

Dreamer: A 45-year-old woman suffering from hysteria and migraine headaches.

Association: She recalled that her uncle had touched her inappropriately as a child. She also recalled that her mother had recently told her that when she was an infant she had bitten her mother's nipple and made it bleed. After that, her mother refused to breast-feed her again.

Interpretation: The dream is an allusion to her uncle's molestation. The vampire suggests the brutality of the incident from her child's eyes. The uncle's sleeping in the same room and the fact that she calls on him to rescue her represents her wish that he had been a different kind of man. The oral nature of the fantasy also refers to the stage of oral-sadism, when infants first get their teeth and bite their mother's breast; in her unconscious she links her uncle's molestation to oral rage (rage she herself experienced toward her mother, who weaned her during this stage of teething).

Van

Dream: I was riding in the back seat of a van. Two young guys were sitting in the front—handsome construction-worker types in knitted shirts and shorts. The two guys were bantering to each other in a jovial, heterosexual way. I whispered into the driver's ears (as if I were one of the boys), "I'd really like to make that handsome body of yours feel good." He turned around and had a blade in his hand. "I could cut you for that," he said. "I was only making a joke," I replied. "Calm down. Sure, I'm gay." They stopped the van and let me out. The next day I was sitting in a cafe with the driver and we were having a nice chat.

Dreamer: A 29-year-old man with ego-dystonic homosexuality.

Association: The day before the dream he had almost been hit by a van. He thought at the time that he was feeling suicidal and wanted to be hit. He had recently been rejected by a lover.

Interpretation: The van symbolizes masculinity (a phallic symbol). The dreamer hates his own homosexuality and all it connotes to him, and hates heterosexual men who spurn him. He wants them either to accept his homosexuality or kill him. In his adolescence he had similar feelings toward his hostile father, who had disdain for him and called him a "sissy" and "Mama's Boy." However, in the ending of the dream, his wish to be accepted is fulfilled.

Vein

Dream: I was in a cave looking for gold. Sharon was with me. Suddenly she said, "Look, there's a vein of gold." I shined my flashlight and saw something hanging down the wall of the cave. But it didn't look like gold, it looked like a human vein, with blood rushing through it. I held it in my fingers and sure enough it had a pulse.

Dreamer: A 48-year-old man.

Association: Recently he had complained to his wife, Sharon, about his frustrated ambitions. An aspiring actor, all his life he had dreamed of being rich and famous, but had not found the "golden" role that would advance him to stardom.

Interpretation: The vein in the cave, which is not of gold but of human blood, is perhaps a message to the dreamer from his unconscious that he is looking for gold in the wrong place. Contentment comes from within, not from without.

Video

Dream: I was visiting a gay friend. He was showing his friends a new video. In the video, he and his lover were having anal sex. Then he takes a pistol from the table and shoots his lover. After the video was finished, he asked for feedback. I wanted to tell him that the way he presented homosexuality was stupid, stereotypical, but I didn't want to hurt his feelings.

Dreamer: A young woman with latent homosexual impulses.

Association: She recalled a former lover who had rats for pets and would take them to bed with him.

Interpretation: The video symbolizes both the homosexual man's and the dreamer's unconscious. It reveals not only the man's homosexual and violent tendencies, but also her own rage at men (the former lover who took rats to bed) displaced onto her friend. Her critique—that his treatment of homosexuality was stereotypical—denotes her inner struggle with her own homosexuality.

Vines

Dream: I was sitting against a tree when vines came out and wrapped themselves around me. I couldn't get free.

Dreamer: A young, schizoid woman.

Association: She had argued with her mother about moving out.

Interpretation: The vines represent her mother's clinging, the tree her mother (mother nature). The dream reflects her real-life situation.

Volcano

Dream: Bob and I were driving somewhere in his car. Suddenly I looked over toward some mountains, and they suddenly turned into volcanoes. Three or four of them rose up and erupted, spewing out beautiful configurations of lights that looked like fireworks. We stopped the car on the side of the road and watched with amazement, and then suddenly we were making love and it was very exciting, as if the fireworks had inspired us.

Dreamer: A 30-year-old woman.

Association: On the day before—July 4th—she had seen a fireworks display. She had had the thought that there were no fireworks in her relationship with her boyfriend, and regretted that it had become so routine and boring.

Interpretation: The volcano emitting fireworks indicates the dreamer's wish that her boyfriend would become more potent and passionate (like a volcano).

Vulture

Dream: A vulture swooped down into the back yard while Bill was mowing the lawn. He rushed inside and I hugged him.

Dreamer: A 34-year-old woman.

Association: She was angry that Bill had had an affair.

Interpretation: She wishes death (the vulture) for her husband because of his philandering (mowing the lawn). Hugging him symbolizes her guilt for having the death wish.

Wall

Dream: I was in some kind of yard. There was a high brick wall all around, but I didn't know if it was to keep me in or keep others out. Maybe both. It was cold inside, but I had some animals in a stable—sheep, pigs, and chickens—which I could kill and eat. I made a chicken broth and it was delicious.

Dreamer: A 33-year-old man with schizoid features.

Association: He thought maybe the wall was the wall he put around himself.

Interpretation: The wall connotes the dreamer's schizoid withdrawal from other people. Raised in a dysfunctional family, he had erected an emotional wall to protect himself from the aggression that he projected onto external objects. The animals that he kills perhaps represent members of his family, whom he devours (oral-incorporation and introjection). The dream also is a wish to be self-reliant and self-nourished (the broth).

Dream: For some reason I went to my job at night. I thought I had forgotten something. When I got inside, I found that there was graffiti all over the wall. Tom was with me and I said, "Look at all of this. I wonder who did it." Then I couldn't remember what I had come there for.

Dreamer: A 32-year-old businesswoman.

Association: Things had been going badly at work and she was feeling anxious about it.

Interpretation: The wall with graffiti was a warning: the dream was telling her to pay attention to the "writing on the wall." She was on the verge of being fired because she had been chronically coming late to work.

Dream: My mother and I were walking on a street. Suddenly we saw a man on the wall of a skyscraper. He was making his way up the side of the building. Police were telling him to come down, but he wouldn't. He waved everybody away.

Dreamer: A 37-year-old man suffering from anxiety.

Association: His mother was nagging him constantly.

Interpretation: The dream was confirming for him that his mother's constant nagging was making him feel like "climbing the wall."

War

Dream (fictional): ". . . she was among hordes of war-crushed people for whom she was responsible." She awoke, saw the strong light in the chintz curtains, and thought, "That's France, but what about the concentration camps in Germany?" Then she fell into another feverish sleep and saw herself in Germany, "holding back brutality there, but tormented that she was forgetting France, or Russia, or some other place for which she was responsible."

Dreamer: Doris Lessing, British novelist, through her heroine, Martha Quest, in *A Ripple from the Storm* (1964).

Associations: This novel and the four other novels of the series called *Children of*

Violence are all autobiographical. A guilt-ridden obsessive, Quest had the above dream while sick with fever and delirium. She had joined a Communist political organization and now felt pressured by her responsibility.

Interpretation: The protagonist of the novel (Lessing's alter ego) had fallen sick from worry over her responsibilities. In the dream, the hordes of war-crushed people, the concentration camp victims, perhaps all symbolize the weight of not only the responsibilities she felt in her present life, but also harked back to guilt that first manifested itself in her childhood—hence the nervous breakdown. As a child she had felt guilty about not being able to save her parents; now she transfers that guilty attitude to the world in general. Yet, no matter how much good she tries to do, it cannot resolve her irrational childhood guilt.

Watching

Dream (daydream): The dreamer watched a certain young woman named Stefanie when she was strolling on the street. She was two years older than he and of a slightly higher social standing. He felt that he not only loved her but could see into the depths of her personality. He never spoke to her, but knew that one day he would speak to her and look into her eyes and in that instant she would know that she was to be his wife.

Dreamer: Adolf Hitler, dictator of Germany, when he was 17 years old, as reported by Cross (1973).

Association: His adolescent friend, Kubizek, noted that Hitler used to have many grandiose daydreams such as the one above. However, he never actually approached any girls, and, according to this same friend, he never even masturbated. Upon discovering his body after his suicide at the end of World War II, Russian doctors discovered that he had only one testicle.

Interpretation: Hitler's adolescent daydream belies the narcissistic grandiosity that would characterize his later rise to leadership. He imagines that he can know everything about someone without ever having talked with her, by merely watching her. "Watching" apparently signifies a kind of spiritual intercourse. He also imagines that one look from his eyes will cause her to fall under his spell. It may be that his congenital lack of a testicle contributed to his developing what Adler would call organ inferiority—that is, an inferiority complex related to this deficiency, for which he would compensate through grandiose ideas.

Water

Dream: I was in a village near my home. A little girl was with me. I called Frank and he was home. We went to a lake. It was dark blue. I jumped in but it was shallow. I had to press my stomach against the sand to be covered by water. I was disappointed it was not deeper.

Dreamer: A young, oral-dependent woman who had been physically abused by her father from earliest childhood.

Association: The little girl reminded her of herself as a girl. She recalled many dreams of water. Frank is a gay friend.

Interpretation: The dark blue water denotes her mother's womb, where she had floated safely. From the time she entered the world, her father had terrified her, and her mother had not protected her. The dream is a wish to return to the womb and safety. Frank represents the brother she always wished she had.

Dream: I was walking in the woods. I saw a dark pond. I jumped in and sank to the bottom. I was afraid of drowning, but suddenly I found I could breathe. I looked around and saw you there, beckoning to me.

Dreamer: A 23-year-old phobic woman who had just begun therapy.

Association: She talked of her fear of what she didn't know.

Interpretation: The woods represent the psychotherapeutic journey; the dark pond is the unconscious. She hopes her therapist will help her overcome her fears, including claustrophobia (fear of reengulfment by her mother).

Dream: I was floating in a pond of water and a flower sprouted out of the top of my head.

Dreamer: A 23-year-old man.

Association: He had felt that his creativity was blocked.

Interpretation: Water is the wellspring of creation—all life sprang from it. The flower growing out of the dreamer's head as he floats in a pond represents his wish for creative inspiration.

Dream: I saw myself in the ocean and then it was as though I *was* the ocean. The water of the ocean was going right through me and I was the water of the ocean.

Dreamer: A 33-year-old schizoid woman.

Association: She considered herself to be psychic. Water is one of the four ancient elements.

Interpretation: The dream is an allusion to what philosophers call the *oceanic feeling*; it is an expression of the dreamer's wish to lose herself (that is, her self-consciousness) and merge with nature. At the root of this desire is an unconscious need to return to the symbiosis of the early relationship with her mother, in which she experienced her mother and herself as one.

Dream: Water began flowing out of an old ruin.

Dreamer: A 42-year-old woman.

Association: She feared she was too old to get pregnant.

Interpretation: The ruin which sprouts water is the fulfillment of her wish to be pregnant.

Whip

Dream: The dreamer was riding on a narrow Alpine path, precipice on the right, rocks on the left. The path grew narrower, so that the horse refused to proceed, and it was impossible to turn round or dismount, due to the lack of space. Then, with his whip in his left hand, he struck the smooth rock and called on God. The whip grew in length, the rocky wall dropped like a piece of stage scenery and opened out a broad path, with a view over hills and forests, like a landscape in Bohemia; there were Prussian troops with banners. He thought that he must report it to the King.

Dreamer: Otto von Bismarck, nineteenth century Chancellor of the German Empire. Reported by Freud (1900).

Association: Bismarck was at that time feeling pressured about decisions he had to make as Chancellor.

Interpretation: The dream has at least two levels of meaning. On the surface it probably alludes to his present predicament. The path with no way out symbolizes his sense of being caught up in a hopeless position as Chancellor. The wish is that by praying to God and waving his whip (as Moses in the *Bible* struck a rock with a rod to get water for his thirsting people) he can open up a path and the Prussian troops will appear waving banners of victory. On a deeper level, it is perhaps a masturbation fantasy; he takes the whip in hand (masturbates) and it grows in length (becomes erect and powerful). Such fantasies of erectile prowess are common during the phallic narcissistic stage of development (3 to 4 years old); hence this fantasy may point to Bismarck's phallic narcissism.

Wings

Dream: I saw many animals following one another. When they stretched their wings they proved to be dragons. I flew over their heads, but I brushed one of them.

Dreamer: Emanuel Swedenborg, the Swedish scientist who suffered from paranoia, as reported by Gutheil (1951).

Association: Swedenborg believed the dragons signified deceitful love, which hid its dragon-like character until one saw its wings. He had had an emotionally incestuous relationship with his mother.

Interpretation: The deceitful dragon that the dreamer touches is his mother, whose emotional incest castrates him.

Dream: I dreamed that I sprouted wings and could fly above myself. Yet I was still there walking along as I flew above.

Dreamer: A 24-year-old woman with a schizoid personality.

Association: She felt frustrated by her limitations.

Interpretation: The dreamer wishes to transcend herself and achieve a higher level of consciousness.

Dream: I had secret wings that could emerge from my armpits. Someone discovered them and plucked them out.

Dreamer: A 34-year-old alcoholic man.

Association: His wife was always on his case about drinking.

Interpretation: The wings symbolize the liberated self, or masculinity, that sprouts when he is drunk. His wife is the culprit who "clips his wings."

Witch

Dream: I was accused of being a witch and a younger woman had also been accused. It was as if I had made her be a witch. Her brother was the town manager. He held us in a vat of boiling oil. If we survived, we proved we weren't witches. He threw his sister into the vat and she was instantly killed. He put me into the oil and I woke up.

Dreamer: A 30-year-old passive male who had grown up in a dysfunctional family environment.

Association: He recalled a fourth figure in the dream who was running things, but he could not remember who it was. The night before he had seen a television documentary about the Salem witch trials.

Interpretation: The witchery in the trial stands for the dreamer's perverse sexual thoughts and murderous wishes toward his family. The younger girl in the dream is actually his own sister, whom he had bullied as a child. Her brother in the dream is actually his older brother in real life, who used to bully him. The shadowy figure running things is the dreamer's mother. The dream depicts in symbolic form the feelings of persecution he experienced as a child, the vat of boiling oil suggesting the tortures he endured, with the shadow of his mother calling the shots.

Dream: I'm in a room with several other men, and we're all playing with ourselves. A woman who is some kind of witch sits in the corner on a throne. She orders us to keep playing with ourselves. Soon my cock grows a foot long. She orders me to keep masturbating until it's two feet long.

Dreamer: A 23-year-old man with a masculinity complex and voyeuristic and exhibitionistic features.

Association: When he was 3, his mother and older brother teased him about putting his underwear on backwards.

Interpretation: In the dream, the witch (his split-off bad mother) and the other men (his brother and father) support his masculine strivings rather than negate them, as they did in reality as he was growing up. It is a reparative dream.

Dream: I was at Kathy's house. I was astonished to see Kathy begin acting like a witch. She laughed maniacally as she stuffed huge gobs of white pudding into her mother's mouth. Her mother didn't complain. Kathy brought in one bowl after another of the pudding, and soon her mother was so fat she fell off her chair.

Dreamer: A 27-year-old woman with anorexia nervosa.

Association: Kathy sometimes reminded her of her mother.

Interpretation: The witch symbolizes the dreamer's mother (displaced onto Kathy), who in real life continually nags the dreamer about eating. The dream is a reversal; now the daughter stuffs the mother and makes her grotesquely fat (which is the daughter's worst fear about herself). The white pudding may stand for milk.

Wolf

Dream (fairy tale): One day her mother said, "Come, Little Red Riding Hood, here is a piece of cake and a bottle of wine. Take them to your grandmother." She warned her not to run off the path and fall down and break the bottle. Just as Little Red Riding Hood had entered the woods, she met a wolf. He asked her where she was going and she replied, "To my grandmother's house." The wolf ran ahead to the grandmother's house, where he quickly devoured her. Then he put on the grandmother's dress and bonnet and lay in bed waiting for Little Red Riding Hood. When she arrived, she noticed something different. "Grandmother, what big eyes you have," she said, and then, "Grandmother, what large hands you have," and then, "Grandmother, what large teeth you have," and before she could say more the wolf had jumped up and eaten her. The wolf fell asleep and a huntsman came by and heard him snoring. He stepped inside and, suspecting that the wolf had eaten the grandmother, cut open his belly. Out came Little Red Riding Hood and her grandmother. Little Red Riding Hood quickly filled the wolf's belly with stones, and when he tried to get up, the stones were so heavy that he collapsed and died.

Interpretation: The wolf in this classic children's story represents lecherous males.

The red of Little "Red" Riding Hood symbolizes menstruation—a girl coming of age and now having to deal with sexuality. The warning not to run off the path so as not to break the bottle is a warning about the danger of sex and losing her virginity. The male (wolf) is portrayed as cunning and cruel and the sex act as cannibalistic. Thus the story corresponds to the nightmares of little girls who, due to adverse factors in their environment, develop a fear and loathing of men and sexuality. However, revenge is exacted on this loathsome wolfman by having him suffer a "Caesarean birth," after which he is killed by stones, the symbol of sterility.

Dream: I watched in horror as a wolf ran into my neighbor's back yard, picked her up, and carried her in his jaw.

Dreamer: A 39-year-old obsessive-compulsive man.

Associations: He is continually expressing concern about the welfare of his mother and sister, overly protective about them, and fearful that they will injure themselves.

Interpretation: The wolf that runs into the neighbor's back yard represents the dreamer's aggression, which he generally disowns and projects onto others. His concern about the neighbor parallels his concern about his mother and sister, and hence is a displacement of that concern. However, the concern masks a death wish for the two women in his life, toward whom, unconsciously, he feels rage.

Dream 1: I see many female figures and a voice within says, "I must first get away from Father!"

Dream 2: I dreamed of a veiled woman.

Dream 3: I see the veiled woman with her face uncovered.

Dream 4: This unknown woman stands in the land of sheep and points the way.

Dream 5: I see a skull changing into a red ball, then into a woman's head which emits light.

Dream 6: I see a globe. An unknown woman stands upon it and prays to the sun.

Dream 7: An unknown woman follows me. I keep running in a circle.

Dreamer: A young man, as reported by Jung (1971).

Associations: None reported.

Interpretation: Jung interprets the father in the first dream as consciousness, conservatism, and rigidity, standing in the dreamer's way. The veiled woman symbolizes the dreamer's anima (the projection of his unconscious femininity) and his unconscious. The land of sheep is childhood. The skull that changes into a woman's head emitting light and the woman standing on a globe praying to the sun represent the collective unconscious attempting to unite with the collective conscious (the sun) in order to achieve spiritual integration. The woman following the dreamer as he runs in a circle suggests both his integration of his anima and his collective unconscious.

Women's Clothes

Dream 1: I am in some sort of legitimate setting where wearing women's clothes is part of a test project. I'm trying on a woman's nightgown. A lot of people are there. It is too small for me and won't fit. I think that there should be some regulation about the impossibility of getting a fit. . . .

Dream 2: I am wearing women's clothing and someone is coming down the hall who might see me, a woman. I wonder how to get the clothing off without being seen.

Dream 3: I am supposed to be baby-sitting for somebody but I'm not there. I'm somewhere else talking; perhaps I've gone to get some women's clothes.

Dreamer: A 39-year-old male transvestite, as reported by Socarides (1980).

Associations: Each of the above dreams was precipitated by a recent rejection, or the memory of a rejection, by a woman. The dreamer had experienced much maternal deprivation during his early childhood.

Interpretation: These dreams are very much like the dreamer's actual perversion. In his waking life he wore women's underclothing whenever he felt picked on by other men or frustrated by a woman. The clothing was a substitute for the presence of women (and his mother), and offered erotic satisfaction while also making him feel less lonely. It also had a compensatory function of narcissistic restoration and a defensive function of warding off threats of castration.

Xenophobia

Dream: I was at a party but all the people there were strangers. I kept going from room to room looking for somebody I might know, but there was nobody. I decided to leave but couldn't find the front door. I woke up feeling anxious.

Dreamer: A young woman who suffered from multiple phobic symptoms, including xenophobia.

Association: She recalled a recent party at which she had felt estranged from people, even though she knew them.

Interpretation: The xenophobia dramatized in this dream harks back to a period in the dreamer's infancy when she experienced *stranger anxiety*. Her mother, a socialite, had "abandoned" her to a succession of nannies, whom she had then fired in quick succession. Each nanny must have felt like a stranger to the infant and toddler, like the strangers in the dream. The dreamer's lifelong xenophobia is linked to a fixation during this phase of development.

Yellow

Dream: My father and I were rock climbing together. We had to go over this really steep and jagged part of a cliff. He was ahead and I was tied to him by a rope. Suddenly he waved for me to pass him by. As I did, I noticed that he had turned yellow. His whole body was yellow. I said, "What's wrong?" He said, "Nothing. Go on, I'll catch up." I had to climb over by myself and pull him up. It was really difficult but I finally got him up to the top.

Dreamer: A 27-year-old passive male.

Associations: His father had often gone rock climbing in his younger days, but would not take the dreamer with him. He believed his father went rock climbing to get away from his wife, who henpecked him.

Interpretation: The dreamer perhaps sees his father as yellow (a coward who can't face his wife). The dream shows his wish to surpass his cowardly father and attain the self-assertion and mastery he needs (climbing the mountain/phallus).

Youth

Dream: I saw a youth bowling. He was bowling with one finger.

Dreamer: A middle-aged man.

Association: He was going through a midlife crisis.

Interpretation: The youth who bowls with one finger represents the dreamer's wish to regain his youth and potency.

Zoophilia

Dream: I was in a basement. I saw a cat in the corner, large and puffed up, the way cats get when they are purring. It was a female cat, and she was looking at me strangely. Her eyes were like human eyes, like she wanted me to feel sorry for her.

Dreamer: A 28-year-old male zoophiliac.

Associations: As a child, his mother often locked him in the basement when she thought he was naughty. Sometimes she would lock his pet dog with him, and he developed the habit of letting the dog lick his genitals. An only child, he was not allowed to play with other children. He had a stuffed cat as a toddler.

Interpretation: The dream is perhaps a wish that his mother (the cat with human eyes) will take pity on him. The basement stands for the memory of being locked in the basement, and perhaps for his mother's "cold" womb. The cat represents both a sexual and transitional object.

Dream: I saw a tiger jump over the fence and trot up to my cat. He had escaped from the zoo. As I watched, he mounted my cat, and I could see my cat's breasts grow larger. They looked two human female breasts. I woke up excited.

Dreamer: A 32-year-old female with zoophiliac features.

Association: She engaged in sexual acts with her dog.

Interpretation: The cat with human breasts represents the dreamer, who wishes to be ravished by a dog.

Glossary of Dream Symbols

A

Abdomen: 1. Frustration of oral needs such as hunger, thirst, warmth, safety (pain in abdomen). 2. Sexuality. 3. Pregnancy (growth in abdomen).

Abyss: 1. Imminent danger. 2. Death. 3. The unconscious.

Airplane: 1. The penis (masculine assertion). 2. Liberation, transcendence. 3. Sexual intercourse (flying).

Airport: 1. The need for escape. 2. Confusion, abandonment (lost or stuck in airport). 3. Turning point (leaving airport).

Albatross: 1. Bad luck. 2. Imminent danger.

Albino: 1. Innocence, purity, peace. 2. Death and mourning (in the East).

Alien: 1. Bad father, mother, sibling (menacing alien). 2. Good father, mother, sibling (rescuing alien). 3. The unconscious self (disowned sexuality, aggression, masculine or feminine side). 4. The shadow or anima/animus (Jungian).

Altar: 1 Marriage. 2. Sacrifice.

Amputation: 1. Castration (Freudian). 2. Loss (object relations).

Anchor: 1. Security. 2. Restraint, restriction (anchor dragging).

Angel: 1. Good mother, father. 2. Savior. 3. Death. 4. Omen of good fortune.

Animals: 1. One's family. 2. Sexuality or aggression disowned (wild animals). 3. Sexuality or aggression accepted (tame animals). 4. Projected guilt. (See also listings for individual animals.)

Antique: 1. Childhood. 2. The unconscious.

Antler: The penis or masculine strength.

Apples: 1. Breasts (two). 2. Male genitals (three). 3. Sin (the *Bible*).

Arm(s): 1. Warmth, love (arms outstretched). 2. The penis (extra arm). 3. Ability, strength (strong arms). 4. Castration (loss of arm).

Armor: 1. Wish for safety. 2. Emotional numbness.

Arrow: 1. Love or romance (Cupid's arrow). 1. Trouble ("slings and arrows," Shakespeare).

Ashes: Death.

Avalanche: 1. Imminent danger. 2. State of being besieged by problems, emotions.

Awakening: 1. New ideas, awareness. 2. Aliveness.

Axe: 1. Death. 2. Losing a job (getting the axe). Castration (chopping down tree).

B

Baby: 1. Vulnerability, innocence. 2. Pregnancy. 3. One's true self or feelings. 4. One's inner child. 5. The id (Freudian). 6. Rebirth, creativity.

Baggage: 1. Repressed emotions or memories. 2. Troubles or responsibilities.

Balloon(s): 1. Happiness or the wish to escape from sadness (several balloons rising). 2. Sexual or spiritual liberation. 3. The male genital (one balloon rising). 4. Breasts (two balloons). 5. Oral sex (blowing up balloons).

Banana: The penis.

Bank: 1. Stored emotions. 2. The unconscious. 3. Money, financial success.

Baseball: 1. Masculinity. 2. Male genitals (two balls and bat).

Basement: 1. The unconscious. 2. Sexual or aggressive feelings. 3. The womb. 4. The past.

Basket: 1. Female. 2. The vagina or womb.

Bat (animal): 1. Engulfing mother. 2. Abusive father. 3. Incest. 4. Rape. 4. Omen of bad luck (black bat).

Bathing: 1. Spiritual redemption. 2. Masturbation. 3. Sexual intercourse. 4. Emotional cleansing.

Beach: 1. Mother's lap. 2. Happiness.

Bear: 1. Good man or father (cuddly bear). 2. Bad man or father (scary bear). 3. Unconscious "animal" instincts. 4. Animus (Jungian).

Beheading: 1. Castration. 2. Guilt.

Bird(s): 1. Female. 2. Spiritual or sexual liberation (birds soaring). 3. Messenger (mythology). 4. The penis (Freudian). (See also listings of individual birds.)

Birth: 1. Wish for pregnancy. 2. Personal growth. 3. New ideas. 4. Prenatal or infantile trauma (difficult birth).

Black: 1. Death. 2. Depression. 3. The unconscious. 4. Evil. 5. The shadow (Jungian—the dark part of the unconscious).

Blindness: 1. Mental or emotional block. 2. Avoidance or forgetfulness. 3. Castration (Freudian).

Blood: 1. Life. 2. Vitality, passion. 3. Death. 4. Wound. 5. Menstruation. 6. Castration.

Blossoms: 1. Women's genitals. 2. Virginity. 3. Loss of virginity (scattered blossoms).

Blue: 1. Happiness (sky blue). 2. Sadness (the "blues"). 3. Masculinity.

Boar: 1. Aggression. 2. Male sexuality.

Boat: 1. Mother's or father's lap. 2. Womb. 3. Missed opportunity (missing the boat).

Bomb: 1. Rage. 2. Sexual aggression.

Book(s): 1. The past. 2. The unconscious. 3. Wisdom. 4. Women (Freudian).

Bottle: 1. Vagina (Freudian). 2. Emptiness (empty bottle). 3. Loss of virginity (broken bottle).

Box: 1. The vagina or womb (Freudian). 2. The unconscious. 3. Repressed guilt, aggression, sexuality. 4. Evil (mythology: Pandora's box). 5. Trapped (boxed in). 6. The shadow (Jungian).

Breast(s): 1. Mother. 2. Oral or narcissistic needs.

Bride: Marriage.

Bridge: 1. Turning point. 2. The penis. 3. Rebirth. 4. Umbilical cord.

Broom: 1. Redemption (a clean sweep). 2. Evil (witch's broom).

Brown: 1. Earth. 2. Anality. 3. Depression.

Bucket: 1. Female. 2. The vagina or womb. 3. Death (kicking the bucket).

Buddha: 1. Virtue. 2. Wisdom (Eastern religion).

Bug(s): 1. Bad penis. 2. Pesty person. 3. Guilt (swarm of bugs).

Bull: 1. Bad father or man. 2. Masculine aggression. 3. Animal nature. 4. Rape. 5. Confusion, chaos (bull in a china shop).

Bullet: 1. The penis (rape). 2. Conscience (bullet in the heart).

Burglary: 1. Rape (stealing jewels). 2. Castration (stealing money, tools, computers, furniture).

Burial: 1. Death. 2. Frozen emotion. 3. The past. 4. The unconscious.

Bush: 1. Female pubic hair. 2. Omen from God (the *Bible*).

Butterfly: 1. Flight from depression. 2. One's true self (Eastern philosophy). 3. Frivolity. 4. Something temporary.

Buzzard: 1. Death. 2. Omen of bad luck.

C

Cabin: 1. The womb. 2. Serenity (cabin in woods).

Cactus: 1. Aggressive penis. 2. Sterility. 3. Emotional or sexual coldness.

Cage: 1. Feelings of being trapped (person in cage). 2. Repressed sexuality or assertiveness (animal in cage). 3. Blocked creativity, spirit (bird in cage).

Can: 1. Female. 2. The vagina, womb (Freudian).

Cancer: 1. Emotional deadness. 2. Depression. 3. Moral decay.

Candle: 1. Enlightenment. 2. The penis. 3. Impotence (candle going out). 4. Life/death.

Cannibalism: 1. Oral-sadistic needs. 2. Rebirth (snake eating its own tail).

Cannon: 1. The penis. 2. Ejaculation (cannon shooting).

Car: 1. Journey of life (car driving down road). 2. The penis. 3. Intercourse (car driving into tunnel).

Carrot: 1. Achievement/reward. 2. The penis.

Castle: 1. Male. 2. Female (Freudian).

Cat(s): 1. Female. 2. One's inner child. 3. Free spirits. 4. Bad luck (black cat).

Cave: 1. The vagina or womb. 2. The unconscious.

Cellar: (See Basement.)

Cemetery: 1. Death. 2. Buried memories. 3. Ancestors.

Chains: 1. Constrained emotions, sexual passion (person in chains). 2. Constrained aggression (animal in chains).

Chaos: Mental or emotional confusion.

Cherry: 1. Virgin. 2. Loss of virginity (cherry falling from top of ice cream sundae, etc.).

Chicken: 1. Cowardice. 2. Confusion (chicken with head chopped off). 3. Child.

Child: 1. Childhood. 2. Innocence and freedom from responsibility. 3. Emotionalism. 4. New beginning.

Christ: 1. Goodness. 2. Savior. 3. Ideal self. 4. Martyrdom. 5. Spiritual awakening.

Church: 1. Spirituality. 2. Guilt. 3. Wedding. 4. Female genitals (Freudian).

Cigar/Cigarette: 1. The penis. 2. Orality (sucking mother's breast; fellatio). 3. Sometimes a cigar is just a cigar (Freudian).

Circle: 1. Wholeness. 2. Repetition (vicious circle). 3. Mandala (Jungian).

City: 1. Oneself. 2. Home. 3. Woman; mother (Freudian).

Cliff: 1. Imminent danger. 2. Imminent fall (pride goes before a fall).

Climbing: 1. Ambition. 2. Escape. 3. Sexual or spiritual liberation.

Clock: 1. Time. 2. Aging. 3. Failure, regression (clock with hands moving backwards).

Clouds: 1. Depression. 2. Confusion. 3. Impending emotional disturbance (storm clouds).

Clover: 1. Luxury (in clover). 2. Luck (four-leaf clover). 3. Male genitals (Freudian).

Cock: 1. The penis. 2. Male aggression.

Cocoon: 1. The womb. 2. Rebirth. 3. Depression.

Color: 1. Emotionality. 2. Passion or aggression. (See also listings of individual colors.)

Compass: 1. Need for direction or guidance. 2. Spirituality (pointing east). 3. Coldness (pointing north). 4. Warmth (pointing south). 5. Opportunity ("Go west, young man").

Computer: 1. Intellect. 2. The phallus.

Corner: 1. Turning point. 2. Trapped (cornered).

Corpse: 1. Death. 2. Murderous wishes. 3. Fear of death (one's own corpse). 4. Death of passion, spirit (dead bird, cat, etc.).

Couple: 1. Mother and father. 2. Anima/Animus (Jungian).

Cove: Female genitals.

Cow(s): 1. Mother. 2. Fertility (Biblical). 3. Laziness (cow chewing cud).

Cradle: 1. One's infancy. 2. Rebirth. 3. Creation. 4. Mother. 5. Security.

Crocodile: 1. Bad penis. 2. Devouring mother. 3. False sadness (crocodile tears).

Cross: 1. Religion. 2. Martyrdom. 3. Crossroad or turning point.

Crow: 1. Death. 2. Bad luck.

Crowd: 1. Smothering family. 2. Unconscious guilt (menacing crowd).

Crown: 1. Royalty. 2. The ideal (grandiose) self (self psychology).

Cuckoo: 1. Insanity. 2. Silliness.

Cup: Female genitals.

Cupboard: 1. The womb. 2. Repressed memories.

Curtains: 1. The unconscious. 2. Death (black curtains). 3. Secrets (the "iron" curtain).

Curves: 1. Sudden unexpected occurrences (curves on road). 2. A woman's body.

Cyclone: 1. Aggression. 2. Sexual passion.

Cypress: 1. Depression, mourning. 2. Immortality (evergreen).

D

Dagger: 1. The penis. 2. Aggression, anger, murder.

Daisy: 1. Romance. 2. Female genitals.

Dam: Blocked emotions.

Dancing: 1. Sexual intercourse. 2. Cooperation. 3. Happiness, joy.

Darkness: 1. The unconscious. 2. Depression. 3. Death. 4. The shadow (Jungian).

Dart: 1. The penis. 2. Aggressive sexual penetration. 3. Poison (poisoned dart). 4. Romance (Cupid's dart).

Dawn: 1. Rebirth. 2. New ideas.

Dead end: 1. Emotional block. 2. Breakup of relationship.

Decapitation: (See Beheading.)

Deer: 1. Female. 2. Innocence. 3. Childhood. 4. Dear.

Demon(s): 1. Abusive family members. 2. Disowned parts of the self projected onto external objects (Object Relations).

Den: 1. Repressed aggression (lion's den). 2. Perverse sexuality (den of iniquity). 3. The womb.

Departure: 1. Rebirth. 2. Separation. 3. Death (Freudian).

Desert: 1. Frigidity. 2. Sterility. 3. Emotional need or lust.

Devil: 1. Evil. 2. Temptation (the *Bible*).

Diamond: 1. Life. 2. The clitoris (Freudian).

Digging: 1. Searching the past. 2. Psychoanalysis. 3. Looking for evidence.

Dirt: Guilt.

Disorder: (See Chaos.)

Diving: 1. Sexual penetration. 2. Searching the unconscious (diving deep). 3. Plunging into some subject deeply without hesitation.

Dog: 1. Friendliness and warmth (wagging tail). 2. Bitchy or ugly woman. 3. One's animal nature.

Doll: 1. Childhood. 2. Femininity. 3. Voodoo (doll with pins).

Dolphin: 1. Freedom of spirit. 2. Sexual joy. 3. Childhood.

Dome: 1. Intellect (the brain). 2. The breast. 3. Spiritual wholeness (Jungian).

Donkey: 1. Stubbornness. 2. Responsibility.

Door: 1. Opportunity (door of opportunity). 2. The unconscious. 3. Sexual secrets (voyeurism). 4. The vagina. 5. Salvation (Biblical). 6. Impasse (locked door).

Dove: 1. Peace. 2. Love. 3. Messenger from the gods (mythology) or the unconscious (psychoanalysis).

Dragon: 1. The bad father. 2. The devouring mother. 3. Aggression. 4. Sexual passion. 5. Vitality (Chinese mythology).

Driving: 1. The journey of life. 2. Sexual intercourse.

Drowning: 1. State of being overwhelmed by problems, emotions, or unconscious forces. 2. Smothering mother. 3. Tyrannical father.

Duck: The penis.

Dungeon: 1. Traumatic memory. 2. The unconscious.

Dusk: 1. Death. 2. Rebirth.

Dwarf: 1. Stunted potential. 2. Magical creatures bringing good luck and treasure (from fairy tales and mythology). 3. Childhood.

E

Eagle: 1. Courage, ambition, strength. 2. Rising up (from depression). 3. Conflict (mythology—the eagle with snake in its claw represents conflict of opposites).

Ear(s): 1. The need to listen (big ears or no ears). 2. A vagina.

Earth: 1. Mother. 2. Birth. 3. Naïveté (down to earth).

Earthquake: 1. Repressed aggression surfacing. 2. Separation from mother. 3. Sexual passion.

East: Spirituality.

Eating: 1. Oral incorporation of (identification with) somebody or something. 2. Sex (oral).

Eclipse: 1. Sexual intercourse (merger of sun and moon). 2. Foreboding of doom.

Egg: 1. Rebirth. 2. Fertility. 3. Excessive pride (as in the nursery rhyme "Humpty Dumpty").

Eight: 1. Danger (as in "behind the eight ball"). 2. Infinity and eternity.

Elephant: 1. Phallus (the trunk). 2. Strength and vitality (in the Hindu and Buddhist religions).

Emperor/Empress: 1. Mother and father. 2. Anima/Animus (Jungian).

Emptiness: Repression.

Enemy: 1. Parents. 2. Sibling rival. 3. A split-off part of oneself projected onto another dream figure.

Engine: 1. Instincts or drives. 2. Heart.

Entrance: (See Door).

Evening: 1. Serenity. 2. Middle or old age.

Evergreen tree: 1. Eternity. 2. Immortality.

Examination: 1. Fear of failure. 2. Reassurance. 3. Sexuality (playing doctor).

Excrement: 1. Poison. 2. Filth. 3. Money (Freudian). 4. The penis. 5. Baby.

Exit: 1. Escape. 2. Death. 3. The anus.

Explosion: (See Bomb.)

Eye(s): 1. Guilt (eyes looking disapprovingly). 2. Anger (eyes like daggers). 3. Watchfulness (the watchful eyes of the owl). 4. Evil. 5. Awareness (bright eyes).

F

Factory: 1. Life. 2. Responsibility.

Fairy: 1. Homosexuality. 2. Alter ego-ideal.

Falling: 1. Fear of failure. 2. Fear of temptation (falling into sin). 3. Losing control (of emotions, sexual impulses). 4. Fear of death. 5. Orgasm. 6. The unconscious.

Fame: 1. Love. 2. Recognition.

Farm: 1. Serenity. 2. Mother (growing things). 3. The family.

Faucet: 1. The penis. 2. Fertility (running faucet).

Fence: 1. Emotional block. 2. Conscience. 3. Indecision (sitting on the fence).

Ferry: 1. Life change. 2. Death (mythology).

Fetus: 1. Latent creativity. 2. The wish to go back to the womb.

Field: 1. Peace. 2. Freedom. 3. Mother.

Finger: 1. Blame (pointed finger). 2. The penis.

Fire: 1. Sexual passion. 2. Aggression. 3. Bed-wetting (Freudian).

Fish: 1. Fertility. 2. Body of Christ (Christianity). 3. The penis. 4. The vagina.

Fishing: 1. Mating. 2. Striving for approval (fishing for compliments). 3. Searching the unconscious.

Floating: 1. The womb. 2. Lack of direction. 3. Liberation or spiritual transcendence. 4. Orgasm.

Flood: 1. Revenge. 2. End of the world (Biblical story of Noah). 3. Overwhelming eruption of emotion or aggression from within or without. 4. Too much affection (smothering mother). 5. Sadness (a flood of tears). 6. Tyrannical father.

Flower: 1. Female genitals. 2. Virginity. 3. Defloration (broken flowers). 4. Healing (Taoism and Buddhism). 5. The true self (Jungian).

Flute: 1. Seduction. 2. The penis. 3. Oral sex (playing on flute).

Flying: 1. Sexual intercourse. 2. Throwing off inhibitions. 3. Spiritual transcendence. 4. Escaping danger.

Fog: 1. Depression. 2. Confusion. 3. The unconscious.

Foot: 1. The penis. 2. Castration (loss of foot).

Foreigner: (See Alien.)

Forest: 1. Life's vicissitudes. 2. The unconscious. 3. Female pubic hair.

Fortress: 1. Safety, protection. 2. Woman (Freudian).

Fountain: 1. Vitality, rebirth. 2. Ejaculation.

Four: Ancient symbol of wholeness: the four elements (earth, water, fire, wind), the four corners of the earth, and so forth.

Fracture: Castration.

Frog: 1. Male genitals. 2. Guilt. 3. Ugliness.

Fruit: 1. Creativity. 2. Pregnancy. 3. Male or female genitals. (See separate listings of individual fruits.)

Funeral: 1. Imminent death. 2. A wish for someone's death.

G

Gagging: 1. Smothering (smothering mother). 2. Dumbness, inability to speak.

Gangster: 1. Unconscious aggression. 2. Anima/animus or the shadow (Jungian).

Garden: 1. Female genitals (Freudian). 2. Personal growth or creativity. 3. Neglect, decay (garden with weeds).

Gate: 1. The vagina (Freudian). 2. Unsolved problem (locked gate). 3. Opportunity (open gate). 4. Heaven (the *Bible*).

Ghost: 1. Externalization of guilt toward a deceased person. 2. Prophetic messenger. 3. Messenger of death. 4. Mother (Freudian). 5. Father (Christian, "Holy Ghost").

Glass: Female genitals.

Goat: 1. Masculinity. 2. Someone or something blamed (as in scapegoat).

Goblins: 1. Guilt. 2. Aggression. 3. Mischief (folklore).

God: 1. Father. 2. Omnipotence. 3. Animus (Jungian).

Goddess: 1. Mother. 2. Omnipotence. 3. Anima (Jungian).

Gold: 1. Beloved, treasured person. 2. Happiness, joy, vitality (golden sun).

Gorilla: 1. Father. 2. Masculinity. 3. Aggression. 4. Aggressive sexuality.

Grave: 1. Death. 2. End of something.

Gray: 1. Depression. 2. Death. 3. Confusion. 4. Old age.

Green: 1. Youth. 2. Fertility. 3. A go-ahead (green light). 4. Immortality (evergreen). 5. Rot, cancer (gangrene).

Group: 1. Family. 2. Race.

Guitar: 1. Male or female genitals. 2. Oral sex (stroking guitar).

Gun: 1. The penis. 2. Aggression.

Guru: 1. Wisdom. 2. Idealized self.

Gypsy: 1. Sexuality. 2. Shadow or anima/animus (Jungian).

H

Hair: 1. Power (long hair). 2. The penis. 3. Castration (cutting hair). 4. Masculinity (hair on face, body). 5. Aging (gray hair, loss of hair).

Hall: 1. Transition or turning point. 2. The vagina. 3. Umbilical cord.

Halo: 1. Divinity. 2. Purity, innocence.

Hammer: 1. The penis. 2. Aggressive sexuality (hammering a nail). 3. Aggression.

Hand(s): 1. Ability, dexterity. 2. The penis. 3. Restraint, inhibition (hands tied). 4. Guilt (washing hands).

Harbor: 1. Mother. 2. The womb. 3. Home. 4. Contentment.

Hat: 1. Male or female genitals. 2. Lifestyle (changing hats).

Hawk: Aggression.

Head: 1. Intellect. 2. The conscious mind. 3. The penis.

Heaven: 1. Joy. 2. Childhood. 3. Mother. 4. Orgasm. 5. Immortality (the *Bible*).

Hell: 1. Madness. 2. Childhood. 3. The family. 4. Immortality (the *Bible*).

Hen: (See Chicken).

Hermaphrodite: 1. Gender conflict or integration. 2. Consciousness versus unconsciousness. 3. Anima/Animus (Jungian).

Hero: 1. Idealized self. 2. Rescuer (mythology). 3. Archetype (Jungian).

Hills: 1. Breasts. 2. Mother. 3. Obstacles.

Hog: (See Pig).

Hole: 1. The vagina. 2. The anus. 3. Trap. 4. Unconscious.

Home: 1. Family. 2. The self at peace. 3. Mother.

Honey: 1. Sweetness. 2. Nurture (mythology).

Horn(s): 1. The penis. 2. Fertility (mythology). 3. Evil (devils, demons).

Horse: 1. Male sexuality. 2. Gallantry (white horse). 3. Wild emotions (galloping horses).

Horseshoe: 1. Good luck. 2. Male genitals (Freudian).

House: 1. The self. 2. The family. 3. Guilt (haunted house).

Hunger: 1. Sexual craving. 2. Emotional craving. 3. Ambition. 4. Hunger.

Hunting: 1. Sexual conquest. 2. Stalking.

Hurricane: (See Cyclone).

Hyena: Mockery.

Hypnosis: 1. The unconscious. 2. Childhood.

I

Ice: 1. Frozen emotions. 2. Sexual frigidity. 3. Danger (thin ice).

Iceberg: The self (consciousness above water, unconsciousness below).

Icicle: The penis.

Insects: 1. Guilt (swarming). 2. Rape (stinging, penetrating). 3. Creepy men.

Instruments: Male genitals (Freudian).

Invalid: 1. Emotional, sexual, spiritual blockage. 2. Inferior feelings.

Invasion: 1. Controlling parents. 2. Unleashed, overwhelming emotions. 3. Rape.

Iron: Strength.

Island: 1. Isolation. 2. Mother. 3. The womb.

Ivy: 1. Education (Ivy League). 2. Poison. 3. Engulfment (ivy crawling up wall).

J

Jade: Vitality, immortality (Chinese philosophy).

Jesus: (See Christ).

Jewels: 1. Valued person. 2. Male and female genitalia (family jewels).

Journey: 1. Life. 2. An escape. 3. Exploration of the unconscious. 4. A relationship.

Judge: The superego or conscience.

Jug: The vagina.

Jungle: 1. Life's problems. 2. The unconscious.

Junk: Repressed memories.

Jury: 1. The family. 2. Society (social stigma).

K

Kangaroo: Sexual vitality.

Key: 1. Solution. 2. Male genitals. 3. Sexual intercourse (key in keyhole).

King: 1. Father. 2. Idealized self. 3. Animus (Jungian).

Kiss: 1. Sex. 2. Blessing. 3. Death (kiss of death).

Kitchen: 1. Mother. 2. Food.

Knife: 1. Murder. 2. Penis as instrument of conquest.

Knob: 1. The penis. 2. Masturbation (turning knob).

Knot: 1. Problem. 2. Union or harmony.

L

Laboratory: 1. Childhood. 2. Pregnancy. 3. Torture. 4. Creativity. 5. Scientific exploration.

Labyrinth: 1. Problems of life. 2. The unconscious. 3. Smothering or controlling parental figure.

Ladder: 1. Ambition. 2. Communication from above (Biblical). 3. Sexual intercourse (walking up, Freudian).

Lake: 1. The unconscious. 2. Mother. 3. Serenity.

Lamb: 1. Innocence, vulnerability. 2. A child. 3. Sacrifice (sacrificial lamb).

Lamp: 1. Consciousness. 2. Insight.

Landscape: The curves of the female.

Legs: 1. Male genitals. 2. Confidence, support (strong legs). 3. Castration (loss of leg).

Light: 1. Consciousness. 2. Hope. 3. Happiness. 4. Insight.

Lighthouse: 1. Consciousness. 2. Wisdom. 3. Mother. 4. The erect penis.

Lightning: 1. An idea. 2. Sexual excitement. 3. Anger or punishment (wrath of God; Judaism, Christianity).

Lily: 1. Life (Eastern philosophy). 2. Death (funerals).

Lion: 1. Aggression. 2. Sexual passion.

Lips: 1. Oral needs. 2. The vagina.

Lizard: 1. The penis. 2. Castration (lizard with tail that falls off).

Lock: 1. Something imprisoned or blocked (emotions, creativity, sexuality). 2. Chastity.

Locomotive: 1. Aggression. 2. Phallic aggression.

Luggage: 1. The unconscious. 2. Burdens. 3. Past problems.

M

Machine: 1. The mind. 2. The body.

Magic: 1. Childhood magical thinking. 2. Potency. 3. Birth (miracle of).

Magnet: 1. Mother. 2. Family.

Mandalas: 1. Order, harmony (Jungian).

Marriage: 1. Integration of parts of the self (male and female sides).

Mask: 1. Persona (Jungian). 2. Hidden personality.

Maze: (See Labyrinth.)

Meadow: 1. Tranquility. 2. Childhood. 3. Growth, creativity.

Mermaid: 1. Ideal woman. 2. Mother. 3. Seduction.

Merry-Go-Round: 1. Going in circles. 2. Childhood. 3. Joy.

Metal: 1. Strength. 2. Freeing of emotions or spiritual transformation (metal melting).

Meteorite: 1. The unconscious. 2. Externalized guilt or aggression (rain of meteorites).

Milk: 1. Mother. 2. Oral needs (nurture, approval, love). 3. Childhood.

Mill: 1. Masculinity. 2. The unconscious.

Mine: 1. The unconscious. 2. Female genitals.

Mirror: 1. Alter ego. 2. Ideal self. 3. Double (Jungian). 4. Censoring superego.

Mist: 1. Confusion. 2. Tears.

Money: 1. Power. 2. Excrement (Freudian). 3. Wealth.

Monkey(s): 1. Playfulness. 2. Mockery. 3. Burdens (monkey on back).

Monster: 1. Father. 2. Mother. 3. Bad internal objects projected onto the environment (object relations). 4. Aggression. 5. Guilt.

Moon: 1. Fertility (folklore). 2. Woman.

Motorcycle: 1. Male sexual aggression. 2. The penis.

Mountain: 1. Breasts. 2. Ambition, achievement. 3. Grandiosity (standing on top of mountain). 4. The penis.

Mouth: 1. The vagina. 2. Oral needs.

Mud: 1. Excrement. 2. Being stuck (in mud).

Museum: 1. The past. 2. The unconscious. 3. Collective unconscious of humankind (Jungian).

Mushroom: 1. The penis. 2. Magic. 3. Atom bomb.

Muzzle: (See Gagging).

N

Nakedness: 1. Vulnerability. 2. Innocence. 3. Sexuality. 4. Truth. 5. Naturalness. 6. Shame (Judaism).

Nazis: Evil.

Nine: Immortality (as in a cat's nine lives).

Numbness: Blocked emotions or sexuality.

Nun: 1. The Catholic church and Catholic education. 2. Mother. 3. Goodness or purity. 4. Conscience.

Nut: 1. Craziness. 2. The womb. 3. Testicles.

Nymph: 1. Ideal woman. 2. Sensual woman.

O

Oasis: 1. Female genitals. 2. Reward. 3. Goal.

Obelisk: Phallic symbol.

Obstacles: 1. Problems of life. 2. Emotional or mental blocks.

Ocean: 1. The unconscious. 2. Mother. 3. The womb. 4. Creativity. 5. Universal oneness (Eastern philosophy). 6. Death wish (Freudian).

Octopus: 1. Possessive person. 2. Mother. 3. Fertility.

Oldness: The past.

Orange(s): 1. Breasts. 2. Life, vitality.

Orgy: 1. Lust. 2. Perverse impulses. 3. Missing out on life (standing outside of orgy).

Outlaw: 1. Aggression. 2. Disowned and projected part of the self (Object Relations).

Oven: 1. The womb. 2. Mother.

Owl: 1. Wisdom. 2. Death. 3. Evil (mythology).

Oyster: 1. The vagina. 2. The clitoris (oyster with pearl).

P

Paddle: 1. The penis. 2. Locomotion, energy. 3. Stuck (boat without a paddle).

Paradise: (See Heaven.)

Paralysis: 1. Blocked emotions or sexuality. 2. Arrested progress in a relationship or career. 3. Blocked freedom.

Park: (See Garden).

Parrot: 1. Mockery. 2. Imitation.

Path: 1. Direction. 2. Life journey. 3. Career choice.

Peach(es): 1. Breasts. 2. Male or female genitalia.

Peacock: 1. Male sexuality. 2. Pride, vanity.

Peak: 1. The penis. 2. The nipple. 3. Goal.

Pearl(s): 1. The clitoris. 2. Wisdom, spiritual treasure (pearls of wisdom).

Pen: The penis.

Piano: 1. Woman. 2. Sexual intercourse (piano playing).

Pig: 1. Perverse sexuality. 2. Overeating. 3. Greed. 4. Children ("The Three Little Pigs").

Pipe: 1. The male genitals. 2. Oral needs (sucking pipe). 3. Oral sex.

Pistol: An aggressive conquering penis.

Pit: (See Hole.)

Plow: 1. The penis. 2. Sexual intercourse (plowing a field). 3. Creativity.

Plug: 1. The penis. 2. Sexual intercourse (plugging hole). 3. Preventing danger (plugging hole). 4. Constipation.

Pocket: The vagina.

Poison: 1. Guilt. 2. Cancer. 3. Bad internal objects introjected from bad primary objects (Object Relations).

Pole: The erect penis.

Police: 1. The conscience. 2. Father. 3. Mother. 4. Anality (Freudian).

Pomegranate(s): 1. Breasts. 2. Healing and fertility.

Pond: (See Lake).

Porpoise: 1. Freedom and joy. 2. Childhood. 3. Playful sexual intercourse.

Precipice: (See Cliff.)

Pricking: 1. Sexual intercourse. 2. Conscience.

Priest: 1. Spirituality. 2. Father. 3. Superego (Freud).

Prince/Princess: 1. The idealized self. 2. The ideal mate. 3. Anima/animus (Jungian).

Prison: 1. Inhibition. 2. The family (clinging parents). 3. Blocked emotions.

Prophets: Messengers from God (Christianity).

Prune: 1. Dried up sexuality. 2. Old age.

Pumpkin: 1. The breasts. 2. Empty headedness. 3. Magic (fairy tales).

Puppet: 1. Child. 2. Controlling parent (puppet on string). 3. Inhibition, subservience.

Purple: 1. Royalty. 2. Perverse sexuality. 3. Deep embarrassment. 4. Mystery.

Q

Quaker: Peace.

Queen: 1. Mother. 2. Homosexual. 3. Anima (Jungian).

Quiche: Homosexuality.

R

Rabbit(s): 1. Innocence. 2. Children. 3. Fertility. 4. Exploring the unconscious (Rabbit in hole).

Rain: 1. Depression. 2. Fertility.

Rainbow: 1. Hope. 2. Joy.

Ram: 1. Masculinity. 2. Fertility.

Rat(s): 1. One's worst fears. 2. Guilt (gnawing). 3. Turds. 4. An obsessive idea.

Raven: (See Crow.)

Rebellion: Psychic conflict in which internalized bad objects overwhelm the good objects (Object Relations).

Red: 1. Sexual passion. 2. Anger. 3. Blood.

Referee: The ego.

Reindeer: 1. Christmas. 2. Joy. 3. Childhood.

Reservoir: 1. Unrealized potential. 2. The unconscious.

Rhinoceros: 1. The penis. 2. Humor.

Riding: 1. Sexual intercourse (riding horse, bicycle, motorcycle). 2. Losing control (riding too fast).

Right/Left: 1. Consciousness/unconsciousness. 2. Male/female. 3. Mind/body. 4. Activity/passivity. 5. Yin-yang (Chinese philosophy). 6. Anima/animus (Jungian).

Ring: 1. Marriage. 2. Wholeness.

River: 1. Journey of life. 2. Sexual or emotional energy. 3. Making a wrong decision or turn (going against the flow).

Road: 1. Journey of life. 2. Decision or turning point (a road dividing).

Roadblock: 1. External obstacle in one's career or life. 2. Blocked sexual or emotional energy.

Robbery: 1. Rape (stolen jewels, cups, etc.). 2. Castration (stolen money, tools, etc.).

Rock: 1. Stability, permanence. 2. Burden.

Rocket: 1. Ejaculation or erection. 2. Liberation. 3. Escape.

Roller Coaster: 1. Life's ups and downs. 2. Sexual intercourse.

Room: 1. The self or part of the self. 2. A female. 3. The womb. 4. A compartment of the unconscious (house with many dark rooms).

Rope: 1. Umbilical cord (tie to mother). 2. Constraint. 3. A penis (Freudian).

Rose(s): 1. Love or romance. 2. Joy. 3. Completeness (Rose mandala; Jungian).

Ruby: 1. Passion. 2. Anger. 3. Truth.

Ruins: 1. The unconscious. 2. The past. 3. Something that has fallen apart or gotten old (a marriage, etc.)

Running: 1. Escaping. 2. Anxiety.

Rust: 1. Deterioration (of a relationship). 2. Abstinence.

S

Sacrifice: 1. Martyrdom. 2. Guilt.

Saddle: 1. Female genitals. 2. Sexual intercourse (riding saddle). 3. Burden (saddle on back).

Sailor: 1. Male sexuality. 2. Travel. 3. Adventure.

Sausage: 1. The penis. 2. A turd.

Screw: 1. The penis. 2. Sexual intercourse (screwing).

Sea: (See Ocean.)

Sea shell: 1. The vagina. 2. A relic of the unconscious.

Seed: 1. Growth and development. 2. Pregnancy. 3. Truth. 4. An idea.

Seven: 1. Good luck. 2. Completeness. 3. Time for a change (seven-year itch).

Sewer: 1. Anality. 2. The unconscious. 3. Family secrets.

Shadow: 1. The unconscious. 2. Depression. 3. Dark side of one's nature (Jungian). 4. Split-off, projected bad objects (object relations).

Sheep: 1. Subservience. 2. Children.

Shepherd: 1. Good father.

Ship: 1. Mother. 2. The self. 3. Trouble (sinking ship). 4. Sex (ship in canal).

Shoe: 1. The vagina. 2. A penis (high-heeled shoes).

Shooting: Sexual aggression.

Shore: 1. Mother's lap. 2. Sexual intercourse (waves lapping the sand).

Shoulders: 1. Strength. 2. Responsibility.

Singing: 1. Mother. 2. Sexual or emotional passion.

Sinking: 1. Death or depression. 2. Deterioration of one's career or relationship. 3. Loss of courage or determination. 4. Moral degradation. 5. Orgasm.

Six: Wholeness.

Sixteen: Innocence and youth (sweet sixteen).

Skeleton: 1. Death. 2. Secrets (in closet).

Skull: 1. Death. 2. Pirates (with crossbones).

Skunk: 1. A flaw. 2. An offensive person.

Sky: 1. Ambition (the "sky's the limit"). 2. Transcendence. 3. Hope. 4. Heaven (the *Bible*).

Sleep: 1. The unconscious. 2. A dormant aspect of the self. 3. Depression. 4. Death.

Smallness: 1. The past. 2. Childhood.

Smog: 1. Confusion. 2. Depression.

Snake: 1. Evil (Biblical). 2. The penis. 3. Rebirth (snake eating itself).

Snow: 1. Purity. 2. Frozen emotion.

Soap: 1. Impure thoughts. 2. A clean start.

Sparrow: 1. Delicate child. 2. Woman.

Spear: The penis.

Spider(s): 1. Engulfing mother. 2. Seductress. 3. Guilt.

Spring: 1. Rebirth. 2. Youth. 3. Romance. 4. Creativity.

Staircase: 1. Sexual intercourse (Freudian). 2. Ambition.

Stalactite/Stalagmite: 1. Penises. 2. Phallic woman (cave with stalactites or stalagmites).

Star: 1. Hope. 2. Fame.

Statue: 1. Death. 2. Immortality. 3. Rebirth (statue coming to life).

Stealing: (See Robbery.)

Stick: 1. The penis. 2. Authority.

Stone(s): 1. Burden. 2. Persecution (stones thrown at one).

Storm: 1. An emotional outburst. 2. A turbulent period of life. 3. Passion.

Stove: 1. Sexual passion. 2. Anger. 3. Female genitals (Freudian).

Stranger: (See Alien.)

Strangling: 1. Something being stifled in oneself. 2. Smothering mother.

Stream: (See River.)

Suffocation: (See Strangling.)

Suitcase: 1. The unconscious. 2. Past problems. 3. Evil (Pandora's box).

Summer: 1. Middle age. 2. Happiness, well-being.

Sun: 1. Life. 2. Father. 3. God. 4. Intelligence.

Superman: 1. Ideal man. 2. Grandiosity. 3. Strength.

Swamp: 1. Confusion. 2. Depression. 3. An overwhelming emotion or predicament.

Swan: 1. Beauty. 2. Sadness (swan song).

Swimming: 1. Sexual intercourse. 2. Mother's embrace.

Swinging: 1. Sexual intercourse. 2. Masturbation. 3. Childhood.

Sword: 1. The penis. 2. Courage.

T

Table: Female genitals (Freudian).

Taming: Controlling a willful aspect of the self.

Teeth: 1. Aggression. 2. Oral sadism. 3. Loss of power or castration (loss of teeth).

Ten: Completeness.

Thirteen: Bad luck.

Thorn: 1. Suffering. 2. An irritating person or thing. 3. The penis (Freudian).

Thread: 1. Umbilical cord. 2. Precariousness or mortality (hanging by a thread).

Three: 1. Triangle. 2. Completeness.

Threshold: 1. Marriage. 2. Beginning.

Thunder: 1. Anger. 2. Quarreling. 3. Power. 4. Sign from God (the *Bible*).

Tie: The penis.

Tiger: (See Lion.)

Tomb: 1. Death. 2. Womb.

Tongue: 1. Speech. 2. The penis. 3. Dumbness (no tongue).

Tool: The penis.

Torch: 1. Peace. 2. Mourning (carrying a torch; lighting a candle).

Tower: 1. Phallus. 2. Ambition, grandiosity (ivory tower).

Town: (See City.)

Track: (See Path.)

Train: 1. Journey of life. 2. The penis. 3. Sexual intercourse (train into tunnel). 4. Missing an opportunity. 5. Death (Freudian). 6. Escape.

Treasure: 1. Ideal self. 2. Neglected self (buried treasure).

Tree: 1. Life. 2. Strength. 3. Immortality. 4. Mother.

Triangle: 1. Eternity. 2. Triangular relationship.

Trumpet: 1. Phallus or breast. 2. Oral sex (blowing on trumpet or other musical instruments).

Trunk: 1. Female genitals (Freudian). 2. Evil (Pandora's box). 3. The unconscious. 4. The shadow (Jungian).

Tunnel: 1. The vagina. 2. The unconscious. 3. Depression.

Turkey: 1. Bad omen. 2. Loser.

Turtle: 1. Male genitals. 2. Slowness.

Twelve: Completeness (one dozen; twelve days of Christmas).

Twilight: 1. Old age. 2. End of a phase.

Twins: 1. Siblings. 2. Ego and alter ego. 3. Doubles (Jungian).

Two: 1. Mother and father. 2. Male and female. 3. Conflicting forces, opposites.

U

UFOs (unidentified flying objects): 1. Messengers from the unconscious. 2. Grandiose paranoid projections.

Ukelele: 1. The penis. 2. The vagina. 3. Masturbation (stroking any stringed instrument).

Umbrella: The penis.

Underground: 1. The unconscious. 2. Sexuality. 3. The womb.

Underworld: (See Hell.)

Unicorn: 1. Male sexuality. 2. Gallantry (mythology).

V

Vacuum: 1. The womb. 2. Depression. 3. Depersonalization.

Vagrant: Confusion, aimlessness.

Valley: 1. Vagina. 2. Mother.

Vault: 1. The unconscious. 2. Female genitals. 3. Potential.

Veil: 1. Mystery. 2. The unconscious. 3. Women; women's secrets.

Violin: 1. Male or female genitals. 2. Masturbation (playing violin). 3. Peace.

Volcano: 1. Ejaculation. 2. Aggression. 3. Passion.

Voyage: 1. Journey of life. 2. Exploration of unconscious. 3. Relationship.

Vulture: 1. Death. 2. A bad omen. 3. A manipulative person.

W

Wagon: Female genitals (Freudian).

Wall: 1. Obstacle in one's career or life. 2. Defense mechanism that keeps one isolated from others. 3. Sexual or emotional block. 4. Barrier to intimacy.

War: 1. Rage. 2. Psychic conflict projected into the environment. 3. The family; family life.

Watch: 1. Time. 2. The penis (pocket watch).

Water: (See also Ocean.) 1. The unconscious. 2. Sexual energy. 3. The womb. 4. Mother.

Weeds: 1. Obnoxious persons. 1. Rotten part of the self.

Well: 1. Deep emotions. 2. The vagina.

Whale: 1. Mother. 2. The womb. 3. Engulfing vagina (Jonah and the Whale; The *Bible*). 4. Grandiose ambitions (white whale).

Wheel: 1. Course of life (turning wheel). 2. Completeness (Jungian).

Whirlpool: 1. Turbulance of life. 2. Internal conflict.

Whirlwind: (See Whirlpool.)

White: 1. Purity and innocence. 2. Peace. 3. Mourning (East).

Wilderness: 1. The unconscious. 2. Alienation. 3. Abandonment. 4. The shadow (Jungian).

Willow: Sadness.

Wind: 1. Turbulent emotions. 2. Message from God (Christianity).

Wine: 1. Passion. 2. Blood (Christianity).

Wings: 1. Transcendence. 2. Power. 3. Penises. 4. Sexual liberation.

Winter: 1. Old age. 2. Frozen emotions. 3. Sexual frigidity.

Witch: 1. Mother. 2. Animus (Jungian).

Wizard: 1. Father. 2. Wise old man (Jungian).

Wolf: 1. Aggression. 2. Father. 3. Aggressive sexuality.

Woods: 1. The unconscious. 2. Forbidden sexuality. 3. Abandonment, confusion (in the woods).

Worm: 1. Death. 2. Decay. 3. The penis.

Wound: 1. The vagina. 2. Castration.

Wreck: Imminent danger.

Wrestling: 1. Internal conflict. 2. Sexual intercourse. 3. Anima/animus (Jungian).

XYZ

X-ray: 1. Voyeurism. 2. Insight. 3. Mind reading.

Yawn: 1. Boredom. 2. Sexual yearning.

Yellow: 1. Cowardice. 2. Vitality (the sun). 3. Asian.

Yew tree: Death.

Yolk: Birth.

Zero: 1. Nothing. 2. Eternity. 3. Worthlessness.

Zoo: 1. Life's craziness. 2. The family.

REFERENCES

Abrams, M. H., ed. (1962). *The Norton Anthology of English Literature.* New York: Norton.

Ackroyd, E. (1993). *A Dictionary of Dream Symbols.* London: Blandford.

Adler, A. (1917). *The Neurotic Constitution.* New York: Moffat, Yard, and Co.

Alexander, F., and Wilson, G. W. (1935). Quantitative dream studies. *Psychoanalytic Quarterly* 4:523–541.

Aristotle (312 B.C.). On divination. In *The Works of Aristotle,* ed. W. D. Ross. Oxford: Clarendon, 1908.

Bettelheim, B., and Hartmann, H. (1924). On feelings and thoughts in Korsakoff Psychosis. *Archives of Psychiatry* 72:120–129.

Binswanger, L. (1958). The fall of Ellen West. In *Existence,* ed. R. May, E. Angel, and H. F. Ellenberger, pp. 237–364. New York: Clarion.

Binz, C. (1878). *On Dreams.* Bonn: Deuticke.

Bollas, C. (1995). *Cracking Up: The Work of Unconscious Experience.* New York: Hill and Wang.

Bonime, W. (1980). The dream in the depressive personality. In *The Dream in Clinical Practice,* ed. J. M. Natterson, pp. 131–148. Northvale, NJ: Jason Aronson.

Boswell, J. (1791). *The Life of Samuel Johnson.* New York: Dell, 1975.

Brewer, E. C. (1870). *Dictionary of Phrase and Fable,* revised by E. Evans. London: Wordsworth.

Broughton, R. J. (1968). Sleep disorders: Disorders of arousal? *Science* 159:1070–1078.

Cross, C. (1973). *Adolf Hitler.* New York: Berkeley Books.

Delaney, G. (1994). *Sensual Dreaming.* New York: Fawcett.

Donn, L. (1988). *Freud and Jung: Years of Friendship, Years of Loss.* New York: Macmillan.

Dostoyevsky, F. (1868). *Crime and Punishment.* New York: Signet, 1968.

Eissler, K. R. (1953). The effect of the structure of the ego on psychoanalytic technique. *Journal of the American Psychoanalytic Association* 1:104–143.

Emerson, R. W. (1904). *Lectures and Biographical Sketches.* Boston: Houghton Mifflin.

Faraday, A. (1974). *The Dream Game.* New York: Harper & Row.

Ferenczi, S. (1916). The psycho-analysis of dreams. In *First Contributions to Psycho-Analysis,* pp. 94–131. New York: Brunner/Mazel, 1980.

Freud, S. (1900). The interpretation of dreams. *Standard Edition* 4:1–338 and 5:339–627.

——— (1901). On dreams. *Standard Edition* 5:631–687.

——— (1905). Fragment of an analysis of a case of hysteria. *Standard Edition* 7:3–122.

——— (1909a). Analysis of a phobia in a five-year-old boy. *Standard Edition* 10:3–152.

——— (1909b). Notes upon a case of obsessional neurosis. *Standard Edition* 10:153–318.

——— (1910). Leonardo Da Vinci: a study in psychosexuality. *Standard Edition* 11:59–130.

——— (1911). The handling of dream interpretation in psycho-analysis. *Standard Edition* 12:89–96.

——— (1915–1916). Introductory lectures on psycho-analysis. *Standard Edition* 15–16:3–481.

——— (1918). From the history of an infantile neurosis. *Standard Edition* 17:3–122.

——— (1920). Beyond the pleasure principle. *Standard Edition* 18:7–64.

——— (1933). New introductory lectures on psycho-analysis. *Standard Edition* 22:3–182.

Freud, S., and Breuer, J. (1893). Studies on hysteria. *Standard Edition* 2:1–307.

Friedmann, C. T. H. (1980). Nightmares. In *The Dream in Clinical Practice,* ed. J. M. Natterson, pp. 301–315. Northvale, NJ: Jason Aronson.

Fromm, E. (1951). *The Forgotten Language*. New York: Holt, Rinehart, Winston.

Gedo, J. E. (1980). The dream in regressed states. In *The Dream in Clinical Practice*, ed. J. M. Natterson, pp. 193–208. Northvale, NJ: Jason Aronson.

Greenberg, R., and Pearlman, C. (1974). Cutting the REM nerve: an approach to the adaptive role of REM sleep. *Perspectives in Biology and Medicine* 17:513–521.

Grinstein, A. (1980). *Sigmund Freud's Dreams*. New York: International Universities Press.

Guntrip, H. (1975). My experience of analysis with Fairbairn and Winnicott. *International Review of Psycho-Analysis* 2:145–156.

Gutheil, E. (1951). *The Handbook of Dream Analysis*. New York: Liveright.

Hemingway, E. (1952). *The Old Man and the Sea*. New York: Scribner's.

Joyce, J. (1918). *Ulysses*. New York: Modern Library, 1961.

Jung, C. (1971). *The Portable Jung*, ed. J. Campbell. New York: Viking.

Kafka, F. (1912). Metamorphosis. In *Collected Stories of Franz Kafka*. New York: Modern Library, 1952.

Kafka, J. S. (1980). The dream in schizophrenia. In *The Dream in Clinical Practice*, ed. J. M. Natterson, pp. 99–110. Northvale, NJ: Jason Aronson.

Kardiner, A. (1941). *Traumatic Neuroses of War*. New York: Paul Hoeber.

Kaufmann, W. (1953). *Nietzsche: Philosopher, Psychologist, Antichrist*. New York: Basic Books.

Keith, P. R. (1975). Night terrors: a review of psychology, neurophysiology, and therapy. *Journal of the American Academy of Child Psychiatry* 14:477–489.

Klein, M. (1932). *The Psychoanalysis of Children*, trans. A. Strachey. New York: Delacorte, 1975.

Kohut, H. (1971). *Analysis of the Self*. New York: International Universities Press.

——— (1979). The two analyses of Mr Z. *International Journal of Psycho-Analysis* 60:3–27.

Lebe, D. (1980). The dream in acting out disturbances. In *The Dream in Clinical Practice*, ed. J. M. Natterson, pp. 209–225. Northvale, NJ: Jason Aronson.

Lessing, D. (1964). *A Ripple from the Storm*. New York: New American Library.

Levitan, H. (1980). The dream in psychosomatic states. In *The Dream in Clinical Practice*, ed. J. M. Natterson, pp. 225–236. Northvale, NJ: Jason Aronson.

Lewin, B. D. (1948). The nature of reality, the meaning of nothing. *Psychoanalytic Quarterly* 17:70–77.

Lindner, R. (1957). *The Fifty-Minute Hour.* New York: Bantam.

Marmer, S. A. (1980). The dream in dissociative states. In *The Dream in Clinical Practice*, ed. J. M. Natterson, pp. 363–376. Northvale, NJ: Jason Aronson.

McGrath, M. J., and Cohen, P. B. (1978). REM sleep facilitation of adaptive waking behavior: a review of the literature. *Psychological Bulletin* 85:24–57.

Miller, G. H. (1884). *The Dictionary of Dreams.* New York: Arco, 1984.

Miller, H. (1975). *The Nightmare Notebook.* New York: New American Library.

Namrow, A. (1980). The dream in obsessive states. In *The Dream in Clinical Practice*, ed. J. M. Natterson, pp. 149–162. Northvale, NJ: Jason Aronson.

Pao, P. (1980). The dream in manic-depressive psychosis. In *The Dream in Clinical Practice*, ed. J. M. Natterson, pp. 111–130. Northvale, NJ: Jason Aronson.

Piontelli, A. (1992). *From Fetus to Child: An Observational and Psychoanalytic Study.* London: Tavistock.

Plato (420 B.C.). Phaedo. In *The Wisdom and Ideas of Plato.* New York: Fawcett, 1966.

Plutarch (110a). *Lives of the Noble Greeks.* New York: Dell, 1959.

——— (110b). *Lives of the Noble Romans.* New York: Dell, 1959.

Pomer, S. L., and Shain, R. A. (1980). The dream in phobic states. In *The Dream in Clinical Practice*, ed. J. M. Natterson, pp. 177–192. Northvale, NJ: Jason Aronson.

Proust, M. (1928). *Swann's Way.* New York: Modern Library, 1957.

Rangell, L. (1952). The analysis of a doll phobia. *International Journal of Psycho-Analysis* 33:43–53.

Rank, O. (1924). *The Trauma of Birth.* London: Kegan Paul, 1928.

Ravenscroft, K., and Hartmann, E. (1968). *Psychophysiology* 4:396 (Abstract).

Sade, M. de (1814). *120 Days of Sodom.* New York: Grove, 1966.

Schilder, P. (1942). Body image in dreams. *Psychoanalytic Review* 29:128–137.

Schoenewolf, G. (1990). *Turning Points in Analytic Therapy: The Classic Cases.* Northvale, NJ: Jason Aronson.

——— (1991a). *Turning Points in Analytic Therapy: From Winnicott to Kernberg.* Northvale, NJ: Jason Aronson.

———— (1991b). *The Art of Hating*. Northvale, NJ: Jason Aronson.

———— (1994). Buttons. *Voices: The Art and Science of Psychotherapy*. Winter, 1994, pp. 52–61.

———— (1997). Soiling and the anal-narcissistic character. *American Journal of Psychoanalysis* 57:91–103.

Schur, M. (1966). Some additional "day residues" of the specimen dream of psychoanalysis. In *Psychoanalysis: A General Psychology,* pp. 103–112. New York: International Universities Press.

Searles, H. (1979). *Countertransference and Related Topics*. Northvale, NJ: Jason Aronson.

Seinfeld, J. (1993). *Interpreting and Holding*. Northvale, NJ: Jason Aronson.

Shakespeare, W. (1610). *Hamlet*. In *Shakespeare's Tragedies*. New York: Modern Library, 1947.

Shengold, L. (1989). *Halo in the Sky: Observations on Anality and Defense*. New Haven: Yale University Press, 1992.

Socarides, C. W. (1980). Perverse symptoms in the manifest dream in perversion. In *The Dream in Clinical Practice*, ed. J. M. Natterson, pp. 237–258. Northvale, NJ. Jason Aronson.

Stekel, W. (1911). *The Language of Dreams*. Munich: Bergmann.

Stevenson, R. L. (1886). *The Strange Case of Dr. Jekyll and Mr. Hyde*. Clinton, MA: Airmont Classics, 1952.

Swift, J. (1726). *Gulliver's Travels*. New York: Pocket Books, 1957.

Volkelt, J. (1875). *Dreams and Fantasies*. Stuttgart: Bergmann.

Winnicott, D. W. (1953). Symptom tolerance in paediatrics. In *Through Paediatrics to Psycho-Analysis*, pp. 101–117. New York: Basic Books, 1975.

———— (1964). *Boundary and Space: An Introduction to the Work of D. W. Winnicott*, ed. M. Davis and D. Wallbridge. London: H. Karnac, 1981.

Wood, R. (1947). *The World of Dreams*. New York: Random House.

Zolotow, M. (1960). *Marilyn Monroe*. New York: Harcourt Brace Jovanovich.

INDEX OF DREAMS BY
FAMOUS FIGURES

INDEX OF DREAMS FROM PSYCHOTHERAPEUTIC LITERATURE

INDEX OF DREAMS FROM MYTHS AND FAIRY TALES

INDEX OF DREAMS ACCORDING TO PERSONALITY AND PHYSICAL CHARACTERISTICS

About the Author

Gerald Schoenewolf, Ph.D., has been Director of the Living Center in New York since 1979. He is a practicing psychoanalyst and the author of ten books, including *101 Common Therapeutic Blunders* (with R. Robertiello), *101 Therapeutic Successes The Art of Hating, Counterresistance: The Therapist's Interference in the Therapeutic Process,* and *The Couple Who Fell in Hate.*